"G. P. Wagenfuhr and Amy J. Erickson reclaim the Sabbath as a creative force in God's redemptive story, revealing its transformative impact on our identity, our rhythms, and our calling. Theologically profound yet practically grounded, this work casts a compelling vision for individuals and communities striving to live with faithfulness and sustainability amid the hyperactive pace of contemporary life."

Alan Hirsch, founder of 100 Movements and 5Q Collective and author of several books on missional leadership and spirituality

"It is deeply ironic that a people who follow the Lord of the Sabbath, who offers the promise of rest, are so often exhausted. Part of the reason, as G. P. Wagenfuhr and Amy J. Erickson show, is that we have approached the Sabbath as yet another thing to do, another task to accomplish within structures that are often exploitative and unjust. Instead, they offer a fresh vision of Sabbath which calls us, not to stop work altogether, but to take up the right kinds of work. Here is the promise of true rest, not for frantic people on the go, but for hopeful people on the Way."

Ryan Tafilowski, assistant professor of theology at Denver Seminary and coauthor, with W. David Buschart, of *Worth Doing: Fallenness, Finitude, and Work in the Real World*

"This is not a book about one day of the week or retreating into personal rest. G. P. Wagenfuhr and Amy J. Erickson cast a richly biblical and theological vision of Christians living and ministering in God's time, in Sabbath time. They summon and guide the church not into stopping or withdrawing but into being ambassadors of God's rest in and to the world. Far from an individual spiritual practice, Sabbath is community life and mobilization."

W. David Buschart, professor of theology and historical studies emeritus at Denver Seminary and coauthor, with Ryan Tafilowski, of *Worth Doing: Fallenness, Finitude, and Work in the Real World*

"Most Christians know that the Sabbath is the one commandment of the Decalogue explicitly given for our immediate and obvious benefit. Why, then, do so many of us not 'keep Sabbath' (asking for a friend)? In their joint volume, G. P. Wagenfuhr and Amy J. Erickson answer this question and many more. Like the Sabbath journey they describe, this book is a peregrination, as Wagenfuhr and Erickson lead us on an exodus away from dream houses into full maturity and freedom. They worry that the result is 'wildly ambitious and woefully ineffective,' but I believe those fears are unfounded: readers who take this book seriously will learn an immense amount and live quite differently as a result."

Brent A. Strawn, D. Moody Smith Distinguished Professor of Old Testament and Professor of Law at Duke University

"Sabbath is one of those religiously connotative terms. To older generations, it evokes long days at church, strict rules of conduct, and dress-up clothes. To younger generations, it evokes memories of leisure, play, and chores, which bring an end to the weekend. But more than anything, it evokes longing. We're weary and busy. We want rest, deep rest. G. P. Wagenfuhr and Amy J. Erickson's *Sabbath Gospel* engages the topic with rare freshness and insight. Their book does not limit itself to exploring Sabbath as the last day of the week, or the first, as Christians tend to assume. It organizes the entire biblical story as an extended commentary on God's plan to give us rest—the rest of his kingdom rule, the rest of redemption, the rest of community, the rest of a restored Garden of Eden in which we live fully as members of God's household. It is a rest for people who live as exiles, no matter their rank, wealth, and power. I have read many books on the Sabbath. I have read none like this one. It sets a new trajectory for how we think and experience the Sabbath. It is theology at its best: compelling, persuasive, subversive, and livable."

Gerald L. Sittser, professor emeritus of theology at Whitworth University and author of *Water from a Deep Well* and *Resilient Faith*

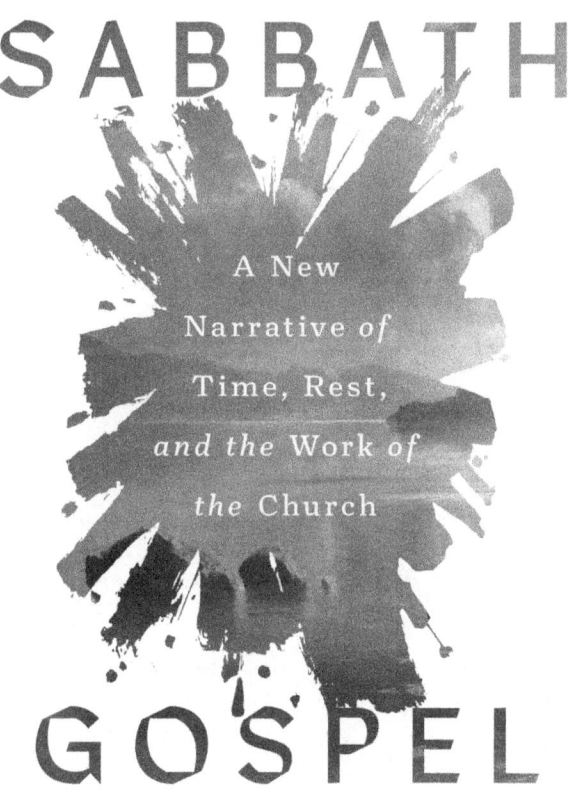

SABBATH GOSPEL

A New Narrative of Time, Rest, and the Work of the Church

G. P. Wagenfuhr

Amy J. Erickson

An imprint of InterVarsity Press
Downers Grove, Illinois

InterVarsity Press
P.O. Box 1400 | Downers Grove, IL 60515-1426
ivpress.com | email@ivpress.com

©2026 Amy Joy Erickson and Gregory Paul Wagenfuhr

All rights reserved. No part of this book may be reproduced in any form without written permission from InterVarsity Press.

InterVarsity Press® is the publishing division of InterVarsity Christian Fellowship/USA®. For more information, visit intervarsity.org.

Scripture quotations, unless otherwise noted, are from the New Revised Standard Version, Updated Edition. Copyright © 2021 National Council of Churches of Christ in the United States of America. Used by permission. All rights reserved worldwide.

The publisher cannot verify the accuracy or functionality of website URLs used in this book beyond the date of publication.

Cover design: Faceout Studio, Tim Green
Interior design: Jeanna Wiggins
Images: Getty Images: © Fine Art Photographic / Stone; © CSA Printstock / DigitalVision Vectors

ISBN 978-1-5140-0954-3 (print) | ISBN 978-1-5140-0955-0 (digital)

Printed in the United States of America ♾

Library of Congress Cataloging-in-Publication Data
Names: Wagenfuhr, Gregory P., (Gregory Paul), 1984- author | Erickson, Amy J. author
Title: Sabbath gospel : a new narrative of time, rest, and the work of the church / Gregory P. Wagenfuhr, Amy J. Erickson.
Description: Downers Grove : IVP Academic, [2026] | Includes bibliographical references and index.
Identifiers: LCCN 2025031549 (print) | LCCN 2025031550 (ebook) | ISBN 9781514009543 paperback | ISBN 9781514009550 ebook
Subjects: LCSH: Rest–Religious aspects–Christianity | Sabbath–Biblical teaching
Classification: LCC BV4597.55 .W34 2026 (print) | LCC BV4597.55 (ebook)
LC record available at https://lccn.loc.gov/2025031549
LC ebook record available at https://lccn.loc.gov/2025031550

---

32 31 30 29 28 27 26 | 12 11 10 9 8 7 6 5 4 3 2 1

For Aristeia and Adeilia

For Addie, Jake, and Austin

Posterity will serve him;

future generations will be told about the Lord

and proclaim his deliverance to a people yet unborn,

saying that he has done it.

Psalm 22:30-31

CONTENTS

PART 1: STARTING FROM WHERE WE ARE

1. A Journey Toward Rest — 3
2. The Dream Home: The Foil of Sabbath — 13
3. The Sabbath Psalm: Beginning in the Middle — 25

PART 2: SABBATH THROUGH SCRIPTURE

4. Sabbath at First — 43
5. A Tale of Two Times — 65
6. Signs of the Covenant — 92
7. Life in God's Household: Lifeblood of the Old Covenant — 119
8. Jubilee Time: The Lord of the Sabbath Arrives — 141
9. Recapitulated Time: Blood of the New Covenant — 155
10. Exodus Time: Entering into God's Final Rest — 169

PART 3: SABBATH NOW

11. Embassy Ecclesiology: Ambassadors of Rest — 191
12. Establish the Work of Our Hands — 213

Conclusion: A Call to Renewal — 243

Acknowledgments — 251

Selected Bibliography — 253

General Index — 256

Scripture Index — 261

PART 1

Starting from Where We Are

A JOURNEY TOWARD REST

CHRISTIANITY IS TIRED, and most of us are tired, too. Some are tired from the frenzy of performative religion with its stages and lighting in slickly polished services. Others are tired of worn-out religious formulas and rituals in straight-back pews stuck in an outdated past. And we're all tired of tribalized factions and bloody infighting. We're tired of revolving mission statements and steady leadership failures. We're tired of small talk and of grand plans. We're tired of people who are too busy for church and churches that are too busy for people. We're weary from posturing as a group that claims unique answers but looks like everyone else.

Western Christianity has been exiled, removed from its formerly privileged status that conveyed material benefits needed to maintain institutional structures. Is Christianity tired because it has been exiled from the secular age, or is the secular age itself an expression of the tiredness of Christianity and its institutions? Either way, everyday experience suggests a looming obsolescence arising from Christianity's own exhaustion.

But you know this already. Christianity is weary because you're weary. That's likely why you picked up a book on Sabbath. And it's maybe not the first. There are lots of books on Sabbath. This book is different. That's because most books on Sabbath fail to diagnose the actual conditions of our tiredness. They end up legitimizing the exploitative structures of the world that the church too often caters to. Instead of reminding us that God is leading slaves out of Egypt, they justify making bricks for Pharaoh.

For Christianity—or, better yet, for *Christians*—to be revived, we must renovate our understanding of Sabbath. In this book we'll touch on the notion of Sabbath as a weekly practice of cessation from paid and deliberate work. But that won't be our focus. The reduction of Sabbath to this practice—and the subsequent fixation on or rejection of that practice—is symptomatic of a deeper malaise that exhausts us. But recovering the real meaning of the Sabbath promises to refresh the church for our time.

There's another way Sabbath promises to help the church. A paradox that we will continue to unravel is that understanding the nature of its true rest is key for the church to understand its true work. We wonder whether one of the reasons that today's church is so weary is that it has been busy with the wrong kind of work. It has been doing the work of building, of laying brick and mortar, of establishing and constructing and restructuring institutions, when it should instead be about the task of sojourning, of breaking and setting up camp again and again, of seeking the city God has prepared.[1] The primary work of the church is not manufacturing, but wayfinding; not creation, but migration.[2] We are not architects; we are wanderers summoned to follow a Lord who calls himself the Way.[3] We must go on a journey—a new exodus—to find rest from our weariness so that we can offer rest to a weary world.

Because this is a different kind of book on Sabbath, it may help to bring to it a different set of expectations than you may have carried with you. It may not quite fit the genre of whatever virtual or physical bookstore section you found it in. If it fits into any, we might call it peregrination literature (from the Latin *peregrinatio*, for "sojourning, being or living abroad, traveling about"). In this it would be joining, rather than pioneering, a well-established genre of writing. It includes authors such as

---

[1] Gen 11:3; Ex 1:14; Num 33; Heb 11:10, 16.
[2] See Brian Brock, *Joining Creation's Praise: A Theological Ethic of Creatureliness* (Baker Academic, 2025).
[3] Jn 14:6.

Augustine, Dante Alighieri, John Bunyan, and J. R. R. Tolkien. On one level the genres of these authors vary widely, from a theology of history, to epic poetry, to allegory, to fantasy. But they share a common, animating instinct: that the human path to truth is just that—a path. That arriving at truth—*true* truth—isn't a matter of mentally grasping and assenting to a set of claims; it is more akin to a discovery of the world that also entails the development of oneself. The journey is a cultivation of not just knowledge but also character—and thus of wisdom. Such a journey not only takes time but transforms the character of time itself. What's more, peregrination books, even if read by individuals, require others: There is no city of God with a population of one, there is no tour of hell without Virgil as guide, there is no arrival at the Celestial City without help along the way, and there is no Frodo without Sam. That a journey demands both time and company, and transforms both in the process, already begins to foreshadow some of the discoveries that await us in Sabbath.

The nature of those discoveries may differ from that of other books. This book isn't going to give you a set of practices, formulas, or strategies. And in fact, we would invite you to resist the urge to evaluate or demand applications until the end. One of the main aims of this book is to outfit the church with navigation tools. Navigation tools aren't shortcuts. They help you discern what steps are in the right direction from the ground under your feet. The concepts and even the vocabulary explored in this book are aimed to help us renew our vision of what God is doing in and for the world so that we can orient ourselves toward *his* work. This book is more like a compass than a map.

So who is this journey for? We wrote this book for people who love the church—or who maybe *want* to love the church, or who maybe even *used* to love the church—but who sense, like us, that something is amiss. We wrote it for ordained pastors—like Gregory—who labor to cultivate a church of healthy, mature disciples of Jesus Christ who are ambassadors of reconciliation. We wrote it for bookish laypeople—like Amy—who long for a church characterized by robust, intimate community that bears each other's burdens. We wrote it for fellow theologians, like both of us, who appreciate a book that can hold water theologically while nourishing a readership outside the confines of the academy.

And we wrote this book for people who are tired. Tired of how the busy pace of contemporary Western culture has colonized and infiltrated even what should be the measured and meditative pace of pastoral life. Tired by the constant noise of measures—our salaries or net worth, our social media influence or sexual appeal, our career accomplishments or children's success—by which our lives are compounded, weighed, and found wanting. Tired of participating in, propping up, or perpetuating institutions that are at best hemorrhaging and unfit for purpose, or at worst exploitative and complicit with the managerialization and atomization of community. We wrote this for those who are wearied by life both inside and outside the church of our time and place and want to hear afresh the good news of the gospel. If you're still reading, we wrote this book, we think, for you. Admittedly, we also wrote it for ourselves. But most of all, we wrote it for the people of God, for whom there still awaits a Sabbath rest at the end of time.

Mapping the Path

So what *is* Sabbath? Sabbath does not simply refer to the fourth commandment in the Decalogue but to a river valley of themes in Scripture connected by a network of tributaries and channels that, taken together, reveal a consistent whole.[4] Sabbath is itself the journey and the destination toward rest and refreshment. Sabbath is bound to the topography of all human experience. It encompasses how we inhabit time and the character of time itself. Throughout this book, we will aim to distinguish between Sabbath as the reality of God's reign and practices or *signs* of Sabbath that point toward that reality. Sabbath might be summed up as *the immediate dwelling presence of the sovereign king of all creation with the united household of God.* We believe that the seventh day of creation

---

[4]*Decalogue* is another name for the Ten Commandments as found in Ex 20 and Deut 5.

is the enduring time in which God himself dwells, the *aiōn* of God (to use the Greek) or *'olam* (to use the Hebrew).[5] Sabbath is less fixated on the "when" of time than on the "so what" of time. Sabbath is ultimately characterized by the Lord of time, the one who takes up the sovereign rest of ruling a dominion of peace.

Like any biblical theme, Sabbath is attached to a specific subset of words (such as *Sabbath* and *rest*) that feeds into and is fed by other words, themes, and images. Because of this, and because of the especially rich and varied nature of Sabbath, our explorations of the biblical portrait of Sabbath will sometimes take us to nontraditional and unsuspecting texts. While it remains to demonstrate these themes in Scripture, we invite readers to set aside the many presuppositions and debates about what Sabbath means—which day of the week, what can and cannot be done, what qualifies as work or rest, and so on. Our task is first to rediscover what Sabbath means in the Bible before considering what this may mean for us as the church in the present.

In the course of our journey we will encounter key terms that will be shown to be intimately related to Sabbath: *household* and the people of a *household order*, the *seventh day*, *signs*, *sovereignty* and *kingship*, and more. At times we will also choose to frame our discussion with original Hebrew or Greek words in order to try to avoid any preconceptions that might be smuggled in with more familiar English ones. Just as we might slowly appreciate the interlaced geological features of a landscape as it naturally undulates at the pace of our travel, we'll encounter and incorporate these terms organically as our exploration unfolds.

In part one, "Starting from Where We Are," we'll take the crucial first steps of our journey. Chapter two, "The Dream Home: The Foil of Sabbath," marks our departure point on our journey. Sabbath requires us to consider what it means to rest. So, to begin our journey, we ask: What *does* it mean to rest? Or perhaps better, what do we *think* rest means? Resting is

---

[5]We purposefully avoid the use of the word *eternity* due to its regular definition as nontime or the state of pure being/nonchange. This Platonic ideal we will critique later.

something that usually takes place at home. Home is where we literally sleep but also where we retreat from the world. In this chapter, we reflect deeply on what kinds of expectations and desires tend to accrue around the concept of a dream home. We'll discover that the notion of a dream home takes on a life of its own as a metaphor for the false gospel that rivals the gospel of Sabbath rest. We'll find that the dream home is our re-presentation of the world, but in a form under our own control.

This false gospel of the dream home prevails today. The Bible labels it with names such as Babel and Babylon, Sodom and Gomorrah, Egypt and Rome. The desire for a dream home is a desire to rest in a structure and project of our own making. The irony is that the attempt to construct our own rest is an illusion; it leads only to restlessness, exploitation, and ultimately death. By contrast, the gospel of Sabbath is a home already built and a rest already created in which the infinite diversities of the creation are held together in relationship to their Creator. This opening theme of the home will be re-encountered throughout our book. In particular, to discuss Sabbath is to discuss matters of economy—or, as the English word *economy* etymologically means from its Greek roots—the household law (from *oikos*, "house," and *nomos*, "law"). Sabbath forces us to ask the question of whose economy we are participating in: the household of God, or a household of our own making? In other words: Whose rest are we seeking?

In chapter three, "The Sabbath Psalm: Beginning in the Middle," we'll launch our exploration of the story the Bible tells about the good news of Sabbath from an unlikely place: the middle. Rather than starting with theological first principles, reflecting on the nature of God in isolation, we begin with Psalm 92, the only psalm dedicated to the Sabbath. Although this psalm makes no direct reference to Sabbath practices, it shows that the biblical authors understood Sabbath as pointing to the sovereignty of God exactly where we find ourselves: in the midst of a hostile, unresting world. In other words, starting our biblical exploration of Sabbath with Psalm 92 helps us to start thinking about Sabbath in exactly the place we find ourselves: in the middle of history and on the far side of Eden.

Part two, "Sabbath Through Scripture," logs critical miles as we follow the trail of Sabbath through the biblical landscape. In chapter four, "Sabbath at First," and chapter five, "A Tale of Two Times," we'll look at the Bible's first pages by considering key Sabbath passages in Genesis. These reveal that while creation was originally intended for God's abiding or resting with his creation as an expression of sovereignty, this sovereign abiding was prevented by human rebellion, an unrest that takes on a life of its own and brings about destruction and death. In these chapters we'll consider how the Bible's prehistory is less the story of a universal humanity than it is the story of the formation of the people of God in distinction from a rebellious, rival line of people. We'll also consider the nature of sin as not primarily individual moral failure but a power that inhabits and distorts human structures and institutions on a collective level.

Chapter six, "Signs of the Covenant," will consider how God responds to rebellion by equipping a covenant people for a journey toward his rest. Practices of Sabbath—ranging from weekly practices of rest through ecological and economic practices of relief in the Jubilee—serve to reveal the nature of God's kingdom and of God's time of Sabbath rest. In other words, signs of Sabbath are a way that God's people participate in God's reality, recognize his sovereignty, and reveal his character to a rival order of time.

Chapter seven, "Life in God's Household: Lifeblood of the Old Covenant," takes our journey to an infrequently visited holy site, to Leviticus and the character of the household of God as it is understood through the sacrificial literature of the Old Testament. Rather than dwelling in arcane ruins of a bygone temple religion, this chapter works to discern the logic of the household of God so we can rightly discern the meaning of Jesus' own ministry, death, resurrection, and ascension as the formation of a new people vivified by the undying life and love of God, who makes himself available to human flesh.

In chapter eight, "Jubilee Time: The Lord of the Sabbath Arrives," our journey continues into the New Testament as we consider how Jesus Christ, as Lord of the Sabbath, is reconciling a rebellious world into his eternal reign of rest by establishing a renewed economy or household characterized not by rest taking but rest giving. In chapter nine, "Recapitulated Time: Blood of the New Covenant," we consider the life, passion, resurrection, and ascension of Jesus Christ through the lens of Sabbath and find renewed language for articulating Christ's atoning and reconciling work. We will see that Jesus recapitulates all of human history, bringing it to its true end, thus gathering all creation to himself.

Chapter ten, "Exodus Time: Entering into God's Final Rest," considers eschatology (the Christian doctrine of the end of time, or last things) by exploring the nature of the final Sabbath rest for which God's people wait. It will consider two main New Testament books—Revelation and Hebrews—that, from either side of God's final Sabbath rest, envision God as leading his people in a great exodus out of the world's crumbling structures of exploitation and enslavement. In the final Sabbath rest, God and humanity will no longer be mediated by constructions and institutions—or in other words, by human work. Instead they will feast on God's generous and free abundance.

If the main chapters of the book are our biblical journey of Sabbath, then the chapters of part three, "Sabbath Now," are our debriefing sessions before we reenter the lives we left behind. Chapter eleven, "Embassy Ecclesiology: Ambassadors of Rest," considers how a deep appreciation of Sabbath might reconstitute the church for our time. What does it mean to be the people of God together who represent the household of God from within the order of our time? Chapter twelve, "Establish the Work of Our Hands," suggests how our account of Sabbath might inform our approach to what we put our hands to in the present. We examine what it means to be a people who do good works, which should inform our approach to work and how we understand ourselves to be contributors of true and lasting value from within the distorted economic systems of the world. Refreshed, we hope, from the journey, we close by calling the church to renewal.

If our journey metaphor holds true, then the map we've just sketched should be just about as exciting as squinting at the contours of a hike on the tangled fold of two-dimensional paper. The real thrill, of course, lies in the journey itself: at the opportunity to stop and marvel at a sunrise-glinted mountain, a thundering waterfall, or a rare animal that has just crossed our path. And no adventure is worthy of the name if we don't encounter the unplanned-for and the unexpected, maybe even the disastrous incident that ends up not in disaster but in a renewed understanding of life's wild unmanageability and grace.[6] We hope the path we just outlined is but a whetting of an adventurous appetite for a full-blooded life of journeying toward the Sabbath rest of God.

A final word about how to read this book. One of its premises is that it's impossible for the gospel to be privatized. Living in the truth of the gospel must be a communal endeavor. If what we encounter doesn't join us to others in Christ, it is not the truth of Christ. This book aims to develop the household of God, not a personal ethic; it's a journey as God's people, not a journey of self-discovery. For that reason, we encourage you to travel the course of this book with others. The end of each chapter has a set of discussion questions you may wish to share. Instead of telling you what to do, this book instead will indicate what kinds of conversations you need to have. Perhaps these will also help you discern as a community what the next steps are on your collective journey toward God's Sabbath rest.

---

[6] A "eucatastrophe," as Tolkien coins it: "Tragedy is the true form of Drama, its highest function; but the opposite is true of Fairy-story. Since we do not appear to possess a word that expresses the opposite—I will call it *Eucatastrophe*. The *euchastrophic* tale is the true form of fairy-tale, and its highest function. The consolation of fairy-stories, the joy of the happy ending: or more correctly of the good catastrophe, the sudden joyous 'turn' (for there is no true end to any fairy-tale): this joy, which is one of the things which fairy-stories can produce supremely well, is not essentially 'escapist', nor 'fugitive'. In its fairy-tale—or otherworld—setting, it is a sudden and miraculous grace: never to be counted on to recur. It does not deny the existence of *dyscatastrophe*, of sorrow and failure: the possibility of these is necessary to the joy of deliverance; it denies (in the face of much evidence, if you will) universal final defeat and in so far is *evangelium*, giving a fleeting glimpse of Joy, Joy beyond the walls of the world, poignant as grief." J. R. R. Tolkien, *Tree and Leaf: Including the Poem Mythopoeia* (HarperCollins, 2001), 68-69.

The call of Jesus is, "Come to me, all you who are weary and carrying heavy burdens, and I will give you rest. Take my yoke upon you, and learn from me, for I am gentle and humble in heart, and you will find rest for your souls. For my yoke is easy, and my burden is light."[7] The Sabbath journey leads to a rest that takes up a new and different responsibility—a yoke—supplied by Jesus himself. Let's head in that direction.

---

[7]Mt 11:28-30.

THE DREAM HOME
The Foil of Sabbath

THE SABBATH GOSPEL JOURNEY BEGINS AT HOME. Home, after all, is where the heart is. Or, as Jesus says, "Where your treasure is, there your heart will be also."[1] Home is the sense of a place where our hopes and dreams are realized in a state of rest in a restful place, a place to dwell, to abide. But, like many journeys, the journey only truly begins when our hopes of home are questioned or made impossible.

Introducing the Dream Home Through the Dream House

This chapter explores the notion of the dream *house* as a doorway to explore a deeper concept: the dream *home*. It's a concept that characterizes the world as we know it. It's also directly at odds with Sabbath. The dream home is a foil *to* Sabbath, and the dream home also *foils* Sabbath.[2] It's a phenomenon we participate in individually and willingly but by which we are also exploited on collective and political levels. In one way or another, we all find ourselves conscripted into making bricks for Pharaoh's dream home.

We'll begin to unpack this phenomenon of the dream home, which is exemplified by the American dream house, but with a disclaimer. Given the

---

[1] Mt 6:21; Lk 12:34.
[2] Thanks to prereader Luke Keenan for this turn of phrase.

rise in housing prices across the Western world as we write, many readers may not be in a position to contemplate buying or building a house. But the fact that some people's dream houses, or ability to contemplate and actually construct such dream houses, operate at the exclusion or neglect of others already begins to direct us to the deeper phenomenon of the dream home. A 2024 *New York Times* article notes a telling trend: Increasing housing unaffordability has not turned ordinary audiences away from escapist real estate television that traffics in the allure of buying the paradisical mansion of a Hollywood star; instead, it has only increased the appeal.[3] The less attainable it is, the more power the *dream* has. *All* are victims in some way of the dream homes of others, just as all of us are guilty of the misguided pursuit of dream homes of our own devising. That's because the dream *home* is more than just a physical *house*. There are many other ways the dream home exerts power not only over our imagination but also over the actual infrastructure of the world we inhabit. But for now, the physical building, the constructed human habitat, is a useful place to start.

The dream home is a place of rest, where one's desires are realized, where an entire artificial environment is constructed exactly to one's specifications. "The Englishman's home is his castle," as the old saying goes. It's a modern consumer conceit that we all could live with a custom living environment all to ourselves. But perhaps modernity has provided the means to create individual versions—at least in a simulated dream form—of something deeply ancient.

The problem is that the dream home has value only as a *dream*. No one who builds their dream home is finally or forever satisfied. The realization of the dream defeats the dream, or at least defers it. The very consumerism that allows us to customize our homes relatively cheaply makes us feel discontented with outdated appliances or decorations.[4] Consider the

---

[3] Debra Kamin, "Real Estate Fantasies," *New York Times*, April 28, 2024, www.nytimes.com/2024/04/28/briefing/celebrity-real-estate-agents-selling-sunset.html.

[4] The work of sociologist Zygmunt Bauman has deftly diagnosed this dynamic of contemporary consumer culture, e.g., in his claim, "The society of consumers derives its animus and momentum from the disaffection it expertly produces itself." Bauman, *Consuming Life* (Polity, 2007), 48.

dream homes built when fireplaces were the central feature of the great room. The hearth had been the central feature of homes since time immemorial. The invention of large, wall-mounted televisions rendered the previously obsolete fireplace into something of a nuisance, easily replaced by looped videos of simulated fire. Its displacement by screens is both literal and figurative. The same virtual mediums have launched a new transformation away from the dream *home* and toward the *dream* home. In other words, the same desire for constructing a building designed to meet one's imagined needs can now be channeled into engineering a domain designed to taste within an entirely virtual reality. Today, houses are often directed to facilitate screen time—that is, to be a real portal to a virtual space.

That this desire to fashion a world to our tastes no longer needs to be concretized but can be achieved in artificial reality may betray something about the nature of that desire. Perhaps it shows that the dream home is valuable only as a *desire*, not as a *fulfilled* desire. Perhaps the recent rise of virtualized spaces shows that the dream home for which humanity has always longed needs to be inhabited only in our dreams. In other words, perhaps what humans have always longed for is to come to rest in a fantasy of our own making—not in the actual world in which we find ourselves.

Certainly not all readers will feel that these descriptions fit their situation or desires. Not everyone plays computer games, is interested in social media, or aims at fashioning a virtual world; not everyone can afford a home, let alone renovate it regularly. But there are other ways in which all humans, of any class, try to reorient reality according to some idea of what would make things better. The dream home is really about how humans aim to change things, about the dreams we cultivate individually and collectively around prefabricated conceptions of what would make the world a better place. What is true of the house is true as well of the human body, the political body, and the planet as a whole.

What does any of this have to do with Sabbath?

As we hope to begin to show at the end of this chapter and perhaps by the end of this book: everything.

The Deep Roots of Our Desire

The dream house is a modern manifestation of an ancient human desire—to come to rest in an environment entirely suited to oneself or one's people. The desire is to arrive, to reach a finality, to have the world fit like a glove rather than laboring to fit into our purposes a field full of thorns or a house full of inconveniently small and island-less kitchens. The desire is rest, to have everything in its right place and a place for everything. We might call this kind of rest *order* or *justice*, but the desire is the same: to live in a safe, well-suited, predictable, stable world—a home. This desire is to be like a god: to form everything according to one's own will, to achieve sovereignty as fellow creators. Because of this desire, the appearance of evil, of pain, of meaninglessness has long militated against belief in God and underwritten the view that the world is chaotic and in need of a major renovation.

When this desire is running at full throttle, it can be difficult to imagine a being one could call God who would not order the universe according to a law of total benevolence. If we were gods, we would not will the world as we find it—so how can there be a God? Thus, any glitch in the system of a restful, controlled cosmos is attached with a label that persists from ancient into modern times: chaos. Like the ancient pagans who first developed literature in the genre of mythology, moderns often conceive chaos as a starting point, the raw matter out of which the godlike exercise their sovereign will to bring about order. This desire to be like God manifests as control to create order and rest. But the comforts of consumerism have left contemporary humanity with few natural monsters to slay. We now need new places to domesticate.[5]

---

[5]Scholars such as Willie Jennings have identified similar features in other fields of study, such as in the concept of race and whiteness. We believe we are identifying something of the fundamental logic of domestication, imperialism, and colonialism that is observable from the earliest of records.

Today technology opens new doors to new realms. As humanity seeks to live in the virtualized *dream* home whose portals are our screens, we create virtual realities in which our bodies can truly be at rest, freed from bodily discomfort to efficiently focus sensory input into our minds. This efficiency bypasses the inconvenience of turning the dream into reality. This retreat is no longer geographical, no longer in the family, no longer staring at a gas fireplace with a glass of wine. This virtual retreat allows escape from even our own inconvenient physicality. And when it comes time to interact with other people in the physical world, there is less desire to give house tours to reveal the extent of one's ability to manifest one's will over the material world. There are other canvases beyond interior decoration. The body, for example, is the site of some people's dream homes, a malleable surface over which control is exerted.

Again, we acknowledge that not all readers are concerned with or able to remodel their body any more than a social media account or a home. There are other forms of the dream, such as a job or relationship. Is it possible that the object of one's dream could never be fulfilled by an actual position or title, or an actual face or name of a real person? Is it possible that, in reality, the job or the person would present challenges, annoyances, and resistances? That dream teaching job can't be guaranteed to be free from pesky administrative demands or unruly students, any more than that dream partner can't be guaranteed not to transgress a pet peeve or commit any number of minor—or major—betrayals. Whatever the object of one's dream, does it have any place in the real world? And if not, where does the desire for it come from?

The Misplaced Rest of Aseity

All of this talk about dream homes, virtual spaces, the human body, and any other object of our fantasies symbolizes something profoundly theological and philosophical: the great desire to come to rest in a cosmos constructed out of chaos. We want to have no needs in the first place and thus no external entities that define us. To experience no needs is to be freed from desire and the discomfort of not having. It is also to be free from interdependency. This desire is to *be* ourselves in and *by* ourselves without reference to others to give us meaning or value. Truly coming to rest, at least according to this desire, is to be free of everyone and everything. This is not simply an individualist notion but one that factors into collective identities and grand projects as well.

Another caveat: We aren't denying that humans can and do want healthy relationships with other people. Nor that humans can and should pursue sacrificial lives of service without reference to themselves, just as they should also rightly set appropriate boundaries around unhealthy and abusive relationships. But we are drawing attention to a strand of the human psyche, this side of God's Sabbath rest, that wishes to construct the self or the world by means of impact analysis—not how we are transformed in mutual ways but in how the self is manifest by causing change in others. This rebellious strand of human behavior animates the desires that fuel our various dream home fantasies. The name we're giving this misguided desire for the dream home is *aseity*.

The Latin term *aseity* literally means "from the self." Let's define it as "self-sufficiency." In theology it is often used of God. Aseity describes how God's existence derives from God's own being, and in such a way that God has no external needs or dependencies. The term *aseity* is not used frequently to describe human desire as we are doing here through the metaphor of the dream home. The desire for the dream home is rooted in a desire to be without needs, to be satisfied to the extent that we no longer think about needs; it's a desire to be independent in the most literal sense of the word. It's a desire to be self-made, *a se*. The problem, of course, is that this desire is entirely misguided and downright impossible for finite creatures. Only God is *a se*; humans can never be. Thus, the desire for aseity can never be *anything but* a fantasy. This desire itself is the hope to realize one's ambition, to make a story come true. The only way to make our own stories come true is to be the author of a fiction or fantasy. But the pursuit of that desire can wreak havoc psychologically, relationally, and ecologically. For that reason, the human desire for aseity is not only misguided. It is also dangerous and destructive.

Aseity in Other Forms

Aseity is something of a game of the scientific method. Control comes by eliminating variables. The simpler the home, the easier it is to build, clean, and maintain. The simpler a system, the more controllable the variables. This simplification happens in many ways.

On an individual level, simplification often takes the form of reducing inputs or stimuli. This can include spiritual methods such as centering prayer, mindfulness, and meditation. Simplification can also mean retreats, quiet places, closed doors, or time management—segregating space and time to control interaction with others. On a collective level, simplification requires that differences be controlled through segregation (walls, property boundaries, zoning, ethnicity, religion, gender), or eliminated through merging (as in ethnic merging in race) or by violence. The twentieth century is a handbook of grand political projects that demanded the total organization of people by both constructive (e.g., large-scale urban planning or environmental engineering) and destructive means. The extermination camps of Nazi Germany are among the most violent examples of aseity on a collective political scale. They are not the only. Consider the Khmer Rouge's killing fields, the millions of deaths resulting from Mao Zedong's Great Leap Forward, Joseph Stalin's collectivization, and dozens of genocides. Even large-scale urban planning and social engineering aim at control by segregation and management of variables in ways that transform people into processes. For all their cruel variety, they also share much in common: the dream of the good achieved by control.

The most advanced way to simplify and reduce human variables is to group them into categories and anonymize individuals, especially those who provide for our needs so that we don't factor them in. We transform variable individuals into corporate constants. States are large-scale versions of this same kind of control through simplification. States assimilate minorities, crush them, or transform them into largely anonymous and manageable category identities.[6] But whether on an individual scale of a personal program of spiritual control or as a global corporate conglomerate or nation-state, the dream home is a version of eliminating variables until all aspects of the environment are controlled.

In this way human aseity truly obtains rest only by a final simplification that ends in sheer meaninglessness. The rest of aseity is the dreamless sleep, the elimination of all variables and all otherness. The final rest is not the peace of an equilibrium but equivocation, *this equals that*. Buddhism calls it nirvana, but it goes by other names.[7] All differences disappear, and with them, all relationships. All of these forms of aseity are irresponsible in the most literal sense of the word. They fail to respond to others and instead try to control or eliminate them as other. These are attempts to solve the apparent problem of complexity, relatedness, of conflict, of otherness, and dependency. And when there are two variables, the self and the other, there are only so many options for resolving the two into one. The rest of aseity is ultimately a form of nihilism; it ends in nothing. For in seeking ultimate resolution to difference we must always come to some notion of stasis, eternity, or eternal recurrence. Resolution of this kind can only result in changelessness. It is eternity conceived as a static serenity, not a harmonious dynamism between living things.

Ecclesiastes 3:11 observes how this desire for rest as changelessness is inscribed in the human heart. The desire for eternity abides at the core of the self. It is a desire for an all-encompassing timeless resolution, an *identity* (this = that). But even though eternity is something God has set in the human heart, Ecclesiastes does not see this as a positive thing for humans to obtain,

---

[6]For a haunting analysis of how this manifests in contemporary capitalist economies, see Shoshana Zuboff, *The Age of Surveillance Capitalism: The Fight for a Human Future at the New Frontier of Power* (Profile Trade, 2019). See also James C. Scott, *Seeing Like a State: How Certain Schemes to Improve the Human Condition Have Failed* (Yale University Press, 2020).

[7]Much of the Upanishads (early Hindu wisdom literature) concerns the relation of brahman (ultimate reality) with the self (atman), with many of them concluding that brahman = atman, as all rivers, though traveling in different directions, eventually enter the sea. Views within Hinduism widely vary on how atman is related to brahman, though many do end up equivocating the self with the universe.

at least not on their terms. God is the one who makes everything beautiful in its time. Humans may desire eternity but were made in time and for time. And that means that we were not made for the rest of resolution or fusion, or for aseity. Time is essential to story, which is the medium of meaning making. Time is not about resolutions, about reaching goals or engineering outcomes; time is about character development through relationships.

The (False) Gospel of Desire and Rest

We could reframe what we've just suggested about the dream home and aseity by telling it as a *story* of desire. Every story has a problem and its solution. The description of the problem determines what shape the solution—or good news—will take. The problem we face is an experience of not-at-homeness in our environment, which feels like chaos and disorder, a feeling we also label *injustice*. Things are out of place. Something isn't right. Something is broken. God can't exist, because how could such a God tolerate the way things are? Therefore the gospel, the story that encapsulates our hopes and values, in which people have lived for millennia, is to attain the rest of cosmic order, justice, making everything fall into place. This is a rest of home. And whatever gospel we live by promises to transform the world into a home for us, a suitable environment in which we do not experience lack, need, injustice, or disorder.

The problem with the dream-home gospel is the problem with nearly every human-made gospel. It narrates a solution in the same terms of solving the stated problem, confirming the reality of the problem and legitimizing the problem. Put another way, our hamartiology (doctrine of sin) determines our soteriology (doctrine of salvation), meaning that such gospels encase us in a closed narrative in which the solution is the problem. But what if, in our desire to attain the rest of aseity, the desire for godlikeness, we misidentify the problem? In other words, what if the environment wasn't a problem to be solved by a dream house, even a paradisal dream house offered by popular religion? What if the problem was this kind of desire itself? In the Bible, this desire is described as a yearning to be like God in knowing good and evil, and through this knowing to devise a rest of our own.

The Gospel of Sabbath

By contrast, the good news offered by the Bible is the hard-to-hear story of a rest we have not created, a solution that upends the very things we see as ultimate goods to achieve. It is a dream home not in the sense of an environment that conforms to our will but an environment that breaks the endless loop of desire for fulfillment of our own devising. It is a *real* home, not a dream in any sense. Rather than dissolving diversity, reducing variables, or simulating freedom and self-expression, Sabbath is a call to a maturity that reconciles our desires with those of others—not by coming to agreement on all points but by learning to live with difference. In God's kingdom, otherness is secured by relationship with the God who alone can relate to all things in infinite diversity. We will find that the good news of the Bible is rest in God rather than in the expression of godlike faculties for the creation of rest. In other words, we'll find that the Sabbath gospel is grace, a gift, not the fruit of human cocreation with God.

The Sabbath gospel does not reform the world in the way we might imagine or desire. The Sabbath reforms *us* and our desire, and in doing so transforms the people of God to be the renewal that creation has long awaited.[8] The Sabbath gospel moves toward relationships of mature responsibility. It is a gospel that describes rest as an adaptation of the self to a nexus of ever-changing relationships. It is not a vision of stasis but a vision of constant discovery of uncontrollable and unmanageable others. Sabbath is the exodus from Babel, the leaving behind of a desire to express unity in concrete ascending forms that secure the oneness of a people through standardized identities. The Sabbath gospel is about the irreducible diversity of the creation, including human beings, who find their unity not in the simplicity of group identities but in giving up the management of complexity in submission to the Creator. Indeed, the goal of

---

[8] Rom 8:21.

creation is not in some final resolution but in a durable relationship of faithfulness. God's plan to dwell with his creation demands that the way be prepared by his people. This is a task of replanting a garden of faithful people in the midst of a wasteland of human sin.

Put another way, the gospel of the Sabbath is the rejection of the dream home by living in the world as it is. It is learning, like all the other creatures, to adapt to it first before growing in maturity to master it and have dominion responsibly.

The first step of the Sabbath journey is to leave behind the dream home—which in Scripture is signified by empires such as Egypt and Babylon—and journey to the wilderness, where the forces of chaos dwell and where we will be tempted, tried, tested, and reformed as we learn responsibility within the environment of our journey rather than by seeking to rest by conforming the world into our own dwelling.

So where is this Sabbath in which we find ourselves at home in a world not of our creating but of God's? Or, maybe more accurately: When is it? As we'll see in chapter three, which focuses on Psalm 92, our invitation to Sabbath rest is issued not from an unfallen creation or the consummated reconciliation at the end of time. Instead, our invitation to belong to God's real home of Sabbath is issued from the very midst of a world that threatens to destroy itself in order to create a home for itself. We may be in the middle of that homelessness, but we are not left there.

The Sabbath gospel is a journey to take with others in order to practice the kinds of responsibility and maturity discussed in this chapter. This implies asking ourselves some questions. What story have we been telling ourselves, and what kind of resolution have we sought? That is, what is our own *dream* home where we come to rest? And if we were to ever attain that dream, what next?

Group Discussion Questions

1. What are some of the dream homes (e.g., dream job, dream partner, dream body, dream life) you have entertained or pursued?

2. What are some of the dream homes your church community may be enamored by?

3. In what ways do you see the surrounding culture, society, or government enlisting you or others into a dream-home project of someone else's devising?

THE SABBATH PSALM

Beginning in the Middle

IN THE LAST CHAPTER, we started our journey toward Sabbath from the place we find ourselves: within the world's misguided pursuit of rest. We looked at the distorted human desire for aseity, which strives for self-sufficiency, epitomized by the notion of the dream home. Sabbath directly resists the dream home by issuing an invitation to a maturity that reconciles competing desires and plans for aseity. Sabbath ultimately encourages unity amid diversity. It is the rest found when all members of a community dwell together in peace.[1]

The next step on our journey toward this Sabbath encounters a fork in the road. The traditional theological path speaks of first principles, of who God is prior to creation—God as God *apart* from creation. We'll briefly tread this path only to demonstrate how it leads astray. Our true course, the Sabbath gospel, transforms how we begin talking about God.

The Road More Traveled: Beginning with God's Aseity

As an academic discipline, Western theology is deeply influenced by Greek philosophy and metaphysics (discussions of foundational principles

---

[1] Ps 133:1.

"beyond physics").[2] This is most evident in discussions about God in isolation from creation. Theologies that begin here often start by describing God in terms such as *omniscience* (God's all-knowingness), *omnipotence* (God's all-powerfulness), and *omnipresence* (God's being everywhere).[3] These terms are imported to the Bible. The Bible does not offer much data on the essence of God, on who God is *a se*—in other words, by himself. Instead, from its opening pages the Bible depicts God in relation, starting with God's very first act of creating.

The Bible's authors begin with God's covenantal relationship with his people, not his aseity. The Bible's foundational discussion of God is a matter of *hesed*, the Hebrew noun used frequently of God's faithfulness. It refers to a love proved *in time*. Throughout the Bible, God's people both praise and plead with God for his *hesed*.[4] And it is not a coincidence that Jesus, when confronting his contemporaries on their misunderstanding of the Sabbath, refers them to an Old Testament passage on *hesed*.[5]

The very biblical definition of God is thus not a question of ontology (of the nature of being) but character revealed in relationship, "I am the LORD your God, who brought you out of the land of Egypt."[6] The "I AM" of the tetragrammaton found in Exodus 3:14 is not a great statement that God's essence is being itself but a statement of God's reliability. "I will be whom I will be" is proclaimed in the same context in which God highlights the relationship of Yahweh to the patriarchs: "I am . . . the God of Abraham, the God of Isaac, and the God Jacob."[7]

This is a God of concrete action, not abstract metaphysics; a God of people, not principles.

---

[2]Plato offers one of the earliest uses of the Greek word *theology* in *Republic* 379a, where it is contrasted to myths about the gods. Here Plato assumes that God is good and the prime mover as he considers the problem of evil and the problematic nature of portrayals of divinity in the old Greek poets.

[3]We aren't necessarily contesting these terms of God, but the problem when theology starts here is that it assumes these characteristics of God a priori instead of deriving them from the biblical witness of God's actual relation with creation in time.

[4]Ex 15:13; 34:7; Ps 17:7; 25:7.

[5]Mt 12:7-8; Hos 6:6.

[6]Ex 20:2.

[7]Ex 3:6.

God reveals himself in kingship, his will to rule over his people in a relation of responsibility, and insists—in a phrase that reverberates through the passages of Scripture—"I will be your God, and you shall be my people."[8] We could say, to paraphrase Philippians 2, that as in the incarnation Christ trades Godhood for servanthood, so in creation God trades aseity for kingship. That he does so makes him no less *a se* as a king than it makes Jesus less God as a servant. But it demonstrates the character of God and what kind of relations are faithful to the kingdom of *this* God-King.

Talk of kingship implicates God's sovereignty, which introduces a tension. The world seems anything *but* under the complete rule of God. Far more prevalent in Scripture than philosophical questions of God's essence are existential questions of God's covenantal faithfulness alongside a volatile and hostile world. The Bible is peppered with questions such as, "Why do the nations conspire?" and "Why does the way of the guilty prosper?" and "My God, my God, why have you forsaken me?"[9] These questions demand not philosophical principles or treatises but a narrative that accounts for why things are the way they are and where they are ultimately headed. Sovereignty is more of a story and a question in the Bible than it is a theological first principle.[10]

But when theology attempts to describe God-in-Godself, it also attempts to get beyond time and history to eternity, where it is assumed God dwells. A theology that begins with God's aseity also tends to make God's rule timeless, changeless, and therefore logically unassailable.[11] This often leads to the view that everything that happens in time *is* the expression of God's will. From this view, God's sovereignty is a type of personified fatalism, potentially confusing the events of history as the

---

[8] Lev 26:12; Jer 7:23; 11:4; 24:7; 30:22; 31:1, 33; 32:38; Ezek 11:20; 14:11; 36:28; 37:23, 27; Zech 8:8; 13:9; 2 Cor 6:16; Heb 8:10.

[9] Ps 2:1; Jer 12:1; Ps 22:1.

[10] So, e.g., N. T. Wright, *How God Became King: The Forgotten Story of the Gospels* (repr., HarperOne, 2016).

[11] This view of God's aseity, especially as paraded by a doctrine of predestination, is often known simply as Calvinism, though its origins are far earlier than John Calvin and are known outside Christianity too. There are internal debates in Reformed theological circles about the extent and character of God's predestining sovereignty. Our point is not to dive into such a debate but to show that it becomes centrally important because of a false theological starting point in aseity and eternity.

expression of God's will. Such a view fails to perceive that the time of God overlaps human history as a different timeline, a different possibility—one that would exist if God were recognized as king.

Jesus suggests in his descriptions of God's kingdom that human history is a realm that God has *ceded* his sovereignty over while he is also *invading* it with his patient love. This is why Jesus instructs his disciples to pray, "Thy kingdom come" and "deliver us from the evil one"—a clear indication that God does not completely rule the present evil age and that human history is not a revelation of God's will. So on the one hand, God isn't found in the timeline of our history. But on the other hand, neither can we escape this history to attain an aerial view of God outside time. Instead, God *invades* history with Sabbath. Sabbath names the alternate timeline of the sovereignty of God intended by his rest, his dwelling, his abiding as a King at peace.

The sovereignty of God, then, is an unfolding story of God's love and covenantal faithfulness (in Hebrew, *hesed*) as he invades human time with interventions of relationship forming. It is not a static description of God's capacities in a state of timelessness. God's sovereignty does not coerce but allows itself to be rejected. And in the face of this rejection, God chooses to work through a chosen and beloved people to reconcile all things to himself. Sabbath names the kind of relationships that will ultimately obtain when God's kingship comes to completion and when all of God's creation will relate to God and one another in accordance with God's character, not through the forced and prefabricated architecture of the dream home. God's character must be learned *in time* as God's people journey to the Sabbath, where his sovereignty has full reign.

If we cannot theologize by abstraction, by working our way up to heaven by ignoring or bypassing earthbound symbols, any truth about God must be revealed.[12] As Jacques Ellul describes the difference between these two modes, religion *ascends*, but revelation *descends*.[13] While a

---

[12]It is on just this point that famous twentieth-century theologian Karl Barth established the foundation of his theological project, in direct resistance to the popular theologies of his time and their confidence in human reason and investigative tools to arrive at truth claims about God on their own merit.

[13]Jacques Ellul, *Living Faith: Belief and Doubt in a Perilous World*, trans. Peter Heinegg (Harper & Row, 1980), 126-56.

revelation-based theological method is nothing new in Christian history, we believe Sabbath reintroduces this insight in a revitalizing way.

Theologies that begin with God's aseity incorporate a weakness in the foundation of their theological edifice. They attempt, like a misguided ivory tower of Babel, to reach God in a state of timelessness through ladders of abstraction and speculation. In fact, these theological projects are themselves attempting to construct a kind of dream home, a falsified blueprint of God's primordial unity that no creature could ever possess. Taking this fork in the road, then, is to take a loop that leads us back to the previous chapter where we started, returning to continually renovate a theological dream home. This is why academic theology can at times, like Christianity itself, seem so tired.

Scripture does not speak of God before or apart from time.[14] Instead, Scripture speaks of God from *within* time. So to take the next steps of our Sabbath journey, we take the fork that begins in the middle of history, in the midst of conflict. The world as we know it, and time as we experience it, is not the actualization of God's will. It is where God's will is resisted.

The Road Less Traveled: Beginning In Medias Res

In the rest of this chapter, we begin in the middle, in the midst of conflict rather than in an imagined time before time.[15] The Sabbath gospel is exemplified by Psalm 92. In it, we'll find that God's people are those who, while being encompassed by enemies, anticipate God's victory and so are like a living organism rather than a static structure or dream house.

To begin a story in medias res is to begin "in the middle of things." It introduces a story from within its unresolved conflict rather than from its chronological start. This artistic choice seemingly grates against inborn notions of order. People have birthdays, journeys have pioneering steps,

---

[14]Eph 1:4 is a possible exception that proves the rule.
[15]After we initially drafted this chapter, we became aware of two other theological publications that also position themselves as a reflection from the middle. See Miroslav Volf and Ryan McAnnally-Linz, *The Home of God: A Brief Story of Everything* (Brazos, 2022); W. David Buschart and Ryan Tafilowski, *Worth Doing: Fallenness, Finitude, and Work in the Real World* (IVP Academic, 2025).

fires have first sparks: Why not start there? But in medias res touches on a universal aspect of human experience: Everyone starts a narrative of life in the middle of things. We find ourselves thrust into our present circumstances with no choice and little explanation. The march of history long precedes our appearance, and the history texts we meet in school barely get us up to speed on what we missed. Our very birth even evades our memory; its story must be told to us. The psychological record of our own lives starts in the middle, emerging haphazardly from the fog of our first years. The road to adulthood feels almost detective-like, unraveling the familial and political events that shaped us and our times while we were unaware or before we showed up. The journey of adulthood can also entail a degree of resignation, coming to terms with things we cannot account for in a world riddled by uncertainty and pain.

Though the Bible starts with the words "In the beginning," its opening chapters are told and heard long after the prehistoric era they relay, from a people in the midst of turmoil. The primordial era remains beyond our grasp despite the Bible's poetic descriptions.

Dietrich Bonhoeffer, reflecting on the inaccessibility of creation, insists that we can't really know what things were like in the now-lost Garden of Eden.[16] We can talk about it, we can read about it, but we can't *think* our way back to a time before the now-defining conditions of our being and our thinking. To try otherwise would be to set ourselves in the place of God. We can read of God's act of creating at the beginning, but only as those who now reside in the middle. There is no return route to paradise, guarded by a flaming sword; there is only forging forward from the place where we find ourselves.[17] In medias res is an experience that begs for rest, for resolution, both by coming to know the beginning and by seeing the story through to its end. As we will see, the Sabbath gospel intervenes within this middle time of conflict by taking us both back to the beginning and forward to the end.

---

[16]Dietrich Bonhoeffer, *Creation and Fall: A Theological Exposition of Genesis 1–3*, ed. John W. de Gruchy, Dietrich Bonhoeffer Works (Fortress, 2004), 3:39.
[17]Gen 3:24.

Psalm 92 also finds itself in the middle of things as a story of combat between the people of God and their enemies. The psalmist is aware that things are not as they should be, as God's good works are threatened by enemies. But by its end, the psalmist indicates how God's people are to comport themselves in the middle of a hostile world. The psalmist shows how Sabbath orients God's people away from a rebellious world's false constructions by grounding them in God's patient sovereignty, which permits rebellious forces to roam free in their own time.

God's people have always lived in contested times. As chapter two noted, most human efforts to achieve aseity are a rebellion against God's rest. But the charge of God's people has always been to establish themselves in God's order and reign as defined by Sabbath, not in their own structures. Sabbath, we will find, is God's mission to replant the Garden of Eden within the wasteland of humanity's misguided constructions. This garden is the community of God's people.

The World According to the Sabbath Psalm

As the only psalm dedicated to the Sabbath, Psalm 92 curiously never mentions Sabbath after the superscription.[18] Nor are any practices or customs commonly associated with the Sabbath alluded to. One even wonders why it has been dedicated to the Sabbath at all.

But if Sabbath is the opposite of misguided human efforts to achieve aseity and rest, then the themes of this psalm are fitting. The threefold movement of Psalm 92 redirects God's people from artificial rest while indicating how Sabbath is a matter of God's replanting his people as a restored Garden of Eden.[19] Sabbath identifies both the coming era when all of God's rebels will be subdued and the ways God's people anticipate

---

[18]Though interpreters do note a sevenfold structure to the psalm, including seven references to God's divine name, which may hark back to the seven days of creation, climaxing with God's Sabbath rest. Jonathan Friedmann, "Psalm 92, Shabbat, and the Temple," *The Jewish Bible Quarterly* 48, no. 4 (2020): 247.

[19]Brueggemann and Bellinger write, "Commentators take a variety of views on what constitutes the parts of the psalm, but a three-part structure seems to be the best option." Walter Brueggemann and William H. Bellinger Jr., *Psalms* (Cambridge University Press, 2014), 398.

that final rest in the present era. They do so not primarily by executing their wills in the world or defeating God's enemies themselves but by respectively celebrating and anticipating God's present and unfolding work. It is by grounding themselves in and receiving God's action that God's people find meaning and bear fruit, even in the midst of a rebellious world. Psalm 92 thus serves as a nutshell presentation of the Sabbath gospel.

Resting in God's Works (Psalm 92:1-5)

The psalm's opening verses display the beating heart of Sabbath from the vantage of a human participant: reveling in the works of God. The Sabbath keeper is primarily one who delights in God.[20] This is the opposite of aseity (self-satisfaction). The psalmist unites words and music by submitting them to the works of God rather than human works. Two Hebrew words for "works" (*po ʿal* and *ma ʿaseh*) appear right after each other in the center of the Hebrew text of Psalm 92:4, as if God's immense work were piling on top of itself in the center of the sentence. Around this monument of God's works is the psalmist's jubilant declaration. One interpreter suggests that this verse does not just state the depth of God's thoughts but acknowledges that God's ongoing design is deeply embedded in the created order. This plan continues to unfold even in the face of its disruptions by God's enemies, and in a manner that escapes human comprehension (see Eccles 3:11).[21] It is just this depth to God's plans that the fool of Psalm 92:5 fails to comprehend. The Sabbath, these five verses attest, is the opposite of trying to fix what we think is incomplete in God's work. Sabbath is instead a matter of actively and gratefully receiving what God has already done and anticipating what God will do.

---

[20]The subtitle of a volume on Sabbath by Jewish scholar Abraham Millgram quite succinctly defines Sabbath this way: It is "the day of delight." Abraham E. Millgram, *Sabbath: The Day of Delight* (Jewish Publication Society of America, 1965).

[21]W. Dennis Tucker, "The Ordered World of Psalm 92," *Old Testament Essays* 32, no. 2 (2019): 365.

The Unrest of God's Enemies (Psalm 92:6-11)

The second section of the psalm casts a long shadow over the opening portrait of personal intimacy and joy with God. Here we learn that God's ways are resisted on earth by wicked evildoers who rail against God as enemies. Enemies are a recurring theme in Scripture, especially the Psalms. On average, the Hebrew term ’oyeb ("enemy," Ps 92:9) appears twice every psalm, though peculiarly these enemies are rarely specified. The closest thing to a general definition of the term appears in Psalm 41:7, which describes enemies as those who "imagine the worst" for you. Otherwise, the term remains polyvalent in meaning. Enemies can be personal, national, or even cosmic. Sometimes context indicates which kind of enemy is in view. In other instances a particular circumstance, such as sickness or war, is the enemy at hand. But the identity of the enemy in some ways does not matter: "The important thing is not the precise description of the enemies, but the theological classification of their work as contrary to God."[22] This will introduce us to the basic dichotomy operative from Genesis 4 onward between the people of God, who live with God as King, and those who do not. What unites these enemies is the rejection of God's sovereignty, so they naturally take many forms, personal and impersonal. These enemies prompt a desire for relief from enemies, a desire found through many psalms and other parts of Scripture.[23] Thus God promises David—a man whose life, like that of Israel, was plagued by adversaries and rivals—that the reign of his son Solomon will be one of peace and rest from his enemies.[24]

These verses are also rich in messianic symbolism and imagery, as they trace a common motif in ancient Near Eastern literature: The victory of a god over his enemies was thought to bring about his enthronement and

---

[22] G. Johannes Botterweck and Helmer Ringgren, eds., *Theological Dictionary of the Old Testament*, rev. ed., trans. John T. Willis (Eerdmans, 1974), 1:213, 215-18. For contemporary readers, the unspecified enemy of the psalms is pastorally ripe; we can fill in the blank with any number of contemporary enemies we might experience today: a school bully, a rival coworker, an aggressive cancer.

[23] Deut 12:10; 25:19; Josh 1:15; 1 Kings 8:56.

[24] 1 Chron 22:9. Botterweck and Ringgren, *Theological Dictionary of the Old Testament*, 1:215.

usually coincided with temple building.²⁵ This psalm similarly refers to God's temple in its final portion. This pattern is also found in other biblical passages, such as the Song of the Sea in Exodus 15, which follow God's destruction of Israel's Egyptian enslavers and assailants and anticipates the establishment of God's house in the Promised Land. Psalm 93 also traces these themes of God ascending his temple throne following his mastery of tumultuous waters.²⁶ The messianic figure spotlighted in Psalm 92:10-11, who anticipates the downfall of God's enemies and the commencement of the figure's reign as God's representative, does nothing actively to effect the destruction of these enemies. God exalts and anoints the author, who in turn simply sees and hears the end of the assailants. This nexus of themes—of God coming to rest on his throne to reign following the defeat of his enemies and at the establishing of his temple—complements our understanding of Christ's passion, which we will explore in more detail in chapter nine.

This psalm is a declaration of faith that God will reign over a world that feels profoundly rebellious. It attests that Sabbath rest is not a matter of achieving a state of comfortable control over one's environment. Sabbath rest is a matter of learning to inhabit the world as it is before engaging in self-willed violence. It is a matter of learning to live within God's time even when it lies beyond human understanding and perception.²⁷ As one commentator articulates, "The chief question that lingers beneath the surface of this particular psalm is not 'Does Yahweh rule,' but 'Is the world

---

[25]Friedmann, "Psalm 92, Shabbat," 238. Basil of Caesarea offers an expected example of a christological reading of this section of Ps 92, although he is tripped up by an ancient textual variant that reads the horn here as belonging to a unicorn. See Quentin F. Wesselschmidt, ed., *Psalms 51–150*, Ancient Christian Commentary on Scripture, Old Testament 8 (IVP Academic, 20), 177. For more on unicorns in the Bible, see G. P. Wagenfuhr, *Unfortunate Words of the Bible: A Biblical Theology of Misunderstandings* (Cascade Books, 2019), 8-9.

[26]Friedmann, "Psalm 92, Shabbat," 238.

[27]This is one way of reading the main outcome of the story of Job, whose individual complaint runs aground in the face of the immensity of God's created order and his relative place within it. Augustine similarly insists that often what humans perceive as disorder of God's creation is in fact a lack of understanding of the role of each element within God's created order. Augustine even wonders whether God intentionally leaves the purpose of things unclear to humans as an antidote to pride (*City of God* 11.22).

in which humans live and over which God rules rightly ordered?'"[28] This psalm suggests that God's people are those who answer yes even as they raise the question. And their yes takes on a particular posture, even as they await God's final action.

Unmasking False Strategies Against the Enemy

Psalm 92 highlights that Sabbath is a matter of sovereignty as it contrasts the reign of God with the experience of being surrounded by enemies, thrown into the midst of a history hostile to the people of God. God's good creation is under assault by enemies who attempt to undermine the goodness, beauty, and peace of God's created order. Psalm 92 also shows that there is another kind of character who inhabits the world stage alongside God's enemies and loyal followers. This person is the "dullard" (Ps 92:6), whose folly cannot fathom that God's antagonists are doomed to failure.

There are two kinds of fools, who straddle the camps of the people of God and the rebellious powers of the world: those who collaborate and those who retreat out of fear. Both lack a whole life–encompassing faithful commitment to God but find solace or consolation elsewhere. Collaborators take the world too seriously and lack the Sabbath vision Hebrews 10–11 discusses. Often collaboration looks as simple as making faith into a set of principles that do not demand fealty to God but are derived from religious wisdom. Collaborators make bricks from faith for the common project of building the dream home of Babel, working for a central goal of a tower. Those who retreat into artificial isolation likewise aim at building some safe space by backing away from the world. This retreat mentality equally builds a dream home, but it starts by building walls first.

God's Response to Enemies

Both kinds of fools fail to perceive the impermanence of God's enemies (Ps 92:7, 9, 11). God's enemies will not last. The impermanent nature of

---

[28]Tucker, "Ordered World of Psalm 92," 358.

God's enemies is illustrated by their comparison to annual grasses that fade with the seasons. This contrasts with the perennial permanence of the righteous, who like trees are deeply rooted. The character of time is revealed by these differing plants: rapid cycles of growth and death of ever new schemes in opposition to the slow growth of mature trees. In Psalm 92:9 the psalmist declares the fate of God's enemies again.[29] They will "perish" and "be scattered." Though the same Hebrew word is not used in Genesis 11, we wonder whether there may be some allusion here to God's scattering the builders of the tower of Babel. God does not destroy the builders of Babel outright, though the act of scattering does eliminate their work to build a construction in resistance to God's plans. As we will see with God's judgment throughout this book, there is an intentional ambiguity to what God's justice will look like. It is spoken of in Scripture with highly destructive imagery but filled with hope that such things need never come to pass.[30] We wonder whether the previous verbs, then, may not necessarily indicate the full annihilation of God's enemies but perhaps the destruction of their *status* as enemies. Perhaps God does not destroy his enemies by annihilating them but by disciplining and reforming them.

The psalm does not say, but the possibility remains open.[31] But even if this prospect remains, neither does this psalm foreclose the possibility of their utter destruction. It may be left to the enemies themselves to determine what their end will be. Either way, whether God's enemies are annihilated or are converted from their status as enemies, true rest resides in God's work to forge peace. This rest is the opposite of the false rest of the dream home, by which humans mistakenly attempt to achieve their own aseity by manipulation and control of their environment. Psalm 92 reminds us that true rest is found in the defeat of God's enemies. And even if this final rest is one for which God's people still wait, it is one they can foreshadow.

---

[29]Together Ps 92:7 and Ps 92:9 straddle Ps 92:8, which forms the hinge and also the pinnacle of the psalm. Just four words in length—literally "you on-high forever Yahweh"—it concisely relays the permanency and extent of God's exaltation.

[30]As in the book of Jonah; 2 Pet 3; and Revelation.

[31]The next chapters will explain how the flood of Noah sets the context for the sovereignty of God to be expressed in delayed judgment.

Replanting Eden Through Sabbath People (Psalm 92:12-15)

If God's foes are as ephemeral as grass, God's followers are as lasting as trees. Both trees mentioned here, the date palm and the cedar of Lebanon, were used to construct and decorate the temple. Psalm 92:13 also describes these righteous-people-as-trees as planted in the temple itself, referred to in the Bible's prevalent parallelism as both "the house of Yahweh" and "the courts of our God." This same temple elsewhere in the biblical narrative is described as God's "resting place."[32] This is where he comes to rest, having put all of creation in order; this is where God is enthroned as King, having taken care of his enemies. Thus, this psalm simultaneously portrays God's people as trees planted in the temple and akin to the trees that themselves decorated or constituted the temple structure. This also indicates that the physical building of the temple is only a sign that points to the reality of God's restful Sabbath reign. The psalmist does not imagine that the righteous ones are actually, physically planted in the courts of the temple, immobilized and never to leave its gates. Instead, they are rooted in the political order the temple points to—of God's reigning and ruling among his people in peace. God's people replace the temple as a kind of garden-forest, a body politic rooted in a common soil that constitutes God's household order.[33] God's very people are his replanting of the Garden of Eden. As trees in an arid or desert environment, their very rootedness fixes the soil, giving a whole environment the stability of rest it needs to thrive.

To this point, Psalm 92 has been largely narrated from a first-person perspective. Its conclusion transitions to a communal dimension. The careful reverberation of the opening verb from Psalm 92:2 (Hebrew *nagad*), translated initially as "declare" but appearing as "showing" in Psalm 92:15, retrospectively casts the whole psalm as a communal statement that is also caught up into the mouth of God's Messiah. The

---

[32] Ps 132:8, 14.
[33] Significantly, other biblical passages throughout the canon suggest that individually and collectively, people are like trees, including Edenic trees. See Judg 9; Ps 1; Ezek 31; Mk 8:24.

psalm closes with a first-person quotation put in the mouth of the collective righteous. This psalm suggests that good works are not a matter of doing or achieving anything but rather of setting up signs that welcome God's work and bear fruit that can yield only from organic connection to God's will and reign.

The close of the Sabbath psalm gives us an image of God's people as solidly grounded even in a climate of erosion. Even in a bare desert, God's people can become great trees that might yet give shade and comfort that invites others into the oasis of God's Sabbath reign. Likewise, in contrast to our description of the dream house, this forest is planted, rooted, nourished, and watered. Instead of building a simplified artificial environment out of lumber, God's people are grown in the rich soil of God's own created environment. Instead of dead wood, dimensionally cut and reassembled with nails and sacrificed to the building of a collective artificial reality, God's people are freed from building houses for others (as in Egypt) to a flourishing life of bearing fruit.

Conclusion: Sabbath Replants the Garden of God

Psalm 92 establishes and distills some of the central threads of this book. First, Sabbath means that the defining characteristic of God's people begins with their grateful and joyful reception of God's work. Such reception sets up signs that direct attention to God's character and action. Second, Sabbath-shaped action occurs even when God's people are surrounded by enemies, agents who resist and rebel against God's work, who in doing so inflict violence and harm. The perennial temptation is for God's people to respond in fear by either compromising with or cowering under these forces. Both responses falsely assume that God's enemies pose a lasting threat to God's order. God's people should rightly long for the full expression of God's will and reign over his creation, and for the quelling of all rebellion and the complete ascendancy of God to his throne. But this will not occur through any action on the part of God's people, whether collaboration or resignation or even activism, but only by taking root in God's time.

The Sabbath-eyed psalmist knows that God's enemies will not last; they are as fleeting and ephemeral as grass in a desert land.[34] God's people, on the other hand, achieve the lasting permanence of stately trees, befitting the temple and the palatial Garden of Eden.[35] We've seen that the metaphorical placement of God's people in Psalm 92 as trees in the temple courtyards renders the building of the temple itself a metaphor. God's ongoing work in creation is not a matter of setting up static institutions or structures but of replanting the Garden of Eden through a community of people. Even in the midst of a hostile world, the people of God can achieve lasting significance not by any of their own efforts but by bearing fruit that is the organic outcome of their connection with his kingdom. God is resowing his garden in a rebellious world as a symbol of the sovereignty that is coming so it will one day be "on earth as it is in heaven." *This* is the hope and promise of Sabbath to which God's people are invited to participate and anticipate even now, from the midst of the middle in which they find themselves, even while surrounded by God's enemies.

In other words, God's people are called to give up their dream home projects of engineering an environment catered to eliminate their needs and dependencies. Instead, they are invited to *be* the foundation species of an oasis garden, creating a living, harmonious ecosystem that bears fruit for the nourishment and delight of others. The dream home is a parade of static, artificial, and infertile renovations, ever new but always cycling through hope and despair like the annual cycle of grasses. A garden is dynamic, communal, and abundant. Psalm 92 indicates that God's people can begin this task even while estranged from their native soil. They can begin to bear fruit that gives a foretaste of life from a different order of time. The image of a fixed garden may seemingly sharply contrast with our metaphor of Sabbath as a pilgrimage gospel. But the

---

[34] See Is 40:6-8.
[35] While many modern gardens are imagined primarily as vegetable, flower, or decorative Italian or Japanese gardens, a Persian *pardes* ("paradise," from Greek), or Assyrian garden of such as that of Sennacherib at Nineveh, was known as an oasis, with water engineering supporting dozens of species of trees.

dissonance is only apparent. The journey of the Sabbath gospel is one that even trees can make, as this is a journey through time, a journey of maturation that creates rest as trees themselves do in their own maturation, bearing in their wood the annual rings of time. As Psalm 1 portrays, to journey well is not necessarily to go far geographically but to be watered by a different time, unfazed by the vagaries of human history and the works of evil.

But in order to allow Scripture to do its work of penetrating human time even while clothed in time-bound language, we need to permit ourselves to inhabit *its* timeline. And although we have rightly begun from the middle, at some point we need to engage its account of time's beginning.

Group Discussion Questions

1. How have you tended to think about God: outside time and creation or in the midst of time and creation? What implications are there of such thinking for how you understand the gospel?

2. How do you think you and/or your community are more inclined to respond to enemies of God's will—through collaboration or retreat? What does this tend to look like? What might a more measured, Psalm 92–like response entail?

PART 2

Sabbath Through Scripture

SABBATH AT FIRST

IN CHAPTER THREE, we took a brief tour down the well-trodden theological path of contemplating the eternal divine in isolation, and we backtracked to begin in the middle with Psalm 92. The Sabbath gospel thus began with an embattled, surrounded, contested sovereignty of the God who works through people formation rather than structural formation. Now we can reread the telling of the creation with the eyes and ears of exiles rather than as would-be carpenters or engineers. Here we will find that God's story is not conquering chaos to build a dream home but that God is the homemaking Father who aims to produce mature members of a household.[1]

---

[1] In this book we choose to retain masculine pronouns for God. While we welcome and applaud the insistence that God is *not* gendered, which finds resonance with Genesis's opening insistence that men and women *together* image God, this book unashamedly uses the expressions of the Bible, confident that they are not perpetuating an ancient form of patriarchy or legitimizing a paternal monarchism any more than they support modern conceptions of feminism, gender fluidity, or sexual identity. The Bible is not timeless. It is a revelation of God's time in human time and bears the accent of that time in the idiom of a foreign one. We do not redeem our understanding of God by replacing male language for female language. But neither do we think that the solution is to avoid gendered language altogether in a manner that demands significant revision of the biblical language by which God is revealed. What is required instead is a renewal of our imagination through our commitment to the biblical story. See also Amy L. B. Peeler, *Women and the Gender of God* (Eerdmans, 2022) which explores a theology of gender that ultimately contends that we should retain masculine and Father language about God so as not to diminish the role of Mary as mother.

The First Creation Account: The Environment of Sabbath

God's sovereignty is a story of love working itself out in time.[2] Any story—or any good one, at least—has a setting, a world furnished with distinct features and populated by particular inhabitants. Genesis 1 establishes the theater in which the story of God's sovereignty will occur. It sets the stage, laying out the landscape of the first Sabbath as well as the pain of Sabbath unfulfilled and the hope of Sabbath completed. Genesis 1 plots God's careful separation and apportioning of the elements of creation—light and dark, earth and sky, tree and plant, sun and moon, fish and birds, animals and humans—across a succession of time periods called *days*. For Genesis 1, there is no space without time. Space is not an empty container but a description of near and distant relations. It's not isolation; it's connection. A static, spatial focus in theology is deficient because it neglects that God is revealed to us only in time, in relationship.

The conjoining of space and time, each described by the relationships of things, creates *place*. Emplacement exposes the lie of aseity that there is some identity to obtain or discover by the abstraction of environment, by the elimination or manipulation of all external variables that might encroach on one's self-referential satisfaction. Environment is instead the very grounds of true sovereignty, love, and freedom. This is why throughout the Bible particular place names are crucial to the meaning of the story: Sodom and Gomorrah, Moriah and Sinai, Meribah and Massah, Gethsemane and Golgotha, Smyrna and Pergamum, Eden and Jerusalem. God's Sabbath does not take place until there is a place for it to occur.

---

[2] Concerning the phrasing "first creation account": Some readers may not be familiar with a reading of Genesis that is commonly accepted by biblical scholars and theologians, that the opening chapters of Genesis do not relay a single creation account but rather two creation stories that have been joined together. This second creation account begins with a new heading in Gen 2:4.

Chaoskampf: Creation Is Not a Battle

As the Bible sets the scene of its story, we might ask: What is the initial condition, or precondition, out of which creation occurs? In Genesis this is *tohu wabohu*, formlessness and nothingness, which is portrayed as the vast ocean. It is important to ask whether Genesis is narrating an order-out-of-chaos story, as so many other creation myths do.[3] We do not believe so. In fact, we think that the *Chaoskampf* ("chaos war") reading of Genesis, which maintains that the opening account of creation is God's ordering of chaos, not only is a misinterpretation but also seriously conflicts with the narrative thrust of both Genesis and the rest of the Bible.[4] What's more, it produces a faulty mission for the people of God that—as in other ancient myths—focuses on pillaging the corpse of creation to fabricate durable structures. *Chaoskampf* is the mythical form and justification of Babylonian-style imperial conquest the Bible labors to expose and undo.

Chaos has its origin in Greek creation myth in which *chaos* is itself the name of a primordial god. Other cultures' creation myths, such as the Sumerian Enuma Elish, have chaos monsters such as Tiamat, who is slain in battle and out of whose corpse the world is formed. Other famous myths of the day, such as the Epic of Gilgamesh or the Heracles cycle, show that the forces of chaos remain in monstrosities and in the untamed natural world, and that these must be slain by the hero to secure safety for civilization to flourish in peace. Not only is Gilgamesh creating *Lebensraum*, but he is "opening the wilderness" to human construction by deforestation.[5]

---

[3]That Gen 1 is *Chaoskampf* was proposed by Hermann Gunkel based on comparison with the Babylonian Enuma Elish. But others, such as Claus Westermann, have rejected this. More recently, JoAnn Scurlock and others offer copious detail in arguing against Gen 1 as *Chaoskampf*. See JoAnn Scurlock and Richard H. Beal, eds., *Creation and Chaos: A Reconsideration of Hermann Gunkel's Chaoskampf Hypothesis* (Penn State University Press, 2021). Also David Toshio Tsumura, *Creation and Destruction: A Reappraisal of the Chaoskampf Theory in the Old Testament* (Penn State University Press, 2021).

[4]So also J. Richard Middleton, *The Liberating Image: The Imago Dei in Genesis 1* (Brazos, 2005), 163-64.

[5]We intentionally use the German term for "living space" because it was a common justification of the Nazi Party for their war of aggression, demoting those, often Slavs, who occupied the

In many ways, these creation myths bear striking similarities to the dream house of artificial reality we previously discussed. But the displacement of creation, undesirable peoples, creatures, and plants is decisively *not* how creation occurs in the Bible.[6] Genesis itself is careful not to narrate any kind of battle. God does not create by violence, nor is the ensuing violence of Genesis 4–11 cosmic in perspective. The creativity that bursts from sex and war in Genesis's account of the lineage of Cain is human alone in its origin. Genesis intentionally sets up the lines of Cain and Seth to contrast the motivating logic of these different perspectives.

Psychologically speaking, chaos is the experience of disorientation and lack of control that leads to despair. What is needed is a change of perspective, of being outfitted with appropriate tools to navigate the experience. This change of perspective is exactly what God invites of Job at the climactic close of that book. Job has spent several dozen chapters despairing of his undeserved suffering, with his so-called friends attempting—unsuccessfully—to rationalize his experience with tidy theological platitudes. God's retort to both is surprising. He exhorts Job to expand his outlook and consider not just his isolated and personal experience but the whole cosmic canvas of creation in which his small story takes place. God insists that Job look at aspects of creation that from the first blush of a human gaze might appear chaotic, unruly, and threatening: a wild ox that refuses to plow, a negligent ostrich mother whose pace can outstrip a horse and rider, the bloodsucking offspring of a bird of prey, and the supposed chaos monsters Behemoth and Leviathan, who refuse to succumb to human weapons or instruments of control.[7] God parades these unbridled and even monstrous creatures to both expose and undo Job's *Chaoskampf*-like vision and to consider them not as grotesque

---

desired space as less worthy of it than the master race, i.e., Germans. This is a relatively common theme across human empires throughout history.

[6]The Israelite conquest as depicted in Joshua might seem to contradict this statement. However, see John H. Walton and J. Harvey Walton, *The Lost World of the Israelite Conquest: Covenant, Retribution, and the Fate of the Canaanites* (IVP Academic, 2017), for detailed refutations of the many assumptions about this text.

[7]Job 39; 40:15–41:34.

inconveniences to or aberrations of human life and purpose but as causes for wonder.

From the misguided vantage of chaos, which is the mirror inverse of aseity, these animals are undomesticated in the literal sense of the word: They do not belong to the human domicile, the human project of the dream home; they are bugs to be eliminated or not factored in. But God insists otherwise. These wild features of God's creation belong to the very world Job must learn to find his place in and call home. This is the lesson Job must master before he can come to terms with his inscrutable suffering and find peace. Growing up in God's household does not mean achieving victory over chaos, or domination and simplification of his order, but instead learning to dwell with wildness. This is mature love. The true defeat of chaos is not cosmos but right relationship under the sovereignty of the Creator. Reconciliation, not domination, lies at the heart of the Sabbath gospel.

Yet much of history is a story of the human attempt to reject creation as home and instead to domesticate or de-monstrate that which is pejoratively considered undomesticated or monstrous. This is why the heroic myths of slaying dragons or other chaos monsters follow the major plot lines of human history, which are shaped by imperialism, colonialism, and now—especially in the contemporary West—commercialism. Each of these isms and the actors that exemplify them—Babylon and Byzantium, the United Kingdom and the United States, Apple and Amazon—are efforts to instill order over perceived disorder by means of simplification, standardization, and force, whether the force of sword, symbol, or finances—or some combination thereof. All of these, in some way, are an effort to impose a kind of dream home, legitimized by a narrative of *Chaoskampf*, so that, civilizationally speaking, chaos is everything unconquered and not exploited by urban empires.

This is not to say that there is no biblical category of some kind of primordial formlessness that God orders. But the order God brings to creation is not over a chaos that implies violence, struggle, confusion, and lack of control. This is cast into relief when Genesis 1 is compared with other creation myths that do involve explicit violence.[8] The Hebrew word *tohu* in Genesis 1:2 denotes preexistent unformed matter in relation to desert and waters being boundaryless space. This is not equivalent to the Greek *chaos*, or that of other ancient Near Eastern primordial gods or goddesses, or even the golden ages of many other religions, because the biblical *tohu* is not a power or force. It doesn't represent the projection of the inverse of the social order.[9]

Tohu instead refers to something unformed and meaningless to which God gives order and meaning. It is like a blank canvas. *Chaos* is like a canvas splattered with wet paint, still able to be reorganized into something meaningful but in its current state indecipherable. *Chaos* describes the difference between the human dream home and the experience of reality. Ironically, it is through the attempt to domesticate the world of supposed and falsely perceived chaos around them that humans risk rendering it into *tohu*—into an uninhabitable void, a canvas so overlaid with competing projects and colors that it becomes again a uniform canvas, not of white but of brown. As Isaiah makes clear, this is not where God is to be found.[10]

This is perhaps one reason why the Hebrew Scriptures do not record any New Year's celebrations. There are no reenactments of the primordial state in the Bible, as seem central to many other religious traditions.[11] Instead, as we will see, the reenactment of a creation story is found in the exodus and Passover: a story not of human civilization overcoming the

---

[8]Examples abound from Norse and Germanic, to ancient Near Eastern, to some Egyptian, Native American, Greek, and others. There are very few exceptional nonviolent or nonsexual creation stories, including some from native North American peoples.

[9]For more on primordial order inversions, see Roger Caillois, *Man and the Sacred* (repr., University of Illinois Press, 2001); Mircea Eliade, *The Sacred and The Profane: The Nature of Religion*, trans. Willard R. Trask (Harcourt Brace, 1987).

[10]Is 45:18-19.

[11]The origin of Rosh Hashanah in rabbinic Judaism is put in Lev 23:23-25, the Festival of *Teruah* ("shouts/blasts"), but this is explicitly stated to be in the seventh month. Thus, later Jewish linking of Rosh Hashanah to creation is an extrabiblical tradition, and scholarship has no settled opinion on what the *Teruah* represents. See Jacob Milgrom, *Leviticus 23–27: A New Translation with Introduction and Commentary* (Yale University Press, 2021), 2011-19.

chaos of the natural order but of God's setting humanity free from the exploitation of human empire by bringing them to rest. This rest occurs in his presence in the wilderness through a *Chaoskampf* in which the waters are parted and the monsters (Egyptian oppressors) are slain.[12] The true *chaos* that must be overcome is not a *chaos* latent in the created or precreated order but of human constructions. God overcomes *chaos* not in creation but on the cross.

If Genesis were narrating a story of God achieving victory over chaos through domination and simplification, then we would see the human mission as participation in joining God against primordial forces of disorder by human order, and we would quickly fall into the projection trap of nearly every other religion—that God and the creation myth are simply the story of our own society writ large into the cosmos. Instead, we suggest that chaos is not an entity in itself. Instead it is a human experience of a lack of control. Chaos, in other words, is not an actual state but a particular perception of reality, and a false one at that. Chaos is a hermeneutical error of transposing a feeling of fear onto the structure of the world itself. There is no chaos to God; there are only rebels and prodigals. God is love, and perfect love casts out fear through knowing and trusting rather than control or conquest.

What if, instead of reading Genesis as portraying God, and humans after him, as forging and maintaining order out of chaos—as both original ancient myths and more contemporary theologies of work would have it—we instead read Genesis as portraying God filling a void and dwelling with wildness?[13] The void is not in a contest with God, for it is over the void that the Spirit of God is hovering, and it is to the trackless wastes that

---

[12]That Ps 74 links the exodus to creation has been observed by, e.g., Michael S. Heiser, *The Unseen Realm: Recovering the Supernatural Worldview of the Bible* (Lexham, 2015), 113-14, but is evident also from the context of these *Chaoskampf* acts being labeled "salvation" in Ps 74:12.

[13]One portrayal of God and humanity as forging and maintaining order out of chaos: "We share in doing the things that God has done in creation—bringing order out of chaos, creatively building a civilization out of the material of physical and human nature, caring for all that God has made. This is a major part of what we were created to be." Timothy Keller and Katherine Leary Alsdorf, *Every Good Endeavor: Connecting Your Work to God's Work* (Penguin Books, 2016), 36.

God brings his people in exodus to meet with him.[14] This is not because God is in *tohu* but because his people must leave behind the dream house, must leave behind their assumptions of what a rightly ordered universe looks like, in order to encounter God. Domination and simplification are expressions of love predicated on control. But love in the void, in the wildness, does not require control. Mature love lives with the other without the need to dominate. With that, we turn to the question of the human task in the creation in which they are made.

Creating a Sabbath Household

Rather than chaos, in Genesis 1, creation is repeatedly, insistently, and rhythmically declared *good*, or *tov* in Hebrew. Note that translators do not render *tov* as "perfect." The word *perfect* invokes an entire philosophical discourse around the notion of perfection. This notion is epitomized by Plato's theory of forms. For Plato, nothing material can be perfect on its own terms. It can be perfect only to the extent to which it conforms to an immaterial blueprint that already exists in the eternal—and thus timeless—world of forms. Every material instance of a type, an instantiation, is by definition imperfect because it is not the same thing as the type and must undergo change. From this Platonic vantage, nothing—at least nothing with which humans could engage—can be perfect; or if it is, it is only barely so, in a derivative sense. True perfection operates on a plane of changeless self-sufficiency and aseity, not in the vicissitudes of time.

For that reason, English Bible translators have been wise to describe God as stepping back after each successive day of creation to declare not perfect but "good," and not *good* in the mediocre sense but *good* in a robust sense—a good that is good not because it measures up to some standard of perfection but because it is suitable and fitting in its time and place. Goodness is a quality of relationship, and in the creation this relationship is the sovereignty of God. The material creation obeyed the word of God and was thus in good relationship both to his will and to the other

---

[14]Gen 1:2.

parts of creation. There is only one entity God declares good in and of itself: the very first creation, light.[15] Every other declaration of "good" is directed at the *community* of created entities God has just fashioned.[16] In this way, the Hebrew *tov* of the Genesis creation account is very akin to the *tov* in Psalm 133, a goodness not of abstraction but of visceral—and, in Psalm 133, even viscous—particularity and community. The goodness of creation is a measure of harmony. God is not creating his dream house but a community of creation where homeness is expressed in belonging relations rather than static structures.[17]

As much as God is creating the environment *with* which he will rest, he is not creating a dream home *in* which to rest. This is a significant theological distinction that will itself become a point of narrative tension throughout the Bible. God's people must constantly relearn that, though God does reveal his presence through created structures, God does not actually require these for his dwelling.[18] God does not *in*habit creation; he *co*habits with it. This is a lesson Israel learns most dramatically when the Babylonians seize and destroy their glorious temple. The Israelites then also learn that, far from abandoning his people after the destruction of the temple, God goes *with* them into exile. It's a lesson that we too can learn from the opening pages of Genesis, where we see God creating not a house *building* but a house*hold*, not an edifice of static structures but a community of belonging relations with whom he chooses to dwell. God does this by setting up a representative within the community of creation who are fashioned in his own image: humanity.[19]

---

[15] Gen 1:4. Note that God does not label the combination of light and dark as good together, but only light; the Hebrew imagination seems cognizant of the scientific fact that darkness is but the absence of light and not an entity of itself. It is, of course, on just this point that Augustine stakes much of his theological thinking around the nature of evil. See *City of God* 11.9-10.

[16] Though with the exception of the separation of waters on day two (Gen 1:6-8).

[17] Richard Bauckham covers the theme of the community of creation at length in *Bible and Ecology: Rediscovering the Community of Creation* (Baylor University Press, 2010).

[18] 1 Chron 17:4-6; 2 Chron 6:18; Mt 12:6; Acts 7:48.

[19] Our understanding of the image seems to accord, at least to a point, with that as presented in Middleton, *Liberating Image*. Although Middleton does not explicitly identify the image with membership in the divine council, he comes close to doing so in his conjunctive reading of Ps 8 (see pp. 37-38). While Middleton understands that humanity's being made in the image is

The Image of God: Other Theological Approaches

Within theological studies, there is a small cottage industry devoted to decoding the phrase "image of God," which translates the Hebrew *bet-selem ʾelohim*, which first features in Genesis 1:26-27.[20] We can't fully account for this vast literature here, but we can identify two influential approaches.[21] The traditional theological approach attempts to explain humanity's divine likeness by a shared capacity through communicable attributes. This perspective contends that it is by sharing a certain designated trait with God that humans maintain the divine image. One such trait often identified in the Christian tradition is rationality.

Recent theological engagements, especially from disability theology and ecotheology standpoints, have rightly exposed the dangerous theological trajectory this establishes.[22] Any capacity-based account of humans as the image of God faces four main problems. One is that it tends to be speculative and by the same token risks rendering the image of God an object of projection. The second is that, by grounding humanity's divine likeness in an internal capacity, it also tends to neglect the context in which humanity's likeness is established at the same moment that humanity is made responsible for the other inhabitants of creation. That is, it tends toward a false individualism and anthropocentrism.

---

tasked as divine delegation to the earth with ruling responsibilities, he is wary that a version of the "royal functional" account of the image tends to underwrite certain (especially Kuyperian) cultural mandates, which we will critique in chap. 12. Unfortunately, Middleton's own endorsement of the image as licensing the very human activities of city building, which our reading in chap. 6 of the subsequent chapters of Genesis will critique, seems to play into the very hands he seems keen to avoid (*Liberating Image*, 56).

[20]We intentionally avoid the common Latin phrase *imago Dei* in order to distance our account of this term from other understandings.

[21]Westermann has a comprehensive, though dated, survey in Claus Westermann, *Genesis 1–11: A Commentary* (SPCK, 1984), 147-58.

[22]For a survey of how anthropology has been reworked within disability theology, see Medi Ann Volpe, "Irresponsible Love: Rethinking Intellectual Disability, Humanity and the Church," *Modern Theology* 25, no. 3 (2009): 491-501, https://doi.org/10.1111/j.1468-0025.2009.01538.x. See also G. P. Wagenfuhr, *Plundering Eden: A Subversive Christian Theology of Creation and Ecology* (Cascade Books, 2020), 73, 92-101; Wagenfuhr, *Plundering Egypt: A Subversive Christian Ethic of Economy* (Cascade Books, 2016), 105-9.

The third problem is that it produces justification by being human rather than being in Christ, or being righteous or holy, and so ultimately misses that Christ is the unique image of God. According to Pauline theology, the image of God is to be obtained by being conformed to Christ rather than by rediscovering human essence. The fourth problem is that capacity-based accounts are either aspirational or baseline. Aspirational accounts are aristocratic or heroic, and thus unobtainable to groups such as women, slaves, barbarians (as in Aristotle), or the "herd" (as in Friedrich Nietzsche). It renders some people more human than others. Baseline accounts are inclusive but thereby fail to make any ethical demands, rendering the concept functionally meaningless beyond appeals to inherent value or dignity that lack content without comparison.

Another popular interpretive approach to the image of God suggests that, just as images of a deity were set up in ancient temples to direct the attention of worshipers to the temple god, so too are humans set up as the images of God to direct worship within the cosmic temple of creation.[23] This interpretive line also notes that this explains why there is such a strong mandate in the Old Testament against the setting up of divine images of Yahweh; to do so would be to encroach on the very role of humanity. While this interpretive approach is not without biblical and cultural backing as well as explanatory appeal, we think it's problematic. Namely, the role it bestows on humanity is still too dependent on a static, institutional vision of creation that neglects the dynamic aspect of creation as God's household. Not only that, but the very institution it depends on—a temple—exists almost ubiquitously in religious traditions as predicated on a form of relationship that requires sacrificial interventions to obtain favor, something many parts of the Bible militate against.[24] This is also an approach that our ongoing account will continue to question.

---

[23] G. K. Beale, *The Temple and the Church's Mission: A Biblical Theology of the Dwelling Place of God* (InterVarsity Press, 2004); G. K. Beale and Mitchell Kim, *God Dwells Among Us: A Biblical Theology of the Temple* (IVP Academic, 2021).
[24] E.g., Ps 50:9-13; 51:16-17; Is 1:10-17.

Royal Advisers on the Divine Council

We propose that the image of God must be understood through a wider selection of texts, specifically Genesis 5:1-3, the very next instance of the concept. It appears again only in Genesis 9 and is not explicitly taken up anywhere else in the Old Testament, though Psalm 8 has clear parallels. Recapitulating the genealogy of the man and woman as the image of God, in Genesis 5:13 the author goes on to say that Seth is in *Adam's* image and likeness, something not said of Cain or Abel. This is because Seth will represent the true character of Adam's lineage just as Cain's lineage narrated in Genesis 4 reveals the spirit of rebellion. The lineages of Cain and Seth represent a tale of two peoples that characterize what will later be identified as the people of God and the *goyim*/nations/Gentiles. In the Old Testament there is a clear understanding that the children do the works of the parent, so that the character of the parent is carried on to multiple generations.[25] So, "image and likeness" refers to the character of a person insofar as a person measures up to the genealogical head or father. Humanity's goal, then, is to grow into maturity as the children of God's household, taking on increasing responsibility for household affairs in dialogue with the head of the household, thus becoming inheritors of a household. The Johannine literature assumes this paternity-based understanding of the "image and likeness" as it refers to Jesus as the *monogenēs* ("unique") Son of God.[26]

In the Old Testament, the term "sons of God" (Hebrew *bene 'elohim*) invokes a distinct cultural concept often overlooked in popular Christian teaching and interpretation.[27] In the ancient Near Eastern context in which the biblical text took shape, the divine council was a group of gods that formed a political ruling class of the cosmos.[28] Somewhat uniquely

---

[25] See Ex 20:5; Jn 8:39.

[26] Jn 1:14; 3:16-18; 1 Jn 4:9. Most notable here is the connection Jesus makes in Jn 8:39-58 with the children of Abraham or the devil doing the works of their respective fathers, in contrast with the insistence of Jesus that he does only the works of his Father.

[27] Heiser, *Unseen Realm*, is an exception here.

[28] In some Ugaritic texts, the divine council is coterminous with the divine household. See Mark S. Smith, *The Origins of Biblical Monotheism: Israel's Polytheistic Background and the Ugaritic Texts* (Oxford University Press, 2001), 54.

for the Bible, humans can be members of the divine council. As in nearly all of the premodern world, religion and politics were embedded. In the imagination of the ancient Near East, the divine council was akin to the medieval knights of the round table or a board of directors. It was made up of a collection of subdeities whose primary task, along with internal deliberations and other matters of military and liturgical duty, was to execute the will of the presiding deity.[29] The divine council makes its mark throughout the Old Testament, perhaps most prominently in the famous opening scene of Job, and in Psalm 82, which is referenced by Jesus in John 10:34-36. Psalm 82 deploys a common ancient Near Eastern term for members of the divine council, "sons of God," which Jesus invokes to justify his own designation as God's Son.[30] In this cultural-linguistic scriptural matrix, we are not far from Paul's conclusion of God's intent that we be "conformed to the image of his Son, in order that he might be the firstborn within a large family."[31]

Jesus also adopts "Son of Man" as a common self-designation. This has origins in the book of Daniel and also connotes membership on the divine council.[32] What's more, Jesus uses this term to explain his title "Lord of the Sabbath."[33] Given that "Son of Man" is related to the divine council and that Sabbath—as we will see shortly—is depicted as the apex of God's resolve to dwell enthroned over creation, this connection of terms is unsurprising. In the ancient Near East, the divine council was affiliated with both the dwelling place and enthronement of the deity.[34]

There is yet one more nexus of biblical terms that connects the ancient concept of the divine council to humanity in the creation narrative

---

[29] E. Theodore Mullen, *The Assembly of the Gods: The Divine Council in Canaanite and Early Hebrew Literature* (Scholars Press, 1980), 205.
[30] Other occurrences of "sons of God" include Gen 6:2-4; Job 1:6; 2:1. Deut 32:8 is a borderline case.
[31] Rom 8:29.
[32] Dan 7:13. Mullen, *Assembly of the Gods*, 161.
[33] Mt 12:8; Mk 2:28; Lk 6:5.
[34] Mullen, *Assembly of the Gods*, 140.

(though in this instance to Gen 2, to which we will turn in chap. 5).[35] Ezekiel 28 indicates that the Garden of Eden is the dwelling place of God and location of the assembly of the divine council.[36] Rather than conceiving of Eden as a cosmic temple with specifically religious functions of sacrifice, it is vital to see that the Garden of Eden is portrayed as a *palace* garden.

The difference between temple and palace may seem like hairsplitting, but the theological ramifications are significant. Temples are secondary institutions to palaces. Temples exist in cultures only in which a strong imperial and urban core has developed, a theme we see even in the Bible, with Solomon's temple following only after political peace has been secured and a central palace complex constructed. Prior to temples are holy high places, shrines, grottoes, thin spaces, and other generally unmanaged locations. Temples are significant in that they represent the captivity of a god for the city and people group. Temples use the gods for civic benefit, for the common good. By contrast, a palace is the dwelling place of a king.[37] Whereas a palace signifies God's unmediated sovereignty, a temple signifies God's domestication. Eden represents not the presence of a spiritual being temporarily dwelling as in a temple, supporting a body politic spiritually, but the presence of a king in his palace, ruling over all matters of a domain. The palace garden is where God meets with his council to conduct matters of state. But a temple is where a god receives supplicants, beggars, and dealmakers. And as we will see, in Jesus—the Lord of the

---

[35] Although this does not begin to exhaust Old Testament references to a divine council; see also Deut 33:3; Ps 89:5, 7; Job 1:6; 15:8; Jer 23:18. That the dwelling place of ancient Near Eastern Ugaritic deities was often described as a tent also casts new light on the significance of the tent of meeting throughout the wilderness period of Israel in the Torah (Mullen, *Assembly of the Gods*, 168).

[36] Mullen, *Assembly of the Gods*, 151-53. This gets transposed onto Mount Zion (see 154-55).

[37] Arguments for the palace versus the temple are many, of which a few are simply noted here: The temple of Jerusalem didn't have gardens, but the palace did (see 2 Kings 25:4; Neh 3:15). The Persian word *pardes* comes into Greek as "paradise" (used by the LXX) and specifically refers to palace gardens. Palaces are linguistically prior to temples in many languages, including Hebrew; these languages rarely use a special word for a temple, instead employing either *bayit* ("house") or *hekal* ("palace/temple"). Sumerian *e-gal* and Akkadian *ekallu* lie behind *hekal*, and in those languages the term means "big house" or "palace."

Sabbath—"something greater than the temple" has arrived in order that God may find friends, not supplicants.[38]

We realize that distinguishing and preferring palace over temple might seem initially at cross-purposes. Aren't palaces exclusive and luxurious, while temples are inclusive and public? Aren't palaces more like opulent museums instead of relational hubs? And why are temples mentioned so much more by the Bible than palaces? Throughout this book, we will trace how God condescends to work through distorted and even mistaken human forms in order to move beyond them. Ultimately, the trajectory of Scripture moves *beyond* temples as sites of transactions between the human and the divine. On its final horizon is God's invitation *into* the very exclusive and luxurious space of his royal council. The Bible is a story of God's converting rebellious creatures who should, by all rights, remain his groveling enemies into God's confidants and friends; it's a story of being converted from those who go to the religious marketplace to make their payments to appease the gods to those who are invited to dine and dialogue at God's table. The real question of God's intention for his people is this: Does he desire servile worshipers who are liturgical specialists, or does he desire people who have attained maturity and wisdom to rule with him? Is the Bible a book that purports to give the one right religion or a book that challenges the legitimacy of geopolitics altogether? These very questions are embedded in the presumed architecture of Eden.

Genesis 1's designation of humanity as being made in the image of God indicates that humanity's purpose is connected to their involvement on a divine council and thus their participation in God's household as children. To conform to God's image is to grow up as God's children who bear the family resemblance and also bear responsibility for all members of the household. This entails growth and maturation in order to dialogue with God about matters of household judgment.[39] To interpret humans as the image of God as participants on the divine council avoids the

---

[38]Mt 12:6; Jn 15:15.
[39]Mt 19:28; 1 Cor 6:3; Rev 20:4.

capacity-based notions of humanity's divine likeness that fail to include taking active responsibility within creation. It also avoids the misguided accounts of humans as divine images with a mission to expand a cosmic temple without transforming humanity such that they do not need a further institution of mediation or sacrifice. It sets a trajectory of active human participation in God's royal rule as executors of his will over the household of creation and anticipates Jesus' conflict about the practice of Sabbath as highlighting rather than dismissing the expectation for humans to take responsibility for other members of creation.[40]

There is one more Sabbath-shaped concept that the divine council draws our attention to. Insofar as humans are to actively deliberate with God about household affairs, their foundational action is intercessory prayer.[41] Hence Jesus wishes to replace the religious marketplace of the temple with a house of prayer and instructs his followers to pray with confidence and authority.[42]

Understanding the image of God as referring to humans as members of God's household or divine council, combined with a transformed understanding of chaos, means that the dominion of Genesis 1:26-29 takes on a different character. While the word *radah* ("have dominion") is usually deployed in rather violent ways, context dictates its meaning.[43] And if Genesis is intentionally avoiding *Chaoskampf*, then it is reasonable to assume that its word for "ruling over" or "having dominion" would bear a similar character to the methods God himself used in the act of creation—speech and not violence. The dominion God commands of his people is not the completion of an unfinished creation but bearing God's

---

[40]Mt 12:11-12. The work of Catherine McDowell on the image of God also accords with our stressing humanity as royal representatives. See McDowell, *The Image of God in the Garden of Eden: The Creation of Humankind in Genesis 2:5–3:24 in Light Of Mis Pi Pit Pi and Wpt-r Rituals of Mesopotamia and Ancient Egypt* (Eisenbrauns, 2015), 136-37. For a more accessible treatment of the image of God that also stresses the human responsibility to care for creation, see Carmen Joy Imes, *Being God's Image: Why Creation Still Matters* (InterVarsity Press, 2023).
[41]This point has also recently been made by N. T. Wright, *Into the Heart of Romans: A Deep Dive into Paul's Greatest Letter* (Zondervan Academic, 2023), chap. 6.
[42]Mk 11:12-25.
[43]E.g., Lev 25:43; Neh 9:28.

character to the creation. Dominion here should mean that God's people bring the presence of God's household to the creation. This is bringing the presence of God's loving care, the kind of care that knows when a sparrow falls or the intimate detail of the numbers of hairs on another's head.[44] Thus God is not commissioning some grand domestication, cultivation, or cultural mandate. God is commissioning presence through mature representatives. And this is often what rulership looks like, especially in the ancient world, where symbolic presence through statuary (e.g., idols) could communicate the presence of a deity or monarch.[45] This comports with Jesus' own commission in Matthew 28, which picks up on the fruitful multiplication language while transforming it into discipleship terms.

Thus the command to be fruitful and multiply is not about culture.[46] Instead, it speaks to the *character* of dominion. Rather than forging an empire of elites, the command to multiply requires a vision of dispersal and decentralized representation. The work of the people of God should be local and particular rather than global and generic. This requires ongoing training to occur with successive generations. We might say that discipleship is itself a Sabbath work, because it leads new generations to grow into characters who can represent God to his creation. Sovereignty or dominion comes from the character of the rulers, not the institutions they cast. Thus Jesus' Great Commission is a recapitulation of Genesis, not a contrast with it.

The task of the image of God is not agricultural activity or productivity, as indicated from the end of this first creation account in Genesis 1:29-30.

---

[44]Mt 10:26-31.

[45]It should be noted that kings and palaces, or "big men" and "big houses," are historically prior to anthropomorphic gods and their temples. The irony of the history of religions, however, is that as monarchical religion becomes so established in the imaginary of a people, there is a reprojection of the gods onto kings in a way that legitimizes kings as divine representatives. The Bible short-circuits the process of projection (or aims to) by its command to not make graven images and by its preservation of heavy critiques of the monarchy even under its most lauded rulers in David and Solomon.

[46]Chapter twelve will challenge the theologies of work that tend to keep company with the emphasis on human creative labor.

God has *given* food to his people as he has to all the other creatures, as Jesus underscores in Matthew 6:25-34. That food is a gift of God and not the fruit of labor shows that the labor God has given to the image of God is political representation rather than manual labor. Food was not intended to be a reward or threat of punishment designed to keep creatures in line but was provisioned to facilitate the main task of representation. This introduces a theme we will see repeated throughout our study of the Bible: Food symbolizes sovereignty. Adam and Eve do not work for food because they are subjects of the Creator's sovereign rule.

The Seventh Day: God's Reign of Sabbath Rest

After God has shaped the primordial elements of creation, confirmed the suitability and fit of its inhabitants, and commissioned humans as vicegerents, the first creation account climaxes with God's cessation of work at creation's completion. The Hebrew verb *shabbat* in Genesis 2:2 is sometimes translated "rest," though it can also mean "stop" or "cease." These verbs might be preferable because God is not resting here because he is tired or worn out. God's rest is not a sign of finitude or apathy but a reflection of God's freedom.[47] By ceasing to create, God determines to relate to creation not only as its Creator but also as its King. A king at rest is a king at peace.[48]

Sabbath is not God's retirement but his enthronement. Psalm 132 showcases the relation between coronation and rest. Psalm 132:14 reads, "This is my resting place forever; here I will reside, for I have desired it."[49] The verb here translated "reside" is a generic Hebrew verb for "sitting" or "dwelling"; it can also refer to an enthronement, a king coming to sit on his throne to take up his rule, a point noted by the translators of the NIV.[50] That this same word can also refer more generically to dwelling in one's

---

[47]See Jacques Ellul, *What I Believe*, trans. Geoffrey W. Bromiley (Eerdmans, 1989), 153.
[48]2 Sam 7:1.
[49]Although Ps 132:14 uses a different root verb from *shabbat*, it does use the same verb used of the rest commanded in Ex 20:11. (It is also the same verb used in Ps 95:11, which is repeated in the theology of Sabbath relayed in Heb 4.)
[50]See also Ps 2:4; 9:8; 29:10; 55:19; 102:12.

household draws together the theme we have been sketching in this chapter: God expresses his rule over the household of his creation by resting to take up residence in it, like a king entering into his throne room.

Insofar as Sabbath is God's enthronement, we could say that Sabbath is the shape of God's sovereignty. It is a sovereignty that does not dominate by force but by lavish capaciousness. God's Sabbath rest is also the ground for humanity's freedom to rest from its own aspirations and plans—and in this to respect the freedom of others.[51] Human freedom and rest is established by God's freedom to rest. And as with God's rest, this is not a freedom *from* others but a freedom *for* and *with* others; this is not the buffered freedom of aseity but the relational freedom that elects to dwell with wildness.

By determining to cohabit with the household of creation in this way and determining not to be a mere cause of creation, God is demonstrating the character of his sovereignty over creation by offering the very gift of himself.[52] Sabbath shows the *character* of God's sovereignty over his creation and the *means* of that sovereignty—presence. This returns us to the definition of Sabbath offered in our introduction: the immediate dwelling presence of the sovereign King of all creation.

Sabbath is the seventh and final day of the first creation account, and we propose that this is a parallel timeline to the one in which we find ourselves, the time of rebellious human history. The seventh day is the cosmic home from which we have become estranged.[53] We live within the sixth day of creation, or at least between the sixth and seventh days. We do not yet see all things submitted to the sovereignty of God, as Hebrews 2:8 indicates. We live within the time before the Sabbath rest, a time within which God's creation has been finished, has been declared "very good" and yet does not participate in God's rest. This liminal space prior

---

[51]Ex 20:8-11.
[52]See Ellul, *What I Believe*, 153.
[53]Here we disagree with Ellul, who suggests that all of human history takes place in the seventh day and fails to account how this is precisely the reality from which we have become estranged (*What I Believe*, 154).

to the great Sabbath rest of the seventh day is the space of human history, which is introduced in Genesis 2–3 and to which we turn in chapter five. There is no mention of God's Sabbath in this account. Instead, humans are fashioned from the dust of the earth and caused to rest in the Garden of Eden.[54]

We suggest that the Garden of Eden in the second creation account is what the Sabbath is to the first; one is put in spatial terms, the other in temporal terms. Both refer to the completed household in which God determines to dwell with and rule over creation. It is from this home that God's people have been exiled so they no longer experience a reality in which God fully rests and abides. However, God has not completely abandoned humanity, confining himself to the Sabbath time; instead, in the exile that is human history, God draws near by tabernacling—by setting up temporary means of communicating his presence. He remains Lord of the Sabbath, even if we are no longer residents of his household of Sabbath rest.

Rediscovering a Sabbath Theology

By beginning with Sabbath, with Genesis 1 presenting to us both the alpha and omega, the first day and the seventh day, the whole biblical history is encapsulated in the first chapter, if only in a suggestive manner. Theology done in light of the seventh day prioritizes the sovereignty of God as the age of God approaching the creation from its endpoint, meeting it in the middle, rather than beginning with a state of perfection and lamenting its loss. Because a Sabbath lens has forced us to be more attentive to the biblical dimensions of time than of space, we focus more on the character of relationships than the nature of things. Theologically speaking, this means a Sabbath theology can functionally do away with the questions of being and essence, because nothing exists in isolation, not even God. Any attempt to find the essence of God or any element of creation is an

---

[54]Gen 2:8, 15. Note that the verb most English translations render as "put" in Gen 2:15, *yanakh*, is related to the verb used of the rest God gives to David in 2 Sam 7:1, again indicating a character of rest that involves a notion of enthronement.

exercise in invention rather than discovery, a pseudo-creation rather than living in God's creation.

Theologically speaking, this means we begin with God as loving his creation through the unique character of his sovereignty or rulership, which will be expressed best in Jesus Christ. While not denying the truth or validity of traditional theological creeds that focus on the nature of God, creedal formulations are limited in their ability to renew and transform. The more profound, more applicable, and more reliable theological conversations will happen surrounding God's character as expressed in the story of God becoming King through his people.

This also means that our primary lived theological questions do not revolve around human nature, flourishing, or "becoming more fully human." The attainment of an ideal definition of the human species is not the task of a theology but of humanistic speculation couched in theological terms. The role of humans as members of the divine council in the image of God suggests that the kind of actions that characterize faithful human work rely more on the dynamic, the relational, and the imaginative than the static or prescriptive. And this will have profound implications as we turn to the work of Jesus. Rather than focusing on the incarnation as the union of divine and human natures, we will demonstrate that God's kingship and presence are described in terms of dwelling with us not as the ideal human being but as a devoted and obedient elder brother who invites us into a new relation of adoptive royal paternity.

But before we consider the work of Jesus as the elder brother in the household of God, we need to better grasp the nature of God's household as presented in the Old Testament. And this includes its formation alongside its rival: the dream home. So we move along on the journey from the beginning Sabbath rest of a creation alive in good, wild, and free community toward the introduction of conflict and the development of the enemies we encountered from Psalm 92 in medias res.

Group Discussion Questions

1. How have you and/or your community tended to understand the term "image of God"? What are the implications of understanding this as referring to a vocation of vicegerency (serving alongside) with God on a divine council?

2. What have you and your community described as chaos, and how might this relate to your understanding of the gospel? What might the role of the church be in light of that gospel?

A TALE OF TWO TIMES

EVERY JOURNEY ENCOUNTERS a choice of direction. There's the easy way and the hard way. Those who choose the easy way tend to focus on outcomes, on efficiency, on reaching a goal sooner. They see the journey as the means to a destination. Those who choose the hard way use the journey to become the kind of person who is prepared to live well when the destination is finally reached. In this chapter we will come across that fork in the road between the wide gate that leads to easy paths and the narrow gate that leads to challenging ways through the text of Genesis 2–11.[1]

In chapter four, we considered how the creation account of Genesis 1:1–2:3 reveals that God's ultimate aim is to abide or rest with the household of creation. God expresses sovereignty by fashioning a people to join his rest as ruling members of his divine council. Sabbath shows the nature of God's household as a relational medium for receiving God's gifts and growing into maturity. In this chapter we journey through the millennia represented in Genesis 2:4 through Genesis 11, paying special attention to the impact of human rebellion.[2] In the Christian tradition this moment in Genesis 3 is often referred to as "the fall," a term we do

---

[1]Mt 7:13-14.
[2]However, we are here skipping the Noah story, which we will treat in chapter six in relation to God's covenant promises.

not use, in part because it sounds too accidental. But more seriously, it has long facilitated a theology that conceives of the immaterial human soul as trapped in a broken material body and world, from which it needs to escape to an otherworldly heaven. More problematic as well is simply that it is a term the Bible itself never uses in reference to sin.[3] *Rebellion*, or "going astray," better captures the active and willful human rejection of God's way for bids at aseity. But Genesis has much more to say about human rebellion than is found in Genesis 3. Genesis 4–11 continues the Genesis prehistory of the people of God that establishes patterns of rebellion and faithfulness that will be recapitulated throughout the rest of the Bible and through the history of God's people to now.

In our reading, the Garden of Eden in this second creation account corresponds to Sabbath in the first creation account.[4] That is, the garden puts in spatial terms what Sabbath puts in temporal terms. Eden is the kingdom of God, while Sabbath the time of its flourishing. Consequentially, Adam and Eve's exile from the Garden of Eden is also their exile from God's Sabbath as the sovereign household of God.

Genesis 2–3 is not primarily telling the story of the origin of the human species through two people. Instead, it's narrating the establishment of a lineage, or household. While this has often been overlooked, the text indicates that Adam and Eve are the first *elect* people, beginning a story that will be recapitulated in Christ and in the people of God time and again. These are people brought out of the barren land of dangerous human history, brought into the Sabbath day in God's courtyard, which the Garden of Eden represents, then exiled back to the dust from which they were formed. In this Adam and Eve are the first to undergo the probationary test of the divine council, the first to receive God's instruction, the first to violate that instruction to wisdom, and also the first to receive God's discipline.

---

[3]While English translations of Rom 3:23 use the language of "fall short," this is a need of rendering into good English what Greek has in one word, *hystereō*, "to be lacking."
[4]See note 2 in chapter four for an approach to the two creation accounts in Genesis.

A Tale of Two Times

This protean history lays the foundation for the whole biblical narrative caught in medias res between creation and the seventh day. This story begins the spiral shape of human history as it is drawn toward the singularity of Christ, who is later revealed to be both Alpha and Omega and the Way, and thus in whose faithfulness the failure and discipline of Adam and Eve are encompassed. In this way Genesis 2 transitions from setting the scene and toward the beginning of the lineage of God's Sabbath people.

The Great Unrest

Adam and Eve, as the first elect people put on probation, are tested by the very goal for which the people of God aim: wisdom for the ability to rightly image God. The tree of knowledge of good and evil—mentioned here in the second creation account in Genesis 2:9, along with the tree of life—becomes the object of conflict. Humans are commanded, even urged (the Hebrew grammar here is repetitive—"eat, eat"), to eat of every other tree in the garden except for this one.[5] This limit on human consumption reveals the gift-given nature of all the other trees and food sources of the garden. In God's Sabbath, food is gratis. Again, *food symbolizes sovereignty*, and the freedom of the provision sets up the test, a test that is in part a determination toward self-sufficiency.

So, to echo Paul's term for the law in Galatians 3:24, the tree of knowledge is a pedagogue, or tutor, that trains humans into maturity by being something of a ruse. It is not the eating of the fruit that matters; it is the obedience to the word that the fruit tests. In this dual aspect of revealing both the gift and responsibility of God's people, the tree of knowledge ultimately reveals that God's people, as his image and prospective members of the divine council, are to remain in a living and dynamic dialogue with God. Jesus will be tested, like Adam and Eve, by food and tempted by a desire for his own sovereignty attained through food production. Jesus will prove to be the true image of God, who

---

[5] Gen 2:16-17.

knows that humans do not live by food alone but by the word of God.[6] It is not the eating or consuming that conveys wisdom; it is the hearing and obedience.

Adam and Eve fail to live into the full maturity of the image of God by denying the gift-given nature of creation. They reject the invitation to responsibility—to *responsiveness* to God's address—by transgressing God's word. Genesis 3 charts a refusal to live in dialogue with God as the foundational characteristic of a member of the divine council. Ironically, Adam and Eve expose their immaturity by an attempt to attain wisdom by the shortcut. One of Eve's reasons for seizing the forbidden fruit is that she saw "that the tree was to be desired to make one wise."[7]

For all the alien descriptions in Genesis 3 of talking snakes and special fruit, there are aspects in which Eve's (and Adam's) reactions in this heightened moment are perhaps not so removed from our own. Eve is described as evaluating the fruit in material and consumer terms, seeing in consumption the path to wisdom. The fruit is "good for food" and "a delight to the eyes."[8] Here Eve regards wisdom as a material valuation of supposedly inherent value. This is the same problem a disenchanted modern consumer economy has perfected. Value is not regarded through relationship but taken as inhering in things that can communicate their value to us by consumption. This is the mistaken logic of homeopathic (i.e., imitative) magic, transposed in our time through markets and mass production but still operative. The fruit could not convey wisdom in itself. Having or consuming something of value does not in itself communicate that value to a person. Instead, it is the kind of relationship we have with material objects that tests, reveals, and imparts wisdom to us. Value is a relationship, not a thing in itself—or *a se*. Instead of ruling the world as responsible overseers, Adam and Eve instead attempt to both find and fashion their own value from it, hiding behind constructed coverings of clothing that aim to project another self from the naked and now ashamed

---

[6]Mt 4:1-4.
[7]Gen 3:6.
[8]Gen 3:6.

rebels. They move from community to domination, from receiving a home to desiring a dream house, from knowing and being known to projecting masks of constructed selves.

Adam and Eve's exchanging their role of ruling the world to deriving value from it is consummated by their ultimate betrayal as members of divine council: their questioning of God's word. Adam and Eve are not alone in this regard. The serpent might also be a member of the divine council who has defected.[9] Elsewhere in the Bible, a kind of serpent often called seraphim are depicted as God's heavenly attendants.[10] Both Eve and the serpent compromise God's word—the serpent first by casting doubt on God's original command, and Eve by adding a stipulation of not touching, which was not contained in the original command.[11] In its final retort, the serpent flatly denies God's warning that consuming the fruit will bring death. The entire exchange is witnessed by Adam, who cements his own disloyal neglect of God's word through silent complicity. All three of these members of the divine council reject their responsibilities. And all three, each in their own way, will bear the consequences of their defection.

Rebellion's Bitter Fruit

God's response is grace. By discipline, God demonstrates that he has not given up on his project of bringing his people into maturity. In fact, if seizing the fruit of the tree of knowledge was in one sense a shortcut to power, God's response at the end of Genesis 3 is to short-circuit this shortcut by withdrawing access from the tree of life and expelling humanity from the Garden of Eden. This is an act of loving exile for discipline that will be repeated often in Scripture, including in Paul's own logic of church discipline.[12] And if the Garden of Eden is a spatial

---

[9]Michael S. Heiser, *The Unseen Realm: Recovering the Supernatural Worldview of the Bible* (Lexham, 2015), 83.
[10]E.g., Is 6:2. In Numbers, God sends fiery serpents (seraphim) among the complaining Israelites (Num 21:6, 8).
[11]Gen 3:1; see Gen 2:17; 3:3.
[12]Prov 3:11-12, quoted in Heb 12:5-6; 1 Cor 5:5.

representation of Sabbath, then God's response to Adam and Eve is to drive them out of the household of God by expelling them from Sabbath and into the messy arena of human history. God responds to humanity by giving them *time*: at least, a certain kind of time.

What is the nature of the time God now gives humanity as a manner of making good use of their rebellion? As Bonhoeffer notes, there is no way to comprehend the quality of time before or other than the time in which we now find ourselves. Thus we cannot have an objective view of the time of human history, nor can we easily speculate on the nature of God's time by simply projecting our desires or removing all the undesirable aspects of our time. The Sabbath time from which we have been estranged is time at its fullest, the enduring enjoyment of peaceful and mature community, the kind of time that creates inhabitable and indelible memories.

Genesis contrasts the Garden of Eden with the dust and thorns of exile. Similarly, we might say that the character of the time of human history is not only that of toil but a toil that seemingly never gets us very far. While generations come and generations go, it feels like time and the world take little notice.[13] Human progress is ephemeral because nothing is learned about ourselves and how to become more mature, even as we develop techniques and technologies to build our dream home. The goal of arrival is an ever-distant mirage because we try to build a paradise around us rather than learning maturity through the journey. Time is now characterized by decay, scarcity, competition, and distorted relationships. It is "being-towards-death," as philosopher Martin Heidegger puts it.[14] Death defines our lives by making everything relative to the scarcity and sorrow it creates. The reality of death and strained relationships among humans, between humans and their work, and between humans and the earth are characteristic of the unrest that is our exile from God's Sabbath order. If Sabbath is about the kinds of relationships characterized in the household

---

[13]Eccles 1:4.
[14]Martin Heidegger, *Being and Time*, trans. John Macquarrie and Edward Robinson (SCM Press, 1962).

of God, then exile from Sabbath inverts these relations. Let's explore the threefold relational consequences of humanity's uprising.

The first relational distortion is between humans, and especially between man and woman.[15] We have already seen that the impulse to manufacture clothing to mediate between Adam and Eve and hide their exposure is indicative of the strained relations between them. This is intensified by God's declaration in Genesis 3:16 in God's address to Eve: "Your desire shall be for your husband, and he shall rule over you." A relationship of power is introduced here between men and women that is symptomatic of their exile and unrest. Their hiding reveals that even in love people relate to each other in competitive ways that demand submission of one's will to another's in a climate of fear. Where there is fear, there can be no perfect love.[16] Here too women are afflicted with additional pain in childbearing. Time is characterized by decay and death even in the very process of bringing about new life. One implication is that the woman's body is transformed in the process of becoming a mother; she must decrease while others increase. In marriage and motherhood, a woman loses sovereignty over her own flesh.

We should be clear on this delicate issue: We are not suggesting that this state of affairs by which women tend to be dominated by men and bear the heavy cost of bringing new life into the world is ordained by God. It is symptomatic of humanity's exiled state. But this does not make this state of affairs acceptable or tolerable. It can provide the natural grounds for maturation of husbands who, as Paul will say, must give wives their very life and love them as themselves.[17] At the very moment that God names this troubling condition, God also promises to use even painful childbirth to bring about his redemptive purposes and to use the offspring of Eve to overcome the bitter fruits of human rebellion.[18]

---

[15]This is why marriage is significant as a sign of reconciling men and women, and thus all humanity.
[16]1 Jn 4:18.
[17]Eph 5:25-33.
[18]Gen 3:15.

The second set of strained relations between humanity and the earth is shown by competitive relationships developing because humans are now dependent on the creation rather than on God. God's curse is that they will now work the land rather than receiving from the land. It isn't that God created agrarian peoples and then made their job difficult; God chose Adam and Eve to receive his provision and then disciplined them with reformative work. This is a cosubjugation, in a sense. Now the land too is submitted to "futility" and will require the revelation of the children of God for creation to realize its hope.[19] In other words, the reconciliation and healing of creation go hand in hand with the reformative discipline of God's people. In the meantime, humans project their unrest onto creation. Creation becomes seen as chaos, a world of threats and too-scarce provisions that must be civilized or domesticated for human benefit. And out of the corpse of chaos, humans begin to forge their own self-made identities and worlds.

The third set of transformed relations involves labor. God exiles Adam and Eve to an environment in which either discipline or disobedience could potentially thrive, depending on how they respond to the demands of labor. They could respond by repentance and using shared suffering as a means of cooperation and care, or they could respond by seeking every means to outsource this labor and avoid discipline.

In this disobedient mode, production and reproduction can be mythologized as a noble struggle against the forces of chaos while seeking to make resources out of all creation and one another to create merit, because possessing surplus makes a person desirable as a potential source of labor savings. This dynamic creates the conditions for enslavement. It incentivizes those who can induce others to produce a surplus through extra work or who can transform land to make it more productive for humans, which almost always means less to sustain other creatures. It also denigrates those who provide services or maintenance rather than production since their value lies not in further value creation but in care for

---

[19]Rom 8:19-21.

what has already been made. Those who advance the cause of conquering chaos through innovation are lionized as heroes, while the servants, slaves, and all too often women are seen as having lower merit since they don't create value but only maintain it.

In other words, humans leverage the conditions God intends as an opportunity for formation and discipline as the opportunity for further rebellion by creating value through competition, specialization, surplus value, and control. This will characterize economic activity henceforth. Now value is seen not in using the gifts of God to form relationships of responsibility and rest giving but in exploiting resources to acquire value through ownership, consumption, and use of other people's or animals' labor. While these are features celebrated in modern capitalism, they are not uniquely modern. From Eve onward, economic value, and thus the value of time, has been measured by scarcity, by taking time, taking rest, and hoarding these to oneself. So capitalism as a belief system or ideology is best understood as ceding responsibility to the market or the invisible hand of providence, which establishes these factors as natural human laws instead of as a human response to rebellious conditions.[20] What is unique about modern capitalism is more that we treat neighbors and even family as once tribal people only treated strangers or enemies. Competitive value now requires hierarchization, the assignment of greater and lesser value to many things. And most of these valuations come not from the things themselves but from imitating the desire of others, revealing a profound childishness to rebellious economic activity that fails to take responsibility as value creators and instead chases trends and fashions, ultimately imitating created things rather than mastering them.[21] This is a point the author of Genesis understands clearly, as we will see when we discuss the rival lineages of Cain and Seth.

---

[20] It is notable that Adam Smith bases much of his foundational claims on human nature as particularly economic, as humans uniquely "truck and barter" (see *Wealth of Nations* 1.2). This is not human nature, as many anthropologists have documented contrasting evidence, but it does show that capitalism as an ideology wants to justify what it sees as laws of necessity.
[21] Paul describes sin in Rom 1 as an imitation of created things.

God responds to rebellion by allowing humans to experience the full consequence of their action. This response is a grace: God disciplines (or trains or teaches) those he loves.[22] God's discipline often comes in the form of natural consequences. As humans try to play god, they get to live in the world they have made. This form of discipline empowers by giving opportunity for repentance and responsibility. It is not the vengeful paternalism of offended honor. God's ultimate act of discipline is to expel his people from Eden in space and Sabbath in time. If God were to remain with them, it would be in a relationship of judgment. God's restriction of his presence is the very judgment of grace that enables life to continue, but it is life characterized by absence of Sabbath and its restful, fully provisioned sovereignty.

Yet even in absence, God does not abandon. He deploys the consequences of human actions as an ongoing invitation to maturity even on the far side of Sabbath. Paradigmatically in Genesis 3:21, he meets humans on their level, stooping to exchange their fig-leaf dress for actual clothes. God may have retracted some of the gifts of creation by requiring human toil for food, yet he determines, still, to give them gifts within their disordered time.

The Nature of Sin: A Rival Household

For all of the dramatic catalog of human folly and failure in Genesis 3, and the serpent's sinister complicity, it remains mysteriously silent on one key theological theme: sin. Genesis doesn't breathe the word until the middle of Genesis 4, in the story of Cain and Abel. Yet even its mention there falls short of the clarity of a clean definition. Instead, it only establishes sin's mystique. To a glum Cain, sulking over the divine acceptance of his brother's offerings over his own, God warns, in words that mysteriously parallel Eve's curse of desiring her husband from the previous chapter, "Sin is lurking at the door; its desire is for you, but you must master it."[23]

---

[22]Prov 3:11-12; Heb 12:5-6.
[23]Gen 4:7.

The animality of sin is palpable. It "lurks"; it even "desires." Whatever "it" *is* remains opaque, but whatever it is, it appears to possess a will of its own. God's comment challenges precise or legal definitions of sin as a mere missing the mark or "any want of conformity unto, or transgression of, the law of God."[24] Even if this potent and obscure force resists the domestication of definition, we can appreciate at a minimum that sin is capable of developing a life of its own.

Marva Dawn, in critical dialogue with Jacques Ellul, helpfully investigated the animate nature of sin as indicated here in Genesis 4 under the rubric of another set of biblical terms: principalities and powers.[25] Dawn suggests that there exist in the world powers that capitalize and energize human sin in a collective direction. These are expressed through human structures and institutions such as money, political power, technology, and addiction, but they are not coterminous with these phenomena. In fact, a common error is to mistake the powers for the human structures by which they are manifest. The very power of the powers as sin is increased by disguising themselves as merely human phenomena. Yet the powers do not have a separate reality of their own. They depend on human belief for their existence, but their existence transcends belief because they take on a real life of their own and exert real determining power far beyond what the demons of folklore are capable. The powers are manifest in and derive their existence from their very mundanity. In other words, there is a force that animates the rival households humans construct in direct resistance to God's Sabbath household. This is the force of sin, which is much more than isolated actions or choices. But acts of sin over time normalize and gather momentum into a concentrated

---

[24] Westminster Shorter Catechism A.14.
[25] Marva Jenine Sandberg Dawn, "The Concept of the 'Principalities and Powers' in the Works of Jacques Ellul" (PhD diss., University of Notre Dame, 1992). Walter Wink is another theological voice who is often associated with the notion of principalities and powers, and he in turn was inspired in part by lawyer and lay theologian William Stringfellow, who was himself informed by the writings of Karl Barth and Jacques Ellul. For an appreciative engagement with Stringfellow on the topic of the powers, see Walter Wink, "Stringfellow on the Powers," in *Radical Christian and Exemplary Lawyer: Honoring William Stringfellow*, ed. Andrew W. McThenia (Wipf & Stock, 2006), 17-30.

force beyond individual human control or capacity, taking on a life that indeed can lurk around and have desire. To acknowledge this is to begin to set out on the very path of maturity and *mastery* to which God invites Cain in Genesis 4.

Dawn's work on the powers helps connect the notion of aseity and the dream home detailed in chapter two with our theme of Sabbath by this insight on sin buried in Genesis 4. Let's offer a definition of sin now in terms of Sabbath: Sin is an animate resistance to the household sovereignty of God that manifests as concrete actions and corporate structures. Put differently: Sin is the determination to operate out of one's own value system, or economy (household law), in order to achieve satisfaction (aseity) apart from dwelling with God. It does so through the construction of, inhabitation in, and participation in other structures. Dawn highlights how this takes on a collective and animate nature. The irony of this effort to achieve aseity, as we explored through the theme of the dream home, is that it is never satisfied.[26] The irony continues in that, as we aim to create control through the creation of structures, these structures themselves gain a life independent of our control.[27] We end up subjected to ever more powerful forces that no one can master.

Other parts of the Bible support this portrait of sin as inhabiting rival households to God's dwelling. Proverbs 9 portrays Wisdom as establishing a household opposed by that of Folly. Psalm 1 indicates that wickedness dwells in a house of its own.[28] Throughout the Old Testament narratives, idols are portrayed as households of sin that rival the Sabbath household God aims to replant through the line of David, a theme we explore more in chapter six.

In fact, we propose reading much of the Bible as largely a tale of two households, two peoples, and two ways. But before detailing how the genealogies of these two households are launched in Genesis through the lines

---

[26] See Prov 27:20; 30:15-16.
[27] This is the thesis of philosopher Hartmut Rosa, *The Uncontrollability of the World* (Polity, 2020).
[28] The word in Ps 1:1 often translated "sits" and "seat" can also be rendered "dwells" and "dwelling."

of Seth and Cain, it bears highlighting two characteristics of the household of sin that will become more evident in our ongoing interpretation.

Sin is founded on discontent with God's gifts. We have already seen how it was, paradoxically, by seizing the fruit of the forbidden tree of knowledge that Eve effectively rejected the gifts of the whole of creation. By taking what was prohibited, she refused to receive the other elements of creation as God's free gifts. Any household of sin—or human construct fueled by the power of sin—is built on the foundation of discontent with God's gifts. With this insight in hand, we can begin to appreciate why thanksgiving—epitomized in the Sabbath household practice of the Eucharist (Greek for "thanksgiving")—is so significant throughout Scripture and to the people of God.

Furthermore, sin is expressed in self-justification. This is often not explicit but takes the form of praising one's conformity to the structures of one's context or environment—those same structures that are so good at masking the power of sin. In other words, sin is normalization. Sin masks its true sinister nature by making a virtue of necessity. But necessity can simply be a justification for capitulation; being mastered by other economies and logics of value rather than mastering them. We already saw this logic of self-justification at work in Eve's reasoning in Genesis 3, where she places value on material reality without reference to God, as well as in Adam and Eve's self-fashioned clothing, which becomes a medium in their relationship with God. By transforming individual moral actions into systems, institutions, and structures, humans justify sin by making it necessary. The perpetuation of the status quo becomes justifiable because the consequences of doing otherwise are unthinkable.

For example, consider how the vast majority of the world lives in contexts that are locally unsustainable. We cannot eat without transportation of foodstuffs grown at great distances or consuming highly processed foods produced by international megacorporations whose ethical records are dubious. Even if the results of such a system include planetary destruction, obesity, and highly unjust labor practices, these systems are justified as necessary. And currently they *are* necessary, as the modern supermarket system has destroyed local food cultures. How many in the westernized world would be able to survive for a month on only what they grew or gathered? Without supermarkets we die, as does our economy. This is how sin becomes a power greater than any individual choice and how sin is even experienced and excused as the inability to make choices. We boast of abundant consumer choice in supermarkets but often have no real moral choice, nor a choice that seeks to give rest to God's creation or the oppressed people of the world. Yet many moderns congratulate themselves on the progress of civilization, content to exchange the true freedom of choice to be morally responsible for the inferior and largely superficial choices of the consumer. Sin is power, our service to the power, and above all our justification of the power that removes our ability to even bear responsibility.[29]

A Tale of Two Households: The Lines of Seth and Cain

Of course, we don't find grocery stores in the Bible, let alone a critique of them. Yet food symbolically initiates the rebellion with the fruit of the tree in Eden. Food plays a central role in the initial conflict of Cain and Abel. And food will continue to play a central role in the notion of Sabbath. Again, food symbolizes sovereignty.[30] The core question of any household is not leadership but provision: the breadwinner.[31] With an uprising in God's house, there is an uprising in God's economy, for a household *is* an economy.

At this point in the text of Genesis, we might expect Genesis 5 to move the plot forward in a dramatic way. Instead we are met with a genealogy that offends modern tastes in narrative pacing. Yet these lists compress the whole paradigm of the biblical vision. Genesis tells a tale of *two peoples*

---

[29]The notion of necessity and sin as its justification is developed in the works of Jacques Ellul, particularly in *The Ethics of Freedom*, trans. Geoffrey W. Bromiley (Eerdmans, 1976).
[30]Ps 111:5.
[31]This notion animates the portrait of the wise woman in Prov 31, which also subverts modern ideas of patriarchy. In fact, all of Proverbs might be read as animated by the idea that the wise person, in harmony with wisdom, is one who cultivates a healthy home life.

who walk two separate paths: the people of God, who are being shaped into God's image, preparing to return to and even take charge with God over God's household, and those who are seeking to establish a household of their own, on their own terms, to a destructive end.

There are well established theological precedents in reading the biblical story, and all of human history, in this binary way. Preeminent is Augustine's *City of God*, which reads both the biblical text and the ancient history of empires up until his contemporary Rome as a story of the overlapping city of God and city of man, animated by rival loves: the love of God and the love of self. But Augustine's commitment to the concept of city lends his account a slightly more institutional and less organic, even ecclesiological, inflection than we are seeking here. And where Augustine distinguishes these two domains by their love, we are instead proposing that these two peoples are defined by two kinds of rests: the peaceful relations that come only when God is king versus the self-referencing aseity that seeks satisfaction on its own terms but never finds it.[32]

To suggest that the people of God are those who are being conformed into God's image is a key feature of Pauline theology.[33] It also echoes another significant figure in the Christian tradition. Athanasius in *On the Incarnation* spells out Christ's mission as God incarnate as primarily an image-restoration program. Unlike Paul, however, his account of the image remains more individual than communal. Understanding God's image instead as related to the establishment of God's household of Sabbath rest begins to indicate the role and purpose of the church. To be in God's image is to be active residents of God's household, to be subject to his sovereignty, to belong to his family, and so to be formed by God's positive paternal relationship. Jesus is both our brother and our King.[34] Understanding Sabbath as membership in God's household and God's

---

[32]This notion of God as the one in whom humanity alone finds rest is arguably the heartbeat of Augustine's corpus, distilled in his trademark phrase: "You have made us for yourself, and our heart is restless until it rests in you." Augustine, *Confessions*, trans. Henry Chadwick, Oxford World's Classics (Oxford University Press, 2008), 3.
[33]See Rom 8:29; 1 Cor 15:49; 2 Cor 3:18; Col 3:10.
[34]Jn 18:37; 20:17.

kingdom, then, means that Sabbath is a political concept. To talk about Sabbath is to talk about the formation of a people, not a personalized day off.

Biblically, this reading of Genesis also finds resonance with the Johannine theme of rebirth. Because we have been cast out from our original household of Eden—of Sabbath—we need a new paternity, an adoption, even a rebirth.[35] Genesis gestures toward this rebirth at the very start of its postrebellion genealogy. Genesis 4:1-2 echoes the opening creation account's description of humans as created in God's image. But Genesis 5:3 presses the point that Seth was born in *Adam's* likeness and image.[36] This creates a clear trajectory for the line of Seth: to return to the image and likeness of God by calling on him and walking with him.

A second look at the story of Cain and Abel reveals how this tale of two peoples begins to take shape. Consider the location of Cain's fratricide. After their rebellion, Adam and Eve are kicked out of the *garden* that is located *in* Eden. But they are not yet evicted from the land of Eden itself.[37] It is outside the garden but not yet outside Eden that we meet Cain and Abel in Genesis 4. They are both offering sacrifices to God, although no such offering had been commanded. That Cain's sacrifice is rejected and Abel's accepted with no explanation suggests that any attempt at reconciliation with God cannot be achieved on human terms.[38] It is this misunderstanding and even rejection of God's terms and God's economy that leads to Cain's violence.

God's dialogue with Cain offers further clues of the kinds of terms that God *does* expect from his people. God's interrogative questions highlight relationship and responsibility. Yet Cain refuses to take responsibility both for himself and his emotional state, as well as for his brother.[39] In Genesis 4:9,

---

[35]Jn 1:12-13; 3:3.
[36]Gen 5:3.
[37]Gen 3:23; cf. Gen 2:8.
[38]Hebrews explains that Abel's sacrifice was accepted because of his faith, underscoring that it is not the sacrifice as such—or any institution or work—that achieves reconciliation with God (Heb 11:4).
[39]Gen 4:6-7, 9.

when he denies that he is his "brother's keeper," he employs the same Hebrew root word used to detail Adam and Eve's responsibility to serve and keep the Garden of Eden (*shamar*).[40] This is the opposite of an overlord; it denotes a careful attention to the interests and well-being of another. Cain is rejecting here the very task that was intended for humans living in God's Sabbath reign—to attentively seek out rest for and with others.

Cain completes his rejection of responsibility by murdering his brother. But as with Adam and Eve, God does not abandon Cain. Here again, God's discipline is an act of grace and an invitation to ongoing growth. God disciplines Cain by exiling him from Eden to the land of Nod, or "wandering."[41] But Cain rejects the discipline of homelessness. Instead he attempts an alternate path by establishing a city named after his son Enoch.[42] The rest of the chapter details the descendants of Enoch's line, outlining a family tree of artisans who are transforming the world to forge their own rest. Thereafter Genesis describes the birth of Seth and Seth's firstborn, Enosh ("humanity"), when people began to call on God. Here is the germination of the people of God.[43] Seth is the one who prays, who initiates again the act of seeking God's word. This dual genealogy indirectly introduces the crucial biblical question: Whom shall we serve? Will we be the line of Cain or the line of Seth?[44]

These two lines reveal their completion or perfection in the seventh generation of each. Lamech is the seventh generation from Adam through Cain. His line of city builders and craftsmen models formation through work, institutions, and the fashioning of artifices. Just as Cain took God's promise of complete protection as complete (sevenfold) vengeance and built a city instead of wandering, so Lamech brings this rejection of God's sovereign justice to its completion by executing vengeance for himself. Whatever God promised to give to Cain, Lamech will achieve for

---

[40]Gen 2:15.
[41]Gen 4:12, 16.
[42]Gen 4:17.
[43]Gen 4:26.
[44]In some ways this is the question that drives the narrative plot of John Steinbeck's *East of Eden*.

himself—and seventy times better.[45] Whatever God created, those who are born into the line of Cain believe they can do better by their own works, by their own progress, and by bringing to "perfection" that which they considered as raw material. Lamech will protect himself with violence perfected in the preemptive strike and hegemony through a monopoly of violence, the very living symbol of imperial ambition.

Seth's descendant in the seventh generation of Adam is Enoch, who offers a bright contrast. Beginning by calling on God, the perfection is in walking with God, journeying with him. After walking with God for 365 years, he is simply taken away by God, as if death were both an unnecessary and overly abrupt interim in an organic, lifelong formation terminating in reunion with God. It seems Enoch entered into God's rest, the final destination of the one who walks with God. Seth's lineage is conspicuously silent on their civilizational achievements.

While this is just the beginning of the Bible's story of the tale of two peoples, many of the key themes are already contained within. The people of God are willing to accept the discipline of God, to wander, and to bear responsibility through maturity to arrive at the rest of God, ready to take up their role in the divine council as image bearers of God's own character. God's enemies seek to create their own artificial realities of satisfaction and rest, built on monopolies of violence and on the development of powers that dominate with structures that prevent even the possibility of responsible choice. The line of Cain is the line of perpetual unrest by constant outsourcing of responsibility to objective structures. The line of Seth is the way to peace through mature relationships of responsibility. Genesis here is something of a genealogical rendition of Psalm 1: a diptych that sets the organic, patient way of the righteous with the dry, fruitless, and temporary machinations of the wicked. And in this way, as much as Genesis tells a genealogy, it is not an ethnocentric one. The Bible is well aware that siblings can take different paths, that trees can branch off—and be grafted on.[46]

---

[45]Note the parallel logic used in Jesus' own statement about forgiveness in Mt 18:21.
[46]Rom 11:17-21.

Babel: The Construction of Unrest

After the flood, the descendants of Noah's sons come together to form an empire epitomized in the city of Babel. As with the whole of Genesis 1–11, reading these as simple moralistic tales occludes the narrative flow and purpose of this biblical prehistory. Perhaps nowhere is this more obvious than Genesis 10, which concludes the story of rebellion and is in a sense the rounding out of the movement of history away from God. This movement will continue to play out in countless later generations. After the flood, a great fear that the people will be scattered and thus powerless inspires them to a grand construction project.

Reprising the story of Cain, the story of Babel displays a people's rejection of walking with God in their state of exile. They opt instead to construct a walled-off enclosure centered on a ziggurat that symbolizes a holy mountain on which a god would live and accept sacrifices. This artificial god-dwelling perfectly exemplifies the nature of sin as the powers. A human construct takes on a life of its own, projecting the need for value giving and command giving on human institutions. The gods are artificial simulations made real by the real sovereignty given to them. There is often a mistaken interpretive tendency to focus on the tower, as though God were spatially threatened by people climbing a stepped pyramid. A more compelling interpretation understands the tower as representing the religious ambitions of a city to create its own world. In ancient times, cities were often built on sacred sites. The most important sites might have even been seen as the center of the world, its navel, attaching the world of humans to the umbilical lifeline of the gods. Power radiated from these sites, and construction projects often focused most intensely on capturing the latent power of these sites for human use through religious means.[47]

---

[47]For a basic introduction to the sociological link between city, cosmos, and cosmology see Mircea Eliade, *The Sacred and The Profane: The Nature of Religion*, trans. Willard R. Trask (Harcourt Brace, 1987), 32-53. The social construction of space and time through enacted myth is a well-documented phenomenon across premodern cultures. See, e.g., Richard Seaford, *Cosmology and the Polis: The Social Construction of Space and Time in the Tragedies of Aeschylus* (Cambridge University Press, 2015). Others have noted that modern technology has not eliminated the structure of this manner of thinking, and the sacred has moved from religion into other

Babel represents nothing short of the Cainite project of creating an artificial reality—safe, secure, approaching the gods on its own terms through sacrificial bargains. The builders of Babel believed that unity would come through common objective projects, by the creation of identities beyond the familial, by the standardization of language. Social bonds could be cemented through the polis, the city, which would be projected into a united national identity—they would make a name for themselves.[48] Rather than being named, they would *make* a name, and thus construct an identity, by conflating themselves with their dream home.

God's opposition to this project has often been seen as a sign of either arbitrary or insecure spite—as if God felt threatened by this human bid for collective power. But considering this story within Genesis 1–11 reveals that God's judgment on Babel is specifically designed to show what God will do in judgment after his promise not to destroy at the end of the flood. When Cain's project is attempted again, God's response is to undermine the plausibility structure of the whole edifice. Rather than attacking the material reality of the city, God undermines the myth of unity that the city was designed to concretize. We might suggest that God demythologized Babel and that the confusion of their language is really about the lack of a shared moral framework due to a lack of shared identity. They were no longer "us," no longer a coherent household.

At the same time, we see that God punishes Babel with diversity. Babel, like all empires regardless of their propaganda stating otherwise, achieves unity only by uniformity of sacred moral values. Even the contemporary championing of diversity as a value is really a project of conformity, normalization, and commodification of culture.[49] And just as God's

---

areas such as the state and technology. See, e.g., Jacques Ellul, *The New Demons*, trans. C. Edward Hopkin (Seabury, 1975); William T. Cavanaugh, *Migrations of the Holy: God, State, and the Political Meaning of the Church* (Eerdmans, 2011); G. P. Wagenfuhr, *Plundering Eden: A Subversive Christian Theology of Creation and Ecology* (Cascade Books, 2020).

[48] Gen 11:4.

[49] This idea that modern appeals to diversity are actually an attempt at homogenizing may be a new one. For more, see Wagenfuhr, *Plundering Eden*, 117–18.

punishments on Adam and Eve and later Cain were designed to invite them into maturity through discipline, so too Babel's discipline is diversity. The only way unity can be achieved amid diversity without devaluation is by *love*, a kind of relationship that cannot be objectified or concretized. It can be actively lived out only by people with *other* people. Love is a union of heterogeneity. Empire is the crusade of homogeneity. The two cannot coexist and each cannot tolerate the methods of the other. Empires must grow, centralize, and move toward a cult of personality as it worships a single identity. But love cannot grow beyond the relational capacity of people, a capacity formed by time. Empires want to be timeless and strive after static visions of eternality, the golden age. Love lives and dies, and learns to love all the more in the face of death.

As we will see, the kingdom of God stands in stark contrast with Babel in the New Testament, particularly in Revelation. But what we find both with the God of *hesed* and the kingdom of God in Jesus is a characterization of a king who chooses to love his enemies in the face of death. Babel ascends: "Let us build . . . a tower." God descends in love and judgment: "Come, let us go down."[50] And yet, it's not God alone who descends but the whole divine council ("us") who attends him and will attend him, and who thus must engage in the same pattern of divestment that also refuses to respect the accomplishments of bitumen and mortar. This is the very language of making bricks that will haunt the people of God in Egyptian slavery.[51]

God has a personal relationship with every individual creature, unmediated through group or species identities. This means the story of God's sovereignty, the story of Sabbath, is not the conquest of seemingly chaotic difference but of becoming mature enough to love the wild things of the world, including the wild people. God will achieve his victory when Babel is finally defeated, when human myths of unity through self-created identities concretized in economic and political structures are rendered

---

[50]Gen 10:4, 7.
[51]See 1 Cor 6:2-3; Ex 5.

entirely implausible because God's people have loved their enemies enough to undermine their myths.

We could say, then, that an indication of the difference between God's people and Babel lies in the mediums of their union. Babel tries to achieve rest through uniformity of construction; God's people through diversity of relationships of love. The project of Babel, which is the project of aseity—the dream home—will usually be characterized by static structures that are uniform and derivative. The household of God, by contrast, will usually be characterized by the fluid medium of language, which is more thoroughly creative, finding its substance in time and relationship. To reach for ancient philosophic terminology, the difference here is between mimesis and poesis: between that which simply replicates and that which is genuinely original.

Put differently: The worldly empires of aseity are marked by the monuments they build; God's people by the songs that they sing, just as early church history reveals. The lands where the gospel first spread—Jerusalem, Ephesus, Rome—contain plenty of structural ruins of the Roman Empire, that is, crumbling arenas, theaters, palaces, and fortresses. But one will find almost no architectural remains of the church, at least not from its fledgling centuries. The early church didn't build structures, but they did move in together, practicing shared life as the maturing household of God.[52] Their shared lives were distinctive and concentrated enough that Christian neighborhoods were specifically targeted during Nero's persecutions in response to the great fire of Rome in AD 64.

Yet it is just a few decades prior, just after Christ's ascension, that we might detect the starkest difference between the buildings of Babel and the creations of God's people. Acts 2 describes the day of Pentecost, when the Holy Spirit descends on God's people to reverse the judgment of Babel. This happens not by a return to a universal human language but by the gift of interpretation and communication between diverse tongues. The

---

[52]For more on the architectural differences between the Roman Empire and Jesus' first followers, see Eugene H. Peterson, *The Jesus Way: A Conversation on the Ways That Jesus Is the Way* (Eerdmans, 2011), 204-5.

Holy Spirit–empowered church does not *erase* difference; it *reconciles*. The unity of God's people is not found in artificial structures or enforced conformity but in the true unity in which diversity is grounded in a common faith expressed in active love. The Holy Spirit enables the church's diversity. The church of early Acts is the material expression of Christ's statement, "My kingdom does not belong to this world."[53]

But it is still a long road from Babel to Pentecost. More immediately in the biblical story, Babel sets the stage for the next installment of the people of God: God's calling of and covenant with Abraham. The mention of buildings and bricks prefigures their slavery in Egypt and, much later, their occupation by Babylon and Rome. But more universally, it showcases a pattern of God's engagement in history. Misguided human attempts at self-sovereignty are countered by God's own sovereign intervention as an ongoing grace.

Sin, Death, and Corruption

This notion of sin as a power whose existence is predicated on human rebellion fits well with much of the biblical literature, but we must confront the fact that the books of Exodus through Deuteronomy have quite a detailed religious mechanism that complicates but also complements our working definition of sin here. This will help us understand how Jesus fits into the Sabbath gospel.

We will explore this understanding of sin in chapter seven in more detail. But it is worth noting now in brief that the logic of the household of God is the logic of the life giver or the "author of life," while the logic of the household of sin is the logic of death, exploitation, and corruption. These life-and-death relations are played out not only through symbolic forms found in rituals but in a whole economy oriented around using the power of death to advance and gain influence. Thus, while the signs found in rituals might seem arcane, they point toward a household order in which sin is taken seriously as a corrupting power and influence that is

---

[53]Jn 18:36.

about far more than personal legal guilt. It is about a force that actively subverts the economy of the household of God.

A Tale of Two Times

Sabbath highlights how the Bible tells a tale of two times. With the rebellion of Adam and Eve, time becomes fractured into disparate timelines. For the Bible, as for much of the ancient world, the experience of time was related to the character of dominating factors and people rather than objective units of measurement. Time is about character, not about quantity or duration. These times were known as ages. Each age corresponds to the sovereignty of a particular ruler, and where there are competing rulers, there are competing and potentially overlapping ages. The time of Sabbath overlaps human history. This means that each household has a different experience of time. Human history under the household of sin, of Cain, is characterized by conquest, competition, exploitation, and capitalizing on death. The Sabbath is characterized by liberation, giving rest, abundance, and life.

This contrasts with the typical way in which Christian theology has discussed time in comparison with eternity, which is the expression of aseity in terms of time. It's not that God invades time with eternity, denigrating time or change, as though time were of less value than timelessness. God invades an age of rebellion with a time of Sabbath.

The tale of two times takes shape as a story of the sixth and seventh days of creation, of the time of God's patience and the time of God's rule. The sixth day, taken by itself as a self-enclosed universe, as seen by Cain's walled city or by Babel, is ultimately meaningless. It must construct its own meaning: This is the dream home. This is Babel and the myths of unity that sustain it. This is the great hope of Cain's line: to give an authorized history of the universe that needs no external referent apart from human empiricism, rationality, and advanced techniques of observation. This is a false hope, however, because the only way to control time is to abandon time, to move beyond beginnings and ends, stories and relation, and move to a place of stasis that can only exist in the artificial realities of managed systems. Eternity is the dream home, and the time of Cain is the hope of endless structure.

But Sabbath is the time of God. Meaning comes to the sixth day by its advancement to the seventh. This is not a necessary progress, because time itself is not sovereign; God is. The advent of God's reign is not a fact of history—it is the fact that will make history meaningful.

Conclusion: *Felix Culpa?*

In this chapter we explored the shape of human rebellion against the house of God. This narrative relays both a real rebellion *in* history and a pattern *of* history. As we examine the Bible through the lens of Sabbath, with our minds attentive to the shape of time within, we have seen that what the historical drama Genesis 3–10 describes is the origin of history itself (not the universe) and the shape of the historical time with which we are familiar. This is the dialectical nature of time in which children improve the works of their parents, taking them to ever more complete conclusions, but leading nowhere. The true wandering of history is like the land of Nod, of wandering, in which Cain built his city. The attempt at building the dream home is frustrated by time, death, and disillusionment . . . and yet we ceaselessly labor to build—if not utopia, then at least some mirage of stasis and durability. We concretize our values and so try to extend our will beyond the confines of the self or the natural lifetime. All of this is aimless wandering.

The story of Cain, of vengeful Lamech, of Babel, encapsulates the entirety of life in a regressed sixth day of creation, endlessly spiraling in circles of progress but never attaining what the sixth day was pointed toward: the Sabbath. This spiral of time, always curving in on itself just like the individual sinner, characterizes human experience. For this reason many traditions have sought to express time itself as a cycle.[54]

---

[54]These cycles of time are seen in karma, metempsychosis (transmigration of souls), and Nietzsche's eternal recurrence and *amor fati*. "Curving in on itself" refers to a phrase coined by Luther, *homo incurvatus in se*, derived from Augustine's theology of sin as self-love. See Matt Jenson, *The Gravity of Sin: Augustine, Luther, and Barth on Homo Incurvatus in Se* (T&T Clark,

These are attempts to build time itself into a house, into an architecture that is to be loved and lived within. Such time is either something to escape or to be embraced and loved, monstrous as it is.[55]

We will find that the Bible offers a third option, which has been hinted at throughout this chapter—a new parentage and maturation through discipline. In seeking to build heaven on earth, humans have unleashed hell when all along God has been calling us to a form of purgatory here and now in the shape of reformative discipline.

While we may not want to go so far as to describe sin as *felix culpa*, a "happy/lucky fault," as some theologians have previously done, because only by the rebellion of Adam has Jesus come, we can agree that God was not surprised by the rebellion or the shape it took.[56] God will make good out of evil, but not through summary judgment and conclusions. God will make good out of evil because he will raise up people who are rooted in God's Sabbath time. These people live in time when others escape it. They embrace the fate of discipline and death in a posture of Abrahamic trust that God can bring about new life. They become "more than conquerors" not because they have made a name for themselves but because they have been crucified with Christ, suffered with him to be raised with him, and so will come before the throne of God prepared for the responsibility of inheriting a kingdom and shared sovereignty.[57] The mission of God's people will be to reconcile the house of God as they themselves are reconciled to God.

Rather than *felix culpa*, we might suggest *felix disciplina*. Discipline is the essence of discipleship, and the line of Seth are those who embrace

---

2006). Our point has been to demonstrate that this takes civilizational form and is not restricted to the individual.

[55]For time as something to escape, see "axial age" movements in Plato, traditional folk Christianity, Islam, Buddhism, Hinduism. The axial age is Karl Jaspers's hypothesis in the history of religions that posits that a revolution occurred in Persia, the Mediterranean, India, and China, with second-generation beliefs arising that questioned the nature of reality and the old pagan conceptions. As a theory, it has not been widely accepted or rejected, but it is a useful term that does identify shifts in belief. See Jaspers, *The Origin and Goal of History* (Yale University Press, 1953).

[56]E.g., Alvin Plantinga, "Supralapsarianism, or 'O Felix Culpa,'" in *Christian Faith and the Problem of Evil*, ed. Peter van Inwagen (Eerdmans, 2004), 1-25.

[57]As suggested by Jesus in the parables of the talents and minas. Rom 8:37; Gal 2:19; Phil 3:10-11.

discipline, the line of Cain those who reject it. The people of God are those who wander as strangers, exiles, pilgrims and who do not seek to build a home but to inherit one far greater, one that is built not of palaces, temples, and walls but on love for the other and for the community of God's creation with all its diversities. To reach for the wisdom of J. R. R. Tolkien, who may have had a prescient theological sense in the *Lord of the Rings* trilogy, perhaps "Not all those who wander are lost."[58]

Group Discussion Questions

1. How have you and/or your community tended to understand sin? What are the implications of conceiving of sin as a power that inhabits human structures?

2. What are features of the household of sin that you can identify in your context?

---

[58] J. R. R. Tolkien, *The Fellowship of the Ring: Being the First Part of the Lord of the Rings* (Del Rey, 2018), 193.

SIGNS OF THE COVENANT

A TRAILBLAZER IS SOMEONE who makes marks to indicate where trail builders should follow and prepare a way. Along our Sabbath journey, the direction of travel along the narrow path toward maturity of character that arrives at the Sabbath rest of God is determined by God himself. In the Bible, trailblazing happens through covenantal signs. These are indications of how God wants his people to relate to him, to others, and to his creation. When the prophet Isaiah and later John the Baptist call on the people to prepare the way of God's arrival, making straight paths, this is a call to follow the blazed signs and make a trail. The best way to make such a trail will be for the people themselves to simply travel the path laid out by God himself. There is also a tradition established on some famous trails that mark those who have traveled it, a sign that one bears to indicate purpose, like the seashell of the Camino de Santiago. In this way, a trail itself makes a visible mark that travelers bear to show others their character and purpose.

In this chapter we will explore how the practice of Sabbath serves as a *sign*, an embodied action that points beyond itself, within a range of key signs of the Old Testament. Our main claim in this chapter is that God seeks to establish his economy of Sabbath by forming a people who bear signs that point to his sovereign order from within this rebellious world. We'll begin by reviewing some of the key themes from the past few chapters, which will continue to resound in the following ones even as we organically encounter and integrate more themes on our journey.

We started with an invitation to think of creation as God's household. In any household, one of the central activities is the sharing and distribution of food. This is also how the head of the household—the breadwinner—demonstrates the ability and concern to provide. In other words, *food symbolizes sovereignty*.[1] This is encoded in our language: The English word *lord* comes from Old English *hlaford*, meaning "bread-keeper" ("loaf-ward"). Not surprisingly, the giving of food is one of the culminating aspects of the creation account.[2] We'll watch as food continues as a central feature of Sabbath practice, next in the provision of manna as daily bread and eventually in the key ecclesial meal of the Lord's Supper.

But there is another, more dramatic event that forms the climax of the first creation account: God's resting on the seventh day. This divine Sabbath underscores the purpose of the household of creation: to serve as the scene of God's indwelling presence with creation. The first Sabbath shows that God wills to be more than just a distant or ongoing Creator, forever tinkering at his next project. Instead, God wills to be and relate *with* creation. In other words, God's essence isn't known through the act of creation itself, nor is God knowable by the fact of creation. God is not a grand architect of a building or empire but a Father of a household.

Humans are commissioned with a special responsibility within the household order of creation as fashioned in the image of God. We proposed that the image of God reflects an ancient Near Eastern concept of the divine council, a political body whose members would dialogue with a divine being or king on matters related to the administration of a realm. The Bible indicates that at creation, humans are commissioned to serve as members of a divine council with God, taking active responsibility in dialogue with God as overseers of creation. If the Old Testament only hints that being in the image of God entails joining God's extended household,

---

[1] Ps 111:5.
[2] Gen 1:29-30.

this is developed in more detail in the New Testament, where "image" language properly belongs to a child who imitates the father, as Seth does Adam in ways Cain does not.

Sabbath Economy

Another way of understanding the role of humans on the divine council is that of a household manager. Humans are to act maturely as responsible for the running of the household of God's creation, attending to the health and well-being of its members. As mentioned in the introduction, the word *oikonomos* is a compound word that literally means "house law."[3] From it derive the English words *economy* and *economist*. Sabbath is about the economy of God and of God's people.[4] It is about the patterns that govern the flow of gifts between the elements of creation as the material community that enjoys God's presence. Sabbath is unavoidably economic.[5] And *economy*, as with *Sabbath*, applies to the wider groupings humans have imagined as an extension of the family household, namely, the nation (*natio* is Latin for "birth/race"), the politic (*polis* is Greek for "city-state"), and the homeland/fatherland/motherland.

Ecology, like *economy*, is a compound Greek word. It shares the prefix *eco-*, which derives from "house," but in place of *nomos* it contains the suffix derived from the Greek word *logos*—"word" or "logic." *Ecology* is a modern word, but like *economy*, it refers to the material rules that govern

---

[3] Lk 12:42; 16:1.
[4] We aren't the first to draw attention to the economic implications/inflections of Sabbath. At least as far back as 1839, P. J. Proudhon, early anarchist philosopher, wrote an essay titled "The Celebration of Sunday," with Sabbath as the basis for political and economic well-being. He states, "Every system of laws and institutions needs to be protected by a special institution that encompasses and sums it up, which is its crown and its basis; because the Sabbath, suspending the rude labors of an almost entirely agricultural population, and connecting minds through the connection of persons, a day of public exaltation, national mourning, popular instruction and universal emulation, stopped the speculations of interest and directed the reason towards a more noble object. It softened manners by the charm of a rest that was not sterile, aroused a mutual goodwill, developed the national character, made the rich more liberal, evangelized the poor, and excited the love of the homeland in every heart." Proudhon, "The Celebration of Sunday," 1839, www.marxists.org/reference/subject/economics/proudhon/1839/celebration-of-sunday.html.
[5] This point is not lost on Sabbath scholars, even if the implications have yet to be fully metabolized by the church. See, e.g., Ched Meyers, *The Biblical Vision of Sabbath Economics* (Tell the Word, 2001).

planetary ecosystems. The two words point to a similar phenomenon, even if we've separated them into different domains in modern society—one natural and the other human-made. Their linguistic separation speaks volumes about the breakdown of communion between the household of creation and the houses of human commerce. If Sabbath is about the household reign of God, and if Sabbath is a biblical claim to the shape of all reality rather than a spirituality divided from materiality, we shouldn't be surprised to find that a robust theology of Sabbath will have potent economic and ecological implications in the contemporary senses of these terms.[6]

God's economic order is composed primarily of *relationships*—of the quality of the connection, understanding, and trust that exist between parties. Value is created cooperatively in relationships of love and care. By contrast, human economic order is composed primarily of alienated value—a value imagined to be objective or separate, making us only observers of so-called facts when in reality we are judges who create value by the act of judgment. There is no such thing as objective value, only masked judgment. Both divine and human economic orders can exist in one place. But one will confuse the edifice itself (the house) for the set of embodied relations that inhabit it (the family/household). In their very effort to standardize, stabilize, and utilize, human economic orders refuse to properly see, receive, and respond to the kind of thing that the world and its residents are: gifts, or in other words, *grace*. Human economic orders mistake the world as neutral, isolated *resources* that one earns by craft instead of entering into a living economy of gift giving.

These economic orders of craft naturally calcify into systems of earning regulated and reinforced by institutions. This economic creep is most blatantly evident in the temple. God's people make the mistake of thinking that God dwells in a *house* instead of with a *household*. The temple structure becomes misread as a mark of privilege and entitlement instead

---

[6] Again, at least as early as Proudhon, the link between Sabbath and economic life, including that of the natural world, was observed. "Man is a transient on the earth: the same soil which feeds him has fed his father and will feed his children" (Proudhon, "Celebration of Sunday").

of a gracious sign of God's presence.[7] Institutional maintenance replaces relational health.[8] This pattern is evident within human economic orders in the all-too-familiar way that bureaucratic systems and protocols override common-sense judgments about the well-being of the people they supposedly serve.

Repeatedly throughout Scripture, God identifies with and commits to *people*, not human or natural constructs of nation-states or ecological processes (as with pagan gods). This is the God of Abraham, Isaac, and Jacob; this is the God of living people, not dead structures or lifeless institutions or certain segments of the ecosystem or life cycle.[9] This is why the idea of a Christian nation—as governed by a set of constitutional rules and political arrangements abstracted from so-called Christian principles—is theologically (if not sociologically) impossible.[10] God reigns over *people*, not processes; organisms, not organizations. But human rebellion transforms the former into the latter, the relational into the objective, so that love becomes economic in the worst sense of the word.

Sabbath refers to the quality and character of those relations over which God reigns and with which he dwells. The relational nature of Sabbath is what underwrites its temporal dimension. One does not simply enter into God's household as one walks into a building. One enters into God's household as one is adopted into a family.

Signs of Sovereignty

Since God rules over people, it makes sense that God primarily makes *covenants*, not constitutions, contracts, or universalized philosophical principles. A covenant is an agreement between differing parties, confirmed or sealed with a sign, involving terms of union and dissolution. Entering into a covenant transforms a relationship in ways not implied in a contract. Marriage is the classic example, in which the kiss and the rings

---

[7]Jer 7:4; Is 66:1-2.
[8]Hos 4:8.
[9]Mt 22:32.
[10]The Hebrew word sometimes translated "nation" in Gen 12:2 is better rendered "people."

are signs that confirm a transformation of relationship built on an agreed set of terms guiding the union: the vows. Not only is marriage used throughout the Bible as a metaphor for God's relationship with his people, but it highlights the centrality of signs as they transfigure what might otherwise be domination into a household or family. The household or economy of God is manifest in sign-bearing people. Although in everyday English we may rarely talk about signs other than the traffic variety, the term *sign* has a long and rich biblical and theological pedigree.[11] Just as a spouse bears the sign of marriage publicly in the form of a ring, so too the people of God bear public signs to indicate their relationship and purpose to the world.

By displaying signs of God's covenantal commitment to them, God's people claim an identity that points to a sovereignty beyond the rebellious world's horizon. But humans don't just make signs. Humans *are* signs.[12] This is precisely what humans do as the image of God. They are signs of the presence and reality of God. To be a legible and accurate pointer to God, a human must be mature. To be mature in Christian terms is to be a person whose actions intentionally direct attention to God's household economy (sovereignty) in contextually relevant ways.

Within this household covenant God issues commands to form his people to maturity. The pedagogical function of law is its primary purpose in the Bible.[13] Psalm 119 makes clear that God's commands guide the obedient follower along a path or a *way*. In this, the important thing to note is that God relates to people in a manner that involves *time*. Pedagogy is formative, but it implies a process of maturation. Thus God's commands are diminished by translating them into ethics or rules that have meaning

---

[11] Augustine famously discusses the distinction between signs and things as a foundation to his account of biblical interpretation, and in so doing established the Western discipline of semiotics, or the study of signs. See especially Augustine, *On Christian Doctrine* 1-2.

[12] For an excellent theological reflection on Augustine's semiology that develops the notion of humans as a sign of God, see Susannah Ticciati, *A New Apophaticism: Augustine and the Redemption of Signs* (Brill, 2013).

[13] So Paul seems to think in Gal 3:24-25, which comports with the Shema as a summary of the Ten Commandments in Deut 6, which states that these laws are to be displayed in ways that encourage pedagogy.

outside the covenant. These are not objective principles to be obeyed for their own sake or even for achieving a static vision of a well-ordered commonwealth. That would be legalism—the assumption that human morality is about conforming to static ethical principles rather than pointing to the divine authority of a living God as it forms individuals more into his image. Legalism creates an arid work-reward economy of merit rather than a verdant ecosystem of receipt, return, and growth. Legalism imagines that good work merits reward as compensation in a kind of implicit employment contract. The economy of God works in the opposite direction—faithful relationships produce good fruit.

As we will see shortly in this chapter and continue to explore in coming ones, "sign" language is key for making a critical distinction between *practices* of Sabbath and the *reality* of Sabbath. It also shows how the practices of God's people are a kind of language. The language of the gospel a church proclaims is only as good as the language of the life it lives as a witness to the gospel.

We could say that there is a kind of story, or at least a journey, in the biblical signs. The covenantal signs begin as physical markers that are relatively unchanging—such as the rainbow and circumcision. But with the practice of Sabbath there is a key shift: Sabbath is a *lived* sign that shapes human behavior. It begins to develop the people *themselves* into a sign of God. However, the covenantal signs fail to transform God's people when they become ossified into institutions and rote traditions that do not touch or shape the human heart. The sign has little power outside a living relationship. And even when it is practiced, the living out of Sabbath brings about the reality to which it points only partially, in a shadowy way.[14] Jesus, as we will see later, *is* the light that casts the shadow. He is Sabbath and Jubilee in the flesh, establishing a household, bringing people into it by including them in the economy/household rule of God, which begins with rescuing people from the economies of the world. The story of signs is thus also an exploration of the nature of human work. Just as

---

[14]Col 2:17.

food symbolizes sovereignty, so work symbolizes the master. Just as many employees wear a brand or logo when performing official duties, thus transforming the individual into a representative of the corporation, so too Sabbath must become the embodied sign that transforms our work into the representation of the image of God.

While signs might seem like objective markers that have an independent existence, they serve a purpose only in a specific kind of active relationship. A sign transforms entirely when it points to something no longer living, like old product advertisements in a largely abandoned town that serve only to highlight the decline and loss. Signs can be bitter reminders of what was or could have been. When the sign ceases to perform its intended function, when it points elsewhere, or even when it does nothing but point to its own existence in isolation, the sense of loss is obvious and tangible.

The fragility of signs contrasts with the durable powers of sin. Sin develops momentum until it takes on a life of its own. Signs, however, do not automatically create the reality they signify. Signs are effective only if they operate as the expressions of an organic and living heart. For this reason, the sovereignty of God over the present evil age does not come by the mere practice of Sabbath. Yet the very vulnerability of signs is a feature of their revelatory power, which is of a different order from the oppressive power of the implements of sin. Masks, buildings, personas, and avatars are durable and plastic; these powers of sin ultimately hide and suppress. They inhibit and quash real relation rather than cultivate them. Signs reveal; the powers conceal. Thus the method of confronting the powers is through the sign-based covenant.

Rainbow: Sign of God's Patience

The story of biblical signs began already with the image of God, as discussed. From there we come to perhaps the most famous covenantal sign: the rainbow. This is one of only three entities in the Old Testament canon explicitly identified as a "sign of the covenant."[15] It is a tangible feature of creation that points to God's commitment and intention in his relation to the world.

As for the nature of this particular sign, consider the second half of the English compound word *rainbow*. In the Hebrew text, what is sometimes translated "rainbow" is simply "bow" (the weapon, not the decoration).[16] Imagine a rainbow as a bow fitted with an arrow and drawn back. The arrow would be shooting *away* from the earth toward heaven. In contemporary terms, the rainbow is like a cocked and loaded gun directed toward heaven. The rainbow at the end of the tale of Noah demonstrates that "God relinquishes the right to use the bow destructively, and instead chooses to offer it as a sign for the covenant of peace and the reconciliation between God and all creation."[17] The bow and its arrows were commonly used to symbolize divine wrath through lightning and plague in the ancient Near East and Mediterranean, as indicated by our word *toxic*, which comes from the Greek *toxon*, meaning "bow."[18] The sign of the rainbow in the story of Noah reveals that God vows not to defeat evil with annihilating wrath. God is committing to work with people. God could easily and rightly determine otherwise. And significantly, the rainbow—unlike the signs that are to follow—does not engage any aspect of human behavior. It is a work of God alone, establishing a foundation of reconciliation with the promise to give the people a new chance. Other signs will engage human effort, though even these will only ever point to or participate in God's action.

---

[15] Gen 9:12.

[16] Gen 9:13.

[17] Jeanette Mathews, "Difficult Texts: 'I Have Set My Bow in the Clouds' (Genesis 9.13)," *Theology* 122, no. 1 (2019): 41.

[18] For comparison, ancient Greek belief held that Apollo's arrows directed at earth brought plague and devastation. Similarly, Rudra in the Indian Vedic tradition shot arrows as lightning and plague. Throughout the Levant, Reshef (with variant names/spellings) was a god of the netherworld responsible for plagues shot from his bow and arrow; he was popular on Cyprus, where he was equated with Apollo. In the Old Testament *resheph* can refer to "lightning," "plague," or "arrow." Douglas Frayne and Johanna H. Stuckey, *A Handbook of Gods and Goddesses of the Ancient Near East: Three Thousand Deities of Anatolia, Syria, Israel, Sumer, Babylonia, Assyria, and Elam* (Eisenbrauns, 2021), 302-3.

At the same time, the story of Noah hinges on a striking example of human work: the building of the ark. If we consider the layers of symbolism and meaning in this story, a portrait of the relation between human work and rest emerges that will continue to develop in the Bible. Noah means "rest." His birth narrative contains a prophecy that Noah will bring rest from the human toil that is the consequence of the cursing of the ground after Adam and Eve's rebellion.[19] There are several possible interpretations of how Noah provides this rest. One is that the incident of the flood is the introduction of rain to water the ground (which was until now in the world's history only spring fed) and thus mitigate the toil of agricultural labor.[20] Another is that Noah provides rest (or "comfort"—another translation) for humans by the introduction of viticulture.[21] Wine may indeed provide temporary relief from toil, a primitive opiate of the laboring masses, but the image of a flourishing vineyard is found often in the Bible as an image of God's household's thriving and providing. God provides not just daily bread but a basic luxury good for all the people in anticipation of the comfort that attends to the rest of attaining sovereignty.

But what we instead take as primary is that Noah brings rest in that he and his ark are the means by which the creation rests from the violence humans have introduced. Noah, of course, doesn't bring this rest himself but is the emblem, the lived sign of God's preservation of a seed of a new beginning in the midst of the seeming chaos of the God-caused storm. God uses this storm to put to death human rebellion. But he also uses people, through a fragile vessel, to bring new hope and life.

Through Noah we see God revealed as both wrathful judge and redeemer. These are not separate acts of God or two faces of the same character. Rest comes through judgment and justice but also through the human work of reconciliation commissioned and directed by God

---

[19]Gen 5:29.
[20]Deut 11:10-11 provides an interesting possible parallel here between the irrigation of Egypt and the rains of the Promised Land.
[21]Gen 9:20. Eccles 2:24 would likely agree.

through his people. As we considered in our reflection on the creation account, it is not the prerogative of human work to bring order to chaos. Throughout the Bible, God is the author of chaos—great storms, plagues, and disasters.[22] God is the one who plays with the wild beasts and chaos monsters. And yet, it is through the obedient work of God's chosen people that God brings his rest. The household of sin brings violence, enslavement, and centralized wealth and power. Rest comes by God's deliverance of a people through the storm. God's work of judgment both condemns and justifies, but God's work of justification will come through human obedience, through *faithfulness*, and this nowhere more obviously than in Jesus Christ.[23] In the story of the flood, we see that God is the cause and faithful humans are the means, the instruments, by which God brings rest to his creation. Faithfulness to God means doing work, but work of an entirely different alignment, work for the household of God.

The story of Noah is about God bringing rest to the creation through both judgment and redemption. But at the end, God swears off direct global judgment, symbolized through the self-pointing (rain)bow that indicates that God will take on himself the toxic arrows of storm and plague to bring rest to his creation through his people. And while the rainbow is a work of God alone, symbolizing God's unilateral promise, it is a sign under which the rest of the story of the Bible and human history can play out in relative safety. God is patient and does not will that any would perish, and so will not act unilaterally again.[24] God will work for reconciliation by the elevation of his image to the maturity that can represent him. Of course, the story of Noah is no hagiography. Noah's drunkenness and his sons' wickedness foreshadow a connection between the false rest of luxury and various immoralities that arise from a refusal to learn discipline through labor. Yet as we will continue to see throughout

---

[22] As in the exodus plagues and miracles, the storm of Jonah, the disasters of military defeat against Israel and Judah (see 1–2 Kings and most of the Prophets), and notably Amos 3:6 imagine that God is responsible for all urban disasters.
[23] The Greek term *pistis*, normally translated "faith," does not mean only or primarily intellectual assent but a whole-life loyalty or faithfulness that does not separate word and deed.
[24] 2 Pet 3:9.

the Scriptures, God can use even a modicum of imperfect faithfulness to bring about his purposes; the smallest of seeds can still grow the largest of trees and bear fruit.[25]

Circumcision: Planting a Household

If the rainbow is the sign of the covenant that assures God's determination to work with humanity to bring about reconciliation and maturation, the next sign indicates how God intends to do so. As with Noah, God chooses to work with someone who shows evidence of faithfulness through responsive obedience. Abraham's faithfulness is far from perfect. Yet in a classic declaration that will ring out into the New Testament and through Martin Luther's pen to form the theological foundation of the Reformation, God considers Abraham upright not because of his perfect behavior but because of the quality of his relationship: that of trust.[26] In the fertile soil of that trust, God will germinate a people who will bless the world.[27]

So God promises to give Abraham a family—a household—and to give those descendants a land. Although God continues to promise and make explicit that Abraham and his wife Sarah will have a child of their own, the promise is not forthcoming.[28] Abraham and Sarah are imperfectly faithful, attempting to engineer the fulfillment of God's promise on their own terms. Tellingly, this attempt at shortcutting God's promise on human terms ends up exploiting another. They arrange a surrogacy with Sarah's slave Hagar, who bears a son but not a child of the promise. God responds in grace by providing for Hagar and her son Ishmael. And God also responds in grace to Abraham by renewing his promise, but this time by also adding a sign for Abraham and his descendants to perform as their acknowledgment of this promise.

This second sign of the covenant is circumcision, an important marker of Jewish identity. For a contemporary audience it is an odd sign. In an

---

[25]Mt 13:31-32; 17:20.
[26]Rom 4:3; Gal 3:6; Jas 2:23.
[27]Gen 12:2-3.
[28]Gen 15:2-5.

ancient imagination it probably more obviously signified fertility and the idea that all of life belongs ultimately to God.[29] Yet even if we appreciate its symbolism as pointing to God as the ultimate author of life, circumcision may still seem patriarchal. A full half of the population is by nature excluded from participation in this sign of the covenant. But to take offense at what seems, at first blush, the exclusive nature of this sign likely only reveals the overly individualized way we think and operate as Western contemporaries. God's promise to Abraham is to fashion a great people through his offspring or, more literally in Hebrew, his seed (*zera'*). The English words *semen* and *sperm* similarly derive from the Latin word for "seed." The sperm that joins with the ovum in the womb to become any single member of the household of Abraham—both male and female—would pass through this sign at the very moment of conception. Even if this sign is borne on an individual body, it is corporate in its import.

Far from patriarchal, the fact that the sign of the covenant is carried on the reproductive member contrasts dramatically with common ancient Mediterranean and Near Eastern religious idolatry of the phallus. For Jews, sex and reproductive members were not a thing to worship, create images of, or view with sacred power. Rather than a sign of valorized genitalia, circumcision was a sign of restriction and dedication, an indelible mark of directed purpose in marriage and procreation. The orgy among pagans, for example, had a sacred power of creating a deep unity. It is easy for moderns eager to rediscover pagan polyamory and worship genitalia to miss the fact that ancient orgies were often not recreational and not necessarily optional. The link between sex and violence both individual and corporate is evidenced in countless myths, rituals, and folk tales. The

---

[29] As a parallel, Lev 19:23-25 describes the first produce of young trees as forbidden to eat because this fruit is to be counted as foreskin, that is, that the trees are metaphorically uncircumcised until the third year. In the fourth year the true firstfruits are holy and consecrated to God. Only in the fifth year can the fruit be eaten. This metaphor shows how the ritual of circumcision was itself a symbol of a belief that all life first and foremost belongs to God. See also Howard Eilberg-Schwartz, *The Savage in Judaism: An Anthropology of Israelite Religion and Ancient Judaism* (Indiana University Press, 1990), cited in Jonathan Klawans, *Purity, Sacrifice, and the Temple: Symbolism and Supersessionism in the Study of Ancient Judaism* (Oxford University Press, 2005), 43.

bacchanalia end in ritual murder. The restriction of sex to marriage and procreation was a radical means of restricting the power of male sexual domination as well as a restraint on the link between sex and violence.

Likewise, Jewish circumcision contrasts with the ancient Near Eastern religious practice of *hierogamy* (sacred marriage), in which a king as the representative of the people would copulate with a priestess or other representative of a maternal deity as a way of producing a good "crop" of a child that would represent the fertility of the whole people and their land. This was the practice at Sumerian New Year festivals, but many other cultures maintained a New Year festival that involved the inversion of social rules and hierarchy, along with otherwise illicit sex, as a means of participating in the yearly re-creation of the cosmos.[30] Circumcision as a sign of the covenant makes all sex acts consecrated to Yahweh for the creation not of an orderly imperial cosmos mediated by a god-king but a household of coheirs and divine representatives of reconciliation. Sex is demythologized, broken in its cultic power of symbolizing a Cainite and Babel-like formation of an imperial dynasty bringing order to chaos and domination through violence. The Jewish sign of circumcision is a symbolic dedication of the whole people to the mission of reconciliation.

Circumcision is a human work; it must be performed by human initiative and by human hands.[31] It's also a work that, as ancient Jewish philosopher Philo points out, ostensibly promotes the very fertility that would facilitate the fulfillment of God's promise by giving semen an unobstructed path.[32] But at the same time that circumcision is a human work that recognizes and even facilitates God's promise, it also acknowledges the limit of human effort: It is only God who can produce new life.[33] Circumcision does not produce life, but it does transform human action in

---

[30] See Mircea Eliade, *The Sacred and The Profane: The Nature of Religion*, trans. Willard R. Trask (Harcourt Brace, 1987); Roger Caillois, *Man and the Sacred* (repr., University of Illinois Press, 2001).

[31] See Jn 7:21-24 for Jesus' discussion with the Pharisees on the relation between circumcision as a work and Sabbath.

[32] Shaye J. D. Cohen, *Why Aren't Jewish Women Circumcised? Gender and Covenant in Judaism* (University of California Press, 2005).

[33] Cohen, *Why Aren't Jewish Women*, 62.

such a way that God's people are formed differently from the Gentiles through the power of living their signs.

The biblical language around the work of circumcision is also theologically instructive. Abraham and his descendants are commanded to "keep" (Hebrew *shamar*) the covenant through the sign of circumcision.[34] This is the same verb used to charge Adam and Eve to "keep" the Garden of Eden, and it is employed throughout the Bible to exhort obedience to God's commands, including the Sabbath command.[35] This language of keeping, which also draws in connotations of watching and guarding, emphasizes protecting something that is either already in existence or will be in existence, but not from the direct action of the keeper. This language of keeping, in other words, emphasizes the nature of signs: While they do not ultimately cause the things to which they point, they serve to form the people who will be the agents of the reconciliation God has purposed to bring to completion. Keeping God's signs is the means by which God is accomplishing the dual purpose of forming a people in his image and effecting the reconciliation he has called his people to proclaim.

What circumcision points to ultimately is God's determination to replant—or re*seed*—a new household, a Garden of Eden, in the midst of a rebellious wasteland. And as much as this household is established most immediately through the flesh and blood of Abraham, it is also resolutely not confined to bloodlines. Again, sex is decentered as an imperial activity because the image of God is not about cocreation. Abraham does not create a dynasty, training only elite sons, but a whole people who equally participate in the same formation. Circumcision is commanded not just of Abraham's direct descendants but of all members of his household.[36] Even here the Old Testament prefigures the principle of adoption into God's family, which will open wide the floodgates to the inclusion of Gentiles into the people of God. Paul's close reading of Genesis takes this one step further. He notes that, at telling moments, God's promises to Abraham's

---

[34]Gen 17:9-10.
[35]Gen 2:15.
[36]Gen 17:12-14.

seed are in the grammatically singular form.[37] Jesus Christ is the true seed who is the fulfillment of God's promise and whose very conception *without* the involvement of a circumcised male underscores that it is God alone who fashions life and that the whole point of the people was not their own thriving but their formation for the purpose for which Jesus came. It is through him that we become the true seed of Abraham, marked not by circumcision, status, or gender but by baptismal belonging to his body.[38]

Sabbath: Transforming Sign

The rainbow indicates the global rule of God's patience, his promise to provide the context within which reconciliation can happen. Circumcision is the sign that points to the consecration and direction of the multitude of people God is creating for his purpose. Sabbath is the sign that shapes the household God is establishing. Sabbath is the pedagogy that will grow his people into his image so that they can effect the reconciliation God has called them to. These signs recapitulate the shape of the creation narrative in Genesis 1. God first establishes the global conditions of creation, the space and time to be inhabited. Then God populates the space and time with particular creations. Finally, God creates a household and takes them to the pedagogy of the household-creation in Eden. Sabbath is the replanting of Eden, now contrasted with Egypt. Sabbath is the sign that God's people will bear as they journey out of Egypt and toward the fulfillment of God's Sabbath household in the kingdom of God.

But Sabbath needs to be set in its proper context of the story of Israel's being freed for worship and for rest from exploitation and slavery in Egypt.

Exodus

The exodus is a story about God's people becoming freed servants who no longer rely on the bread of Pharoh but on daily bread from God. Here we

---

[37]Gal 3:16.
[38]Gal 3:26-29.

focus on how Sabbath gives shape to the entire narrative of Exodus and how the exodus in turn tells us something about the nature of Sabbath as a sign.[39]

The exodus is about work, rest, and just and unjust labor. It's a story about economics—the household order we belong to. The drumbeat call of Exodus, posed repeatedly by God through Moses to Pharaoh—whose name, not coincidentally, means "great household"—is "Let my people go, so that they may serve me."[40] The Hebrew verb ʿabad, often translated "service" or "worship," is the same one used of the Israelites' slave labor in Egypt.[41] The question of Exodus, then, is, *Whose servants are these?* And by extension: Whose household do they belong to? Who is the true sovereign who provides their food? Also not coincidentally, the Israelites are building store-cities.[42] They are dependent on Pharaoh for daily bread even as they suffer the exploitation of his economy of accumulation.[43] The exodus is a battle of two rival household orders seeking to claim sovereignty over their residents. And given the nature of sovereignty, it's no surprise that food takes center stage.

Exodus 12–13 contains instructions for both the in-narrative and future celebrations of Passover. A few features of this meal are worth noting, especially in consideration that this meal forms the context for the Last Supper before Jesus' passion as well as the foundation for the church's regular household meal, the Lord's Supper. First is that the context for celebration is at the household level. This ritual does not require gathering en masse at a centralized institution. It reveals and anticipates (as Ex 16 will show) the Sabbath concern with the material conditions of a localized community.[44]

---

[39] Walter Brueggemann, *Sabbath as Resistance: Saying No to the Culture of Now* (John Knox, 2014), also considers the significance of Sabbath for the Exodus narrative.
[40] Michael S. Heiser, *The Unseen Realm: Recovering the Supernatural Worldview of the Bible* (Lexham, 2015), 12.
[41] Ex 1:13; 5:18; 6:5.
[42] Ex 1:11.
[43] Consider Jesus' parable of the rich farmer who builds barns in Lk 12:15-21.
[44] We would be misguided to project more recent notions of the nuclear family onto this scene. On the one hand, the instructions here make explicit directives to gather with neighbors

This meal is also a meal of several signs that indicates a transfer of allegiance from the slavery of Egypt to the sovereignty of God.[45] For the future generations of Israelites, the eating of unleavened bread is "as a sign" that reminds the Israelites to tell of God's redemptive work to the next generation.[46] And within the narrative of Exodus, the blood of the lamb is to be painted on the doorway as an apotropaic (warding-off) sign to God to spare those inside the consequence of the final plague against Egypt.[47] In this way, the meal distinguishes them from the surrounding empire. It will overlay onto circumcision as an identity marker of God's people.[48] These signs of the Passover meal integrate later generations into the same people who had come out of Egypt and thus, like circumcision, reinforce the specific identity of the people according to their relation to God.

One last feature is the relation of the meal to time. It is their last meal as slaves, a liberation feast and an act of resistance, which also looks ahead to their eating it as settled inhabitants in a new and abundant land. But in the context of that new land, it is a meal that looks backward onto God's rescue as the true act of initiation, the beginning of time. Even in the biblical text, it is a meal of recapitulating time; it is both a remembering and an anticipation, living in medias res. This has a bearing on the way the church celebrates its own liberation feast.

The Shape of Sabbath

If Passover is the last meal of Israel as an enslaved people dependent on the bread of Pharaoh, their first meal as a freed people displays that they are now under a new sovereign, showcasing his character. The miraculous manna, the food from heaven, which appears freely on the barren ground of the wilderness, is also their first theological lesson out of Egypt: Food

---

depending on numbers; but on the other hand, a house here would include both extended family and nonrelatives who are part of the household.
[45] Note it is not a "sign of the covenant" on par with the rainbow, circumcision, and Sabbath.
[46] Ex 13:9.
[47] Ex 12:13.
[48] Ex 12:48-49.

is not something humans earn by their labor, technology, or organization, but they freely receive it by God's grace.[49]

But manna is not just an object lesson in divine sovereignty and grace. It is also a training exercise, an opportunity for formation as God begins to shape ex-slaves into free subjects for life in a new household. It is around the collection and storage of their new daily bread that God gives the Israelites their very first commands, culminating with Sabbath rest, several chapters before the iconic issuing of the Ten Commandments. As we'll see in both the instructions around manna and in the subsequent Sabbath commands in Exodus and later in the Torah, far from Sabbath operating as a merely passive or negative activity, Sabbath is profoundly formative. First, Sabbath gives shape not just to one day in seven but to all of time. Second, Sabbath gives shape not just to individuals but to the entire community. Third, as a sign, Sabbath shapes the very identity of God's people.

Sabbath shapes all time. In the account of manna in Exodus 16, there are several commands that precede the command to weekly rest, developing narrative tension. After the Israelites complain about the lack of food, God promises to "rain bread from heaven for you," telling them to gather only enough for each day.[50] God makes clear that this is a test of obedience. It is a test of trust in God's provision and in their ability to practice the economy of God's household. This is a household built not on accumulation, false security, and exploitation but on daily sufficiency. The manna cannot be stored, thus short-circuiting its potential for both wealth and slavery. However, there's a twist. The manna *is* storable, but only for one day a week: the sixth day, which coincides with God's doubling of provision.[51] In addition to being instructed to gather only enough

---

[49]Common words such as *bread* and *meat* have become more highly specified over time. The Greek *artos* can justly be translated generically as "food," as can *lekhem* in the context of manna, which is obviously not a processed or baked food made of harvested cereal crops. *Lekhem* in Hebrew refers to the staple food, which happened to normally be baked bread, but it is used more in the sense of being a staple food than a baked good. There's an immense difference of economic and agricultural social models at play that can be masked by an assumption of baked bread.
[50]Ex 16:4.
[51]Ex 16:29.

for each day, the Israelites are told explicitly to store two days' worth of food on the sixth day. It is not until the Israelites have successfully completed this second command that its purpose is revealed: that the seventh day is to be a day of rest.

As with the later parable of ten bridesmaids, Sabbath is not no-work; it is prework for the purpose of rest, a work that, if neglected, will lead to a failure to enter the rest.[52] And yet some of the people still get up to gather on the seventh day, but they are met empty-handed.[53] This gift of rest proves difficult for an enslaved people conditioned and exploited by imperial economics to receive, and yet this weekly observance is itself a sign pointing forward to the formation of a people who will treat all possession as a temporary and ultimately perishable gift.

Sabbath shapes community. The Sabbath sign is also the fourth command of the Ten Commandments. Whereas the commands around manna gathering have in view only their context in the wilderness, the Ten Commandments are binding instructions for their settled life beyond the Jordan. Here the Sabbath command prohibits conducting any kind of creative economic activity on the seventh day. But the command is not to *take* a rest but to *give* rest to all the members of one's household: children, servants, resident aliens, and even animals.[54] The version of the Ten Commandments in Deuteronomy further energizes this point: "so that your male and female slave may rest as well as you."[55] Elsewhere in Exodus, another injunction to Sabbath rest even goes so far as to suggest that the point of Sabbath *is* to provide rest not for oneself but for those who are inevitably implicated by one's labor.[56] The biblical text is keen for its readers to be aware of the exploitative potential that all our work carries. At the same time, the Sabbath command also invites a reconciling force into the socioeconomic stratifications that often result from this dynamic.

---

[52]Mt 25:1-13.
[53]Ex 16:31.
[54]Ex 20:8.
[55]Deut 5:14.
[56]Ex 23:12.

All members of the household are entitled to equal rest and time off from their labor to enjoy *together*.

Sabbath shapes identity. Subsequent portions of Exodus describe Sabbath as a *sign*. As with circumcision, Sabbath plays an important role as an identity marker of God's people. Like circumcision, Sabbath is a sign that exists apart from the institution of the temple. But unlike circumcision, it is repetitive and ongoing. While circumcision is a marking sign, Sabbath is a *lived* sign, demonstrating the nature of the household order that lives it out.

Sabbath is a sign of three things.[57] First, the practice of Sabbath is a sign that God is the one who makes his people holy.[58] We will explore this notion more fully in chapter seven. For now, we see that the very act of ceasing from human work is itself a declaration that no human work or effort sanctifies. In this way, Sabbath is a sign of grace. Second, Sabbath is a sign of God's work of creating in six days and his resting on the seventh.[59] By declaring God as the source and wellspring of all creation, Sabbath declares that creation is a completed set of relationships or household, and thus it is community to participate within, not a resource to be exploited. At the same time, Sabbath reiterates God's free decision to cease from creative activity in order to dwell with creation.

Third, Sabbath is a sign of God's covenant.[60] In the biblical context, this makes Sabbath a sign of the Sinai covenant and thus of the entire Torah. It is a sign of the demands and responsibilities God places on his people, precisely as the one who redeems and sanctifies them and who created and dwells among them. When Jesus later claims to be Lord of the Sabbath, he is also claiming the commanding authority of Sinai. Sabbath, of course, is just one command among many in the Torah. But in its status as a sign, Sabbath points to the entire Torah in synecdochic form: It is the part that encompasses the whole. Keeping Sabbath keeps Torah, and the Lord of

---

[57] See also Ezek 20:12, 20.
[58] Ex 31:13.
[59] Ex 31:17.
[60] Ex 31:16.

the Sabbath is thus the Lord of the Torah. And we have already seen how Sabbath is more than just a static marker or sign; in its repeated, regular behavior and in its economic implications, Sabbath points to—even if in a shadowy kind of way—God's determination to form a new household out of a freed people he has both created and redeemed.

Torah and Jubilee

Leviticus adds to Exodus the commands of a Sabbath year and Jubilee. These brightly display the nature of the sign to which Sabbath points. In these festivals, the weekly command of Sabbath is transfigured into annual and semicentennial rhythms that exert an even more powerful influence, extending beyond the economic unit of a single household and into the entire economic and ecological order of the entire house of Israel.

The Sabbath year stipulated in Leviticus 25:1-7 further shows that Sabbath is not primarily about taking rest but *giving* rest. Here the Israelites are commanded every seventh year to give rest to the land. During this year they are barred from the agricultural work of sowing and pruning, but not from gathering. In a promise reminiscent of the manna gathering in the wilderness, God assures that the resting land in the Sabbath year will provide enough for all the people and animals. And as with the Sabbath practice in the wilderness regarding manna, the Sabbath year practice in the Promised Land is a reminder that all they receive, including the land itself, is a gift that creates and develops a relationship of mutual responsibility. This outlook, which sees and receives all as a gift, in turn enables the giving of rest to others. It cherishes them as fellow inhabitants in the household of creation instead of objects of exploitation for the shoring up of one's own comfort and reserves, for making bricks for the dream home.

The Jubilee commands that follow in Leviticus 25 serve as another brake on the tendency for human-made economic arrangements to accrue imbalances and injustices. Every fifty years (or every seven times seven plus one, or Sabbath of years), all land is to be returned to its original family of heritage.⁶¹ This section of Scripture spells out a land arrangement by which all land ultimately is leased (though exceptions are made for urban houses to be bought and sold).⁶² Land cannot be bought or sold as property but only leased by years according to potential crops. No one family or individual, then, can accrue an imbalance of wealth that inherently disenfranchises others of the community, even if such economic gaps were the result of misfortune or misjudgment and not exploitation. All return to their ancestral inheritance.

This is a reminder that land is not earned by entitlement but received as a gift from the hand of God.⁶³ This is a very ancient form of gift giving, however, one that is somewhat foreign to modern minds. Ancient societies that did not know of money operated primarily by being mutually indebted to one another, and they showed the value of their relationship through gift giving of storied heirlooms that, by their very transmission from person to person, would gather value as they gathered a people's history into an object. God's gifts of material possession, including the possession of land for produce, are the temporary gifts of heirlooms, to be treasured for their transmission, not to be coveted, hidden, and hoarded.⁶⁴

Overlaid onto these property-law arrangements are instructions about the responsibility of redeemers. These state, in sum, that those in Israel who find themselves in a position of means and who have a relative who has come into poverty to the point of selling either their property or even themselves as an indentured servant are required to reclaim what has been sold, with the price of property or labor set according to the time from the Jubilee. In other words, a designated Israelite is required to take responsibility to provide rest and relief for a fellow member of the household of Israel. Jubilee is an economic order that is driven not by the owning, mastering, and accumulation of things and of wealth but by

---

⁶¹Lev 25:8.
⁶²Lev 25:30.
⁶³Lev 25:23.
⁶⁴For more on premonetary biblical society and ancient culture, see G. P. Wagenfuhr, *Plundering Egypt: A Subversive Christian Ethic of Economy* (Cascade Books, 2016).

mutual support. This is an economy of care, not competition, of bearing one another's burdens, not exploiting another's misfortune.[65]

Note that there is no state management of redistribution according to some principle of equality or justice here. Rather, the community is reshaped and reformed by vacating strongholds of power in property.[66] By returning property to families, any nascent state power through the formation of a growing dynasty is undercut at its source. Put another way, Jubilee ensures that any claims to sovereignty, even by a state, must be abandoned before the true lord: God. Further, the semicentennial declaration of Jubilee is to take place on the Day of Atonement. It is in these terms, as refracted through the prophet Isaiah, that Jesus will define his ministry at the outset in Luke and characterize salvation through economic reconciliation.[67] In this way, the text foreshadows the kind of household God is raising up through the coming seed of Abraham and true Lord of the Sabbath.

Ossified Signs and the Death of Sabbath

In this chapter we've told a story about the development of Old Testament signs that point to God's determination to establish a household east of Eden. The rainbow is an entirely God-made sign that reveals God's commitment to pursue reconciliation with people by restraining total destruction. The sign of circumcision is executed by human hands. It points to but cannot bring about the fulfillment of God's promise to raise a people through the household of Abraham who bless the world, making his seed not an empire but a blessing to all peoples. Sabbath is unique among the signs. It is a practice that begins to bring about the reality to which it points. But it does even this in a subversive way. It is only by the *ceasing* of their efforts of cocreative construction that humans point to

---

[65]This is, of course what it means to "fulfill the law of Christ" in Gal 6:2.
[66]Indeed, we see the opposite of Jubilee in Ahab's attempted seizure of Naboth's vineyard in 1 Kings 21. Naboth's response shows that he cannot abandon his inheritance—a theme, of course, that contrasts with Esau's own cheap alienation of his inheritance.
[67]One of Jesus' only uses of the term *salvation* is in Lk 19:9, to indicate Zacchaeus's reconciliation with his people by economic justice.

the reconciling reality toward which God is directing all of creation. And it is through this behavior that the people are themselves shaped into beacons of this new household order. Sabbath, in other words, is a pedagogical sign. It was given to form the people of God into the image of God so they would join him in his rest and in so doing extend his sovereignty to all creation through reconciliation.

Unfortunately, the signs eventually lose their significance in the life of Israel. Signs lose their meaning in two ways. One, they become perfunctory. They lose their intention and thus their life. Perfunctory signs, instead of pointing to or participating in the reality they signal, instead point back to the sign bearer. This is a legalism that maintains symbolic acts for the sake of one's own righteousness rather than by submitting oneself to the pedagogy of the sign. When circumcision is cut off from its vital link to the Abrahamic covenant, that this people would be a blessing to the Gentiles, it defeats its purpose. Keeping the symbol without being formed into a multitude of reconciling people, a vast household of peacemakers, renders it an empty sign. The prophet Isaiah complains that Israel's Sabbath practice had become a perfunctory mockery of God's ultimate demand for justice and righteous character.[68] The prophet Amos records the people itching for the Sabbath to be over so that they can exploit others for profit in their market trading during the week.[69] The sign of Sabbath was no longer shaping them. Instead they were formed by the same patterns of rebellion that characterize the house of Egypt.

Second, signs lose their significance when they become neglected or corrupted. Ezekiel indicates that Sabbath practice had been neglected by idolatry.[70] The history of the Chronicler, recorded in 1–2 Chronicles, goes even further, stating that the Israelites' exile from the land resulted from their refusal to give rest to the land.[71] The Israelites neglected both weekly Sabbath and also Sabbath years and Jubilee. By refusing to take up the

---

[68] Is 1:13.
[69] Amos 8:5.
[70] Ezek 20:24.
[71] 2 Chron 36:21.

Signs of the Covenant

sign of Sabbath, they also refused to be shaped by the sign and thus refused to give rest. Deformed or missing signs like this end up pointing in condemnation to the sheer idolatry of the would-be sign bearer. The sign of the Sabbath *could* no longer shape them. Idolatry is living by another story, a story in which Sabbath is reinterpreted to redound to the law keeper's rest taking, a point modern readers of Sabbath-as-personal-health principles should take seriously.

Sabbath is not alone in suffering from a crisis of significance, especially as it relates to God's household. In the time immediately before the exile, the temple—"the house of God"—had wrongly become a sign of entitlement, as the prophet Jeremiah critiques.[72] The temple regularly occupied an outsized position by the people of Israel in the biblical narrative. When David expresses his wish to build God a house, God makes it clear that David has misunderstood: it is not David who will build a house (of stone) for God; it is God who will build a house (of people) through David.[73] And while we often think here of a Davidic dynasty, the reality is that in many ancient cultures a king was the father of his people, the whole state being seen as an extended family. The house of David should have been a whole people who had a heart like God's. At the temple dedication, Solomon acknowledges that God has no need to dwell in a building.[74] And yet the temple building is the ossification of God's household, which was never to be constructed of stone but instead of human hearts.[75] The symbol of God's presence itself became and has remained a replacement, an idol, even, of the real presence of God among his people within his dwelling time of Sabbath. Modern churches should take note.

Unlike the temple, the weekly Sabbath was a behavioral sign that promised to fashion the hearts and lives of God's people into a household of rest. The Sabbath also preceded the temple and tabernacle—it was commanded before both the giving of the Torah at Sinai and the entry

---

[72] Jer 7:4.
[73] 2 Sam 7:1-11.
[74] 1 Kings 8:27.
[75] Ezek 11:19; 36:26; 2 Cor 3:3.

and settlement of the people in the land. And Sabbath has long outlasted the temple. Sabbath is the great summation of God's plan, the presence of his kingdom on earth as in heaven, the very expression of which is the complete absence of a temple.[76] Yet ironically, the temple has had an outsized role in our reading of the biblical narrative, which is evidenced in this way: It is primarily through the lens of the temple, priesthood, and sacrifice that generations of theologians have chosen to read the New Testament and especially the cross. It is to the ossified sign of the house that Christians often turn for the gospel rather than to the living Spirit who animates the living household.

What if, instead of reading the life of Jesus through the eyes of the very temple he claimed to replace, we read his life, death, and resurrection through the primary lens of Sabbath? What if Sabbath, not the temple, became our controlling theme not only for Jesus' ministry and passion but for what it might mean for the church today to exist as the household of God under the rule of the Lord of the Sabbath? For "I tell you, something greater than the temple is here."[77] Perhaps ironically, in order to do this, we need to turn further into the priestly logic of the Old Testament to understand that the temple system was not intended to be an ossified sign but a lived expression of the household order of God, one that forms the very foundational logic of Jesus' own ministry.

Group Discussion Questions

1. What's the unifying narrative this chapter tried to provide about three disparate Old Testament signs: rainbow, circumcision, and Sabbath? How does Sabbath differ?

2. This chapter suggested two ways the covenantal signs of God's people can lose their meaning—by either becoming perfunctory or being neglected. Have you seen evidence for either of these in the contemporary church?

---

[76]Heb 4:9; Rev 21:3, 22.
[77]Mt 12:6.

LIFE IN GOD'S HOUSEHOLD

Lifeblood of the Old Covenant

As we've journeyed into the heart of the Old Testament by following the signs that established the people of God's household, we've found that these signs are not just precursors that are superseded by Jesus. Instead, the Old Testament lays out the pattern of time that Jesus will sum up—or, as many English translations render it, "fulfill"—in himself and in turn commission his disciples to inhabit. This order of time is the order of God's household. Recall the connection we've been tracing throughout this book between Sabbath and the concept of home. A home is where we rest (or try to). Our labor is ultimately aimed at fashioning the conditions in which we share and enjoy life with a household. In our opening chapter we used the term "dream home" to designate the illusive and distorted rest we—and our world—seek to establish in misguided bids of control and independence or, in other words, aseity. These worldly projects are ultimately manipulative and exploitative: They recruit others to make bricks for skyward Babels forged with a falsified unity and storehouses for Pharaoh's larders built by exploitative labor. But unlike the construction projects of the world, the household God seeks to establish so he may dwell with his people is one of true freedom, love, and unified peace.

In this chapter we will consider the Old Testament pattern of this household order, or economy, from the midst of the restless economic systems of the world. The people of God are not simply distant signs pointing to God's order, as though the order were not present. Instead, the people bear the reality of the order of God's time within themselves. This was the original task of Adam and Eve as bearers of God's image. The royal ambassadors are signs of royal authority who contain that authority in *themselves*. In other words, ambassadors *live* the reality they represent. While the Old Testament is filled with examples of the failure of God's people to represent him properly, this household order is the standard by which the judgment of failure occurs.

In order to explore the nature of God's household order, which Jesus fulfills, this chapter will examine the gritty (and sometimes graphic) details of the Old Testament sacrificial system. To continue our journey metaphor, this part of the adventure requires some technical climbing. While it is possible to journey to the top of the mountain by other means, such as skipping to the next chapter, we think this technical climb will ultimately transform the view at the summit. And that's because assumptions about the nature of the Old Testament sacrificial system are often projected onto Christ's sacrificial death. Frequently, Old Testament sacrifices are assumed to be a transactional system by which God's people buy off his wrath for their misdeeds through the death of animals. Instead, this chapter proposes that the sacrificial system, with its focus on lifeblood and cleansing rituals, reveals the heart of the character of the household of God. Law and ritual here operate as a kind of training school in which God's people learn to resist and are cleansed from forces of sin and death, which would abuse, neglect, or commodify the life of others. Ultimately, God's people are invited to live in the truth that all life belongs to God. How we understand blood, sacrifices, and rituals will have a significant bearing on how we understand the blood of the covenant Jesus inaugurates before his death on the cross.

A further clarification: Although the Old Testament indicates the pattern of God's household order, we aren't suggesting that its ritual understanding of God, sin, and uncleanness should remain normative. Rather, our task is to discern the underlying reasoning of the Old Testament ritual worldview, which was also operative for the Jewish authors of the New Testament.[1] If we do not understand the Old Testament world, we will not understand the New Testament world (or will impose foreign assumptions onto it), and thus we cannot understand the operative logic of Jesus' death and what it has to do with Sabbath. We are not endorsing a worldview that treats bodily fluids as ceremonially unclean per se. However, contemporary readers should reconsider their hesitancies with the Council of Jerusalem in Acts 15, which still affirms the logic of what follows, namely that blood is life and that sexual immorality, idolatry, and—presumably—murder remain the trifecta of mortal sins. In this way we hope to avoid supersessionist or progressivist tendencies that dismiss the Old Testament worldview outright before coming to understand it.

Enslaved in the Household of Sin

In the unfolding of the tale of two peoples, we've found that the default position of the household of God within human history is in slavery to or exile in the household of sin. The household of sin is characterized by the power of death. Sin constitutes a rebellion against God and his household of life. It also results in pollution, uncleanness, and disease. It's a contagion. It corrupts good things, misuses the sources of life, or treats things with life-giving power with contempt, and all in a way that risks spreading. Hence the Old Testament is concerned with distinguishing between the clean and unclean.

It's tempting to dismiss this ancient cosmology with modern scientific understandings of microbial life, but the Old Testament is fairly precise in discerning between nonmoral forms of corruption and moral ones.

---

[1] This is somewhat fraught, as Milgrom notes: "No single theory embraces the entire complex of sacrifices. . . . All that can be said by way of generalization is that the sacrifices cover the gamut of the psychological, emotional, and religious needs of the people." Jacob Milgrom, *Leviticus 23–27: A New Translation with Introduction and Commentary* (Yale University Press, 2021), 49. Our aim is to make the household just such a generalization that covers this gamut.

The Old Testament does not consider uncleanness or disease to be moral issues, even though these can express the power of death spreading. In general, the ultimate concern that issues of cleanness and vectors of death raise in the Old Testament is one of sovereignty. If the people are faithful to the covenant, if they have clean hearts and hands, if they do justice, love mercy, and walk humbly with God, then God will bless them with abundant life. But if they commit and tolerate grave sins such as sexual immorality, murder, or idolatry (which are of a piece in the Old Testament view), then God will render the temple ineffective at facilitating life for the people.[2] Even the very land on which they live will vomit them out.[3]

The nations with other gods practiced "abominations" (to'ebah), acts that purchased life for some at the cost of others.[4] Put another way, the logic of the world is slavery, which commodifies other creatures into exploitable resources for the benefit of others. This commodification is symbolized in the Bible by the consumption of blood, which represents life.[5] Eating and drinking blood is abominable in the Bible because it represents the twisted logic of seeking personal flourishing by consuming the life of others. In the household of sin, life comes through death. It is by carefully managing the death of others that abundant life is bought with blood turned into money. This kind of household logic—or economy—is evidenced throughout the Bible, from slavery in Egypt and exile in Babylon through Revelation's casting contemporary Rome as paradigmatic Babylon.[6] But it also manifests in countless empires throughout history and into today. The purchase of life at the cost of blood was and remains widespread in the household of sin. The logic of sin is the exploitation of death.

---

[2] See Andrew Remington Rillera, *Lamb of the Free: Recovering the Varied Sacrificial Understandings of Jesus's Death* (Cascade Books, 2024), 84.
[3] Lev 18:28.
[4] This notion of purchasing life for some at the cost of others is enshrined in many forms of consequentialist thinking, not only through what are currently still viewed as semi-extreme notions of eugenics but also in slightly more mainstream expressions in scholars such as Peter Singer.
[5] Lev 17:14; Deut 12:23.
[6] Rev 17-18.

As we turn to consider Israel's sacrificial system with this understanding in place, we should be on guard against a modern triumphalism that denigrates ancient religious practices without attuning to the logic that underlies them. While seemingly abominable to moderns, ancient practices of animal sacrifices are relatively humane when compared to modern factory farming. Leviticus demands that all livestock be slaughtered only for communal feasts, and the blood be returned to God and not consumed by the people. By contrast, moderns have mastered the techniques of efficient death for nameless animals whose only relation with humans begins with artificial insemination, progresses to feed-lot concentration camps, and culminates in death in specialized factory slaughterhouses. But just because the household of sin is technologized, efficient, and largely hidden from our sight does not make it less an expression of the exploitation of life. Our modern practices of meat eating are in stark contrast to the Levitical expectation that the family cow, a named animal who likely shared a domicile, would be slaughtered only in a way that benefited the wider community. All life, according to the Old Testament, belongs to God, and it is the high crime of the household of rebellion that it tries to own life.

So let's consider the household of life to see the character of its logic, even if shrouded in ancient rituals.

Liberation: Passover and Redemption

The founding event of the household of God is the exodus, the liberation of a people by God from oppressive captivity in a place where life was cheapened and exploited. This event is often referred to as a *redemption* or a *ransom*. While we normally use these words to convey a financial transfer to purchase a slave or alienated property, the Bible uses them metaphorically. In the Old Testament there are no instances of God *paying* a ransom or redemption. God does not pay Pharaoh a fee to release his people. When God liberates captives, it is more akin to an act of wartime appropriation than of peacetime bargaining. It's a mission to retrieve hostages, not bribe warlords. This is because to abide by the logic of the household of sin is to legitimize it. Pharaoh had no valid claim on the Hebrew people. Neither should sin or the devil be given the legitimacy of a payment.

Thus, when we arrive at the historic first Passover and the subsequent memorials of the Passover, the logic of the household of God reveals its character. Take the Passover lamb as an example. It is not a sacrificial payment. Instead, the lamb is killed for dinner, and its blood, which symbolizes its life, is used as an apotropaic sign. The blood—that is, life—turns away the power of death unleashed against the Egyptians. This does not constitute an exchange by which the destroyer is paid off by the substitution of the blood of the lamb for the blood of the firstborn son. Blood here is not a currency that meets an external economic demand. Blood operates as a kind of message that results in preservation. In other words, the blood of the lamb *means* something and thus *does* something. It doesn't *pay* something. The blood of the Passover lamb is yet another example of the covenantal signs explored in the previous chapter. God's household, as represented by the destroyer, does not demand blood but brings death to exploiters and bypasses the people who bear the sign of life.

The liberation event that symbolizes blood as protection develops into a memorial festival celebrated annually as a New Year celebration. Time begins with freedom. The annual Passover feast is just that, a feast. The Old Testament distinguishes between feasts and fasts and rituals that accompany them. The people only ever feast at festival sacrifices (*'olah*, or "burnt offering"). When there are sin offerings (*khatta't*), the people do not eat but instead fast, as we'll see below.

The Passover lambs sacrificed at subsequent celebrations after the Passover in Egypt became memorial festival (*'olah*) offerings. The Passover thus became the celebration of the foundation of the people, the national story, like the Fourth of July for Americans. The blood of the Passover lamb becomes a symbol of identity, indicating that the household of

Yahweh is characterized by life and liberation. The character of the household of God here is simple. God uses a common meal with symbolic elements first to enact an event of deliverance and second to commemorate the formation of his people in the event of the exodus. The blood throughout serves as a *sign* of belonging or identity, not as a payment to a bloodthirsty God who demands compensation for every life in the currency of blood.[7]

This accounts for Paul's use of "Christ, the Passover lamb" in 1 Corinthians 5:7. In his letter to the church in Corinth, Paul is addressing a situation in which a man has committed an "abomination," a sin that has no temple-based means of cleansing and posed a liability to the whole community. Paul criticizes the Corinthians' smug tolerance of his behavior and challenges them to act maturely by taking on a role of shared judgment. Paul insists that they should judge the man and exile him, for exile (stoning, in the Old Testament) was the only community safeguard from the infectious sins of murder, idolatry, and sexual immorality. Paul appeals to the Passover lamb to indicate that the death of Jesus signifies the exodus and formation of a new people who are characterized by a household order opposite to the household order of sin and death. For that reason, the church should act like a people who live within the week of unleavened bread, since—like the Israelites in Egypt—the church is also still in the midst of its exodus from the enslaving economies of the world. The behavior engaged by the man in question was a pollutant that threatened the people of God. The tolerance of sexual immorality demonstrated that the Corinthian community had not understood that Jesus has liberated even the Gentiles from the household of sin; they should flee immorality and not tolerate in their community those whose practices endanger the household order.

Jesus thus recapitulates the Passover in his Last Supper, itself a Passover celebration. He also combines the function of blood as a memorial sign with the sign of a covenant. In this way Jesus clearly classifies his Last

---

[7]Ex 12:13.

Supper as a liberation meal, and his flesh becomes the lamb meat on which they feast. Jesus' death is thus first encoded in the language of liberation from the household of bondage. What's remarkable, and what must have surprised his own disciples, is that Jesus does not position himself as a second Moses. Instead, he identifies with the Passover lamb and also with the manna that would sustain them in their journey out of slavery and through the wilderness. By this, Jesus confirms that God's redemption does not pay off anyone, just as Pharaoh received no compensation for his escaped slaves. Jesus redeems *without* payment, just as he forgives without compensation. These are Sabbath/Jubilee-shaped expressions of the economy of God's house. The household of God is formed in liberation from the household of rebellion. This is what we might normally call salvation. Salvation is a rescue of those trapped in slavery, for the "sinners."

Formation and Forgiveness: Covenant and New Covenant

But rescue is only the first stage. Those who are rescued or saved from the household of sin do not automatically obtain a godly character. It takes time for slaves to learn how to live as free people. You can take a slave out of Egypt, but it takes a while to take Egypt out of a slave.[8] Maturity takes time. Pedagogy takes time. And this is a testament to God's patience. Otherwise God would simply have made Adam and Eve mature enough to bear his image by fiat. But God would have people rule with him according to character, not according to nature.

Because of this, the wilderness generation needs to be formed. Formation comes by a covenant designed to educate toward maturity. In the Old Testament, the notion of maturity is ultimately signified through the label *holy*. We have already discussed the law previously, as well as covenant signs, but here we need to discuss the rituals that establish the covenant, since these are the foundation of forgiveness that Jesus relates to his blood in the Last Supper.

---

[8] See Num 11.

The Sinai covenant is confirmed through a specific blood ritual in Exodus 24. As the tribal representatives gather, they offer a *zevakh 'olah* ("festival burnt offering") and a *shelem* ("well-being offering") of oxen. Half the blood is thrown on the *side* of the altar, God's representative piece of furniture; the other half is thrown on the people. This sharing of blood signifies the shared life between them. Although gruesome to modern sensibilities, we might think of this as a wedding band or a blood brotherhood. The blood of the covenant signifies the life of the covenanted relationship itself. In Exodus 24:9-11 the representatives of the people get to see and eat and drink with God. That is, they hold a feast commemorating the establishment of this new relationship.

This covenant relationship is often referred to in marital terms in the Old Testament. When Jesus invokes this same "blood of the covenant" language at the Last Supper, he is similarly eating and drinking with a symbolically representative number of disciples (not seventy but twelve). Crucially, *this blood is not a payment but the mark of a bond, the seal of a relationship, the sign of mutual promises.* This blood transforms the people from a ragtag group of rescued refugees into a people united by a shared governance.[9] But what about this blood makes it critical for the "forgiveness of sins," which neither the Passover nor Sinai ritual mentions?

Forgiveness of sins comes through the renewal of a covenant. It releases former trespasses, canceling their record, and reestablishes a fraught relationship by putting the past behind. The prophet Jeremiah declares this in Jeremiah 31:31-34, when God resolves to make a new covenant with his wayward people:

> The days are surely coming, says the Lord, when I will make a new covenant with the house of Israel and the house of Judah. It will not be like the covenant that I made with their ancestors when I took them by the hand to bring them out of the land of Egypt—a covenant that they broke, though I was their husband, says the Lord. But this is the covenant that I will make with the house of Israel after those days, says the Lord: I will put my law within them,

---

[9]See also Zech 9:11.

and I will write it on their hearts, and I will be their God, and they shall be my people. No longer shall they teach one another or say to each other, "Know the Lord," for they shall all know me, from the least of them to the greatest, says the Lord, for I will forgive their iniquity and remember their sin no more.

The new covenant promised in Jeremiah comes by the sheer determination and revelation of the forgiveness of sins, not by a ritual mechanism for their alleviation. We'll briefly explore what sacrifices for sins were possible in the Old Testament below. For now, we should note that Jesus' blood signifies forgiveness at the Last Supper because it inaugurates the new covenant promised in Jeremiah. Forgiveness happens here by fiat, by the wounded party, not by a blood-based mechanism.[10] It is the king's prerogative to forgive, as is embedded in the Sabbath/Jubilee nexus by which debts are removed simply by the passage of time as determined by the King's law.

Forgiveness without mechanism is affirmed by Jesus' ministry. In Mark 2:5 Jesus forgives the sins of a paralytic based on the faith of his friends. The scribes who object are correct in their reasoning: "Who can forgive sins but God alone?"[11] Indeed, God alone can forgive sins, which Jesus proves by healing. Sin requires *authority to forgive*, not a ritual mechanism required for this authority to become operative. The Bible never commits God to a religio-legal mechanism himself; it is even at pains to do the opposite ("Do I eat the flesh of bulls or drink the blood of goats?").[12] God's presence is never guaranteed; it cannot be bribed or bought or manipulated. Instead, God's presence is predicated on teachable and justice-oriented hearts. God's faithfulness to his covenant promises is expressed ultimately as faithfulness to his *people*, not to the legal mechanisms that support the relationship. A marriage covenant is not the life of a relationship; it represents pedagogy and boundary markers within

---

[10]For a stimulating theological engagement on the fearfulness of God's forgiveness stemming from Ps 130:4 and in dialogue with the rabbinic tradition, see Sarah Coakley, *The Broken Body: Israel, Christ, and Fragmentation* (Wiley Blackwell, 2024), 112-29.
[11]Mk 2:7.
[12]Ps 50:13.

which trust and love are nurtured by the covenanted parties themselves. For renewal to occur in a wounded relationship, it must ultimately come from the covenanted parties, not through their legal structures. So too the renewal of the relationship of God's people depends on the forgiveness of sins, which is grounded by nothing else than God's own character.

This character is shown in Jesus' life and his own description of his death, as well as in his teaching about prayer. The Lord's Prayer indicates that God's forgiving of his people correlates with their extending forgiveness to others so that those who defy the character of the gift of God's covenant by demanding payment rather than forgiveness are excluded from the kingdom.[13] The economy of God's household is characterized by a kind of relationship, not by its legal mechanisms. This is why the blood of the covenant symbolizes the bond of life shared between partners, not a gruesome death that buys life. To assume otherwise is to impose the logic of the world onto the household of God.[14]

Management and Pedagogy

We've considered the importance of the Passover meal in forming the national identity of the people of Israel at their liberation from the household of slavery in Egypt and how this is taken up by Jesus in the Lord's Supper to reform and liberate the people of God from the household of sin and death. We also considered how in both these meals blood signifies life and the renewed relation between God and his people, rather than operating as a payment to a bloodthirsty God. But there are other details of Old Testament purity laws and purgation rituals, many of which also involve blood. While these remain foreign to modern readers, they were well known and practiced by the Jews of Jesus' day. And it is through some of these intricacies that many of the New Testament authors and Jesus

---

[13]See also the parable of the unforgiving servant in Mt 18:23-35.
[14]Girard helpfully contrasts the *logos* of Heraclitus with the *logos* of the Gospel of John, showing that one is built on conflict and violence, the other on *agapē*. René Girard, *Things Hidden Since the Foundation of the World*, trans. Stephen Bann and Michael Metteer (Stanford University Press, 1987).

himself make claims about the meaning of Jesus' death, resurrection, and ascension. There are far too many details to discuss in depth. We will focus on just a few key distinctions in Torah sacrificial practice that frame Jesus' death not as a payment but as a gift for life that demands rest giving.

Paul understood God's law as a pedagogue, a guide for children to grow them up into maturity.[15] The Old Testament assumes that matters of daily life, down to the crude details of interaction with bodily fluids, are implicated by their relationship to God and form an arena in which to nurture God's people into responsible community members who fulfill the injunction to "sanctify yourselves . . . and be holy, for I am holy."[16] Initially, this language of sanctification offends Protestant sensibilities around being saved by grace alone (*sola gratia*) and not by one's own efforts. But we should hear out Leviticus here: Individuals have a shared responsibility to present themselves appropriately before the throne of God. The responsibility of sanctification even resounds in the Sabbath commandment itself. "Remember the Sabbath day, in order to sanctify it."[17] Jesus also echoes this sentiment in his exhortation to "Be perfect . . . as your heavenly Father is perfect."[18] Here "perfect" is better translated "complete" or "mature." Holiness is the telos of God's people; it is by being set apart that they are transformed into representatives of God. This isn't a call to an impossible moral perfection to earn one's place in heaven. Instead, it's a baseline invitation to civic responsibility as a member of God's household. And in the Old Testament, this notion of being set apart for entry into God's household as a responsible member is expressed through rituals for purification.

Purification and purgation. In the Old Testament, certain forms of ritual contamination required special rituals for cleansing. These rituals differed according to the kind of pollution. Touching a corpse required a

---

[15]Gal 3:24-25.
[16]Lev 11:44.
[17]Ex 20:8, our translation. The common English renditions of "keep it holy" evidence a theological prejudice against any being able to sanctify but God alone. There is no "keep" verb here, only an infinitive construct, which can be a purpose clause, as rendered above.
[18]Mt 5:48.

different, if similar, ritual from that of signifying a house was free of mold or a body free of skin disease. These rituals are called *kipper*, or what have unfortunately come to be called "atoning sacrifices."

Kipper in the sacrificial system specifically means "to decontaminate," "to purify," or "to purge." Translations have often rendered *kipper* with the English word *atonement*, which in turn has been associated with salvation and forgiveness. However, this obscures the original meaning. Andrew Remington Rillera clarifies, "*Kipper* does not mean 'reconcile,' nor 'save,' nor 'forgive.'" He writes, "What's more, only holy objects within the sacred dwelling place, or later the temple, receive the ritual action of *kipper*. In other words, when *kipper* happens, what is decontaminated or purified is a holy object in the sanctuary, *not people*."[19] So-called atoning sacrifices do not atone or restore a relationship; they purify. More specifically, they purify the sanctuary from contamination. This is because what *kipper* remedies is an external object or force, not a legal status internal to a guilty person. In the ancient imagination of Leviticus, bad and good are not reduced to forensic or moral categories but involve a belief in powers and communicable substances that effect negative social consequences.

As Rillera points out, much of our confusion about Old Testament sacrifice can be traced back to the English neologism coined by William Tyndale following the Middle English of John Wycliffe's translation. He invented *atonement* to translate the Hebrew *kipper*; but the meaning it has accrued is more akin to a New Testament Greek word for reconciliation (*katallassō*). Unfortunately, this has generated a misunderstanding about the theological assumptions that undergird the entire Old Testament sacrificial system.[20] And this in turn poses problems to our understanding of Jesus' death—at least, insofar as it is taken as a sacrifice, or, that is, as a certain kind of sacrifice.

In other words, there are translation issues that (ironically) cover over important distinctions and functions of the sacrificial system. To begin to

---

[19] Rillera, *Lamb of the Free*, 4, 112-18, emphasis original.
[20] Rillera, *Lamb of the Free*, 4.

chip away at the buildup of theological, historical, and linguistic confusion, we need to reexamine how blood operates in *kipper* sacrifices. Blood in the *kipper* ("fasting") sacrifices acts as a detergent to wipe away pollution. There are a few different and rather technical kinds of purgation sacrifices by which blood clears away lingering uncleanness after encounters with a disease or a dead body. In these cases, the blood signifies life overcoming the death that clings to someone who has had an infection or been in contact with an infected person or corpse.

The two kinds of *kipper* sacrifice that are most crucial to understand are the *khatta't* or "sin" and the *'asham* or "reparation" (traditionally "guilt"). The first is frequently assumed to carry substitutionary meaning. The second involves payment. The *'asham* offering concerns reparations for damages covered in Leviticus 5:14–6:7: unintentional sins, economic crimes, or untruthfulness. Once the debt has been repaid to the victim of the crime (not a sacrifice but victim compensation), a ram or its silver equivalent is brought to the priest, who performs a ritual to end the conflict. This is the only sacrifice that can be converted into silver, in order to cover the range of economic crimes. The priest makes purgation (*kipper*) for the offender. There is no explicit mention of killing the ram, nor any mention of blood. The ram does not function as a death substitute because these crimes do not warrant the death penalty. This accords with the New Testament: "All wrongdoing is sin, but there is sin that is not deadly."[21] The very existence of the *'asham* ritual belies the widespread belief that all sin is worthy of death in the Bible or that blood is necessary for a reconciling ritual.

The *khatta't* offering is more complex. Although it uses blood, a grain substitute is permissible in the case of poverty, which immediately raises suspicions about the standard life-for-life logic used in penal-substitutionary atonement.[22] Also, while it is also the word for "sin" in Hebrew, the *khatta't* sacrifice is required even where no sin has been

---

[21] Jn 5:17.
[22] Lev 14:21-32. Note that in this case the substitution has to do with someone healed from skin disease, not with someone who has sinned.

committed, such as in childbirth, skin disease, genital discharges, or corpse defilement for a Nazirite. To call this a "sin offering" leads to misunderstandings that suggest that ritual impurities are somehow sinful.[23] Perhaps our modern misunderstandings here repeat those Jesus sought to correct in his own ministry.[24] For this reason, scholars variously suggest using the more neutral terms *purgation* or *purification*.[25] Blood in the *khatta't* offering operates to purge or purify that to which it is applied, which in every case is only various parts of the sanctuary, never the offender.[26]

Thus *khatta't* offerings do not purify individual sinners of their sin. This means that what is contaminated by sin is the holy place, not the sinner. And this contamination is not ritual uncleanness (*tame'*) but simply sin (*khatta't*). "What this means is that in the priestly imaginary, sin as a discrete act produces 'sin' as a *substance* that contaminates the sanctuary (not the person). An act of sin generates 'sin' as 'an aerial miasma.'"[27] This sin substance is then attracted to the place of life-giving power, the sanctuary, where it corrupts. Jacob Milgrom calls this the "Priestly *Picture of Dorian Gray*. It declares that while sin may not scar the face of the sinner it does scar the face of the sanctuary."[28] Sin also accrues on the earth itself, since the land can only tolerate so much sin before vomiting out the offending people.[29] In this cosmology, the land is unable to be cleansed, but the sanctuary can be (of some sins). This undermines popular understandings that envision sin as guilt attached to the body of the sinner in a manner that requires the body to be purged either through death or a death substitute, that is, punishment. But this perspective more

---

[23] Rillera, *Lamb of the Free*, 91. Similarly, the *piel* verb form of the word always means "to purge."
[24] Jn 9. Here the use of mud made from his saliva may possibly indicate a novel healing ritual by which the bodily fluids of Jesus do what blood and oil cannot.
[25] Rillera, *Lamb of the Free*; Jacob Milgrom, *Leviticus 1–16*, Anchor Yale Bible 3 (Yale University Press, 1998).
[26] Blood is applied to a person in an ordination ritual and in the '*asham* ritual when used for purifying a person cleansed of skin disease (Lev 8; 14).
[27] Rillera, *Lamb of the Free*, 94, referencing Jacob Milgrom, "Israel's Sanctuary: The Priestly 'Picture of Dorian Gray,'" *Revue biblique* 83 (1976): 392.
[28] Milgrom, *Leviticus 1–16*, 49.
[29] Lev 18:28; 20:22.

likely derives from Western retributive legal frameworks. The evidence of Leviticus does not support this view.

Instead, in Leviticus, the proper detergent for the contaminating substances produced by sin is animal blood. Blood has the power to make things holy, to consecrate. For this reason, it is only ever appropriate for it to touch a priest or be eaten by a priest (a holy person). If the blood is spattered on clothing, it must be washed in a holy place. Clay pots that hold the sacrificial meat must be broken after use. Priests may eat of the animal, but not the part of the animal that was brought into the tabernacle, which must be burned.[30] What we see here is that consecrated blood is only for the sanctuary, and the consecrated animal is only for holy people. In other words, *the blood is not a substitute for the death of a sinner; it is the lifeblood that cleanses the power of sin*. Blood consecrated by sacrificial ritual is holy and makes holy. Death is not the primary element of the *khatta't* sacrifice. That the animal must be killed in order to access its blood is inconsequential. Exsanguination may be deadly, but the goal is access to blood, not the end of the animal's life. This helps us understand the declaration in Hebrews 9:22 that "under the law almost everything is purified with blood, and without the shedding of blood there is no release."[31] Hebrews is referring to the purification of the *khatta't* blood. Its argument is that Jesus' blood is the superior detergent required for the heavenly sanctuary, not that Jesus' blood is required to make a payment to appease a supernatural entity.[32]

We should note that the New Testament very sparingly utilizes *kipper* language, which is found only in 1 John and Hebrews. What's more, in these texts Jesus' blood cleanses the heavenly sanctuary, not sinners. At no point does the New Testament associate Jesus' blood as *khatta't* blood with the Last Supper. As Rillera rightly notes, the linking of Jesus' blood

---

[30] Lev 6:26-30.
[31] Our translation, which serves to highlight that *aphēsis* ("forgiveness/release") here does not have an object, which is often inserted in English translations ("for sins"). English translations often thus conflate the purgation of blood with the forgiveness of sins by an insertion into the text that is not justified. Heb 9 does not mention sin until Heb 9:26.
[32] Rillera, *Lamb of the Free*, 116n72.

Life in God's Household   135

with *kipper* is an advanced teaching, not the foundation of the gospel. The basic "milk" of the gospel, according to Hebrews 6:1-2, includes repentance, faith(fulness) to God, baptism, laying on of hands, resurrection, and judgment. These comprise what we're calling the economy of God's household. For this reason, it's best to view Jesus' death as connected primarily to the blood of the covenant and only secondarily to the blood of sacrificial offerings.

Yom Kippur. To reform our contemporary account of sacrifice, we could begin by considering Yom Kippur as the "Day of Purgation" (or "Decontamination") instead of the Day of Atonement.[33] It was the annual cleansing day when the sanctuary was purged not by the death or suffering of a sacrifice but by the *lifeblood* of that animal. God gave some animals specifically for this purpose, so animals offered on the altar are not so much killed as given back to God.[34] For this reason, the meat was entirely burned up. Unlike with other (festive) sacrifices, the people did not eat the meat; instead, they fasted. The purpose of the Day of Decontamination and related sacrifices was to purge pollution and return the temple to proper working order. Again, these rituals of purification were not for *people* but for the ritual mechanisms themselves, which were, of course, for the people—just as humanity was not made for Sabbath observance but Sabbath observance for humanity.[35] And as with the Sabbath, the main aim of the ritual mechanisms was not to make the people feel more justified but to facilitate the right kind of relationship with animals, the land, and God.

Yom Kippur was a yearly maintenance cycle (or factory reset) for the machine of the temple.[36] Yom Kippur also removed the contamination of sin from the people, though not through blood or death. The sins of the people were put onto a goat released into the wilderness, thus expelling

---

[33]Lev 16.
[34]Lev 17:11.
[35]Mk 2:27.
[36]Joel S. Baden, "The Purpose of Purification in Leviticus 16: A Proposition Pertaining to Priestly Prepositions," *Vetus Testamentum* 71 (2020): 26, quoted in Rillera, *Lamb of the Free*, 127.

sin from the people. The traditional language of the *scapegoat* is based on a mistranslation of the KJV. Some authors prefer "tote-goat" because it carries away sin. The Bible specifies that the goat is sent to "Azazel," which scholars generally assume to be a demon. This is not a sacrifice but an antisacrifice. The goat is released live into the wilderness, but all sacrifice to goat demons, that is, Azazel, is forbidden. In a manner akin to Jesus' own mocking of Caesar in paying taxes, returning to Caesar what is his, this ritual returns to goat demons and idols what belongs to them: sin. Sin is thus returned to its proper place: in the household of sin. Cleaning up sin, like cleaning a house, involves using detergents to move dirtiness to where it properly belongs, to reestablish the boundaries of identity and character of a household.

The notion of a maintenance cycle for the mechanism of the temple seems quite foreign to us if we do not understand how power and pollution worked in the ancient world. We conceive of sin as a single category of moral guilt, and thus we see all forms of purgation through a forensic lens of forgiveness for legal guilt. The purpose of these cleanup projects was not to assuage consciences but teach responsibility through participating in the process of keeping the divine social order running well.[37]

But we do not see in the blood of the *khatta't* sacrifice, or in the goat for Azazel in Yom Kippur, any connection with Jesus' Last Supper, which is not only a Passover feast but a *feast* and not a *fast* and thus not a purgation or atoning event. Thus, it's not Jesus' death as a death that accomplishes his work; it is his life of obedience that constitutes his freewill, nonatoning offering to God. This, we will see, is the living sacrifice God also demands of us.

Jesus shows that his power of life and holiness was not threatened by disease, uncleanness, or even grievous sin. Rather, everywhere he went he effected cures for things that rendered people unclean. From demon possession to skin disease to menstrual blood, Jesus *himself*—not his shed blood—is a force of contagious cleanness, enabling people to be

---

[37]Rillera, *Lamb of the Free*, 118.

reconciled to their communities. So, in John 2 at the wedding at Cana, Jesus turns the water of purification into wine for a party, perhaps a "drink offering," or *nesekh*, in a symbolic indication that Jesus transforms impurity into community. He himself is the ritual detergent par excellence, who brings the dwelling presence of God into that household to share in the celebration of life.

Celebrating Common Life: Festivals, Well-Being, and the *Tamid*

Western Christianity has focused on questions of atonement, collapsing the complex Old Testament cult into the single point of atoning sacrifice. This has served to de-economize the church and fixate on guilt and shame, along with their solution. The solution is often futurized into an abstracted afterlife rather than concentrating on the presence of God in the regular life together of the household of his people. The Old Testament is not concerned with the afterlife; it is entirely focused on God being the God of Israel and Israel his people. For this reason, the temple cult revolved around celebrating the life-giving presence of God in communion with his people.

Beyond the *kipper* and *khatta't* sacrifices, which we have already considered, there were additional rituals that served to express God's presence in the tabernacle and temple. Again, there's a level of complexity that is not necessary to delve into, but generally they included regular invocation offerings (*tamid*), community festivals (Passover, Sukkoth, Firstfruits, etc.), and personal offerings: well-being offerings (*shelem*), freewill offerings (*nedabah*), and votive offerings (*neder*). These comprised different material offerings: burnt animal offerings (*'olah*), drink offerings (*nesekh*), and grain offering (*minkhah*). In short, a person brought food and drink to the feast, but all of these things were first presented to God, and all the blood was given back to God. What's more, in order to participate in any of these kinds of sacrifice, one generally had to be ceremonially clean, as discussed above. This entailed unreserved devotion to the household of God, a theme that eventually encompasses holiness and faithfulness. This did not mean one was holy, like a priest, but simply "clean" (*tahor*). Responsible members get to participate in the feast. Some of the origins of the later New Testament practice of baptism, which we will explore later, are here evident.

Another feature of these sacrifices to note is that, while other ancient Near Eastern cultures viewed it as a human vocation to feed the gods through sacrifices, in the Old Testament these offerings are burned as an attraction or invocation of the presence of God. The only male lamb sacrifice referred to in the Old Testament is one of these kinds of sacrifices (the *'olah* of the *tamid*). Notably, the New Testament sometimes uses the image of a slain lamb for Jesus.[38] When John describes Jesus as the Word tabernacling among the people, he illustrates the point with John the Baptist's "Lamb of God who takes away the sin of the world."[39] John is suggesting that Jesus too invokes the dwelling presence of God. Rather than taking away sin as a substitute (as for Isaac with the ram in Gen 22), or for the sin of the world, or as a confusion with the tote-goat of Yom Kippur, the Lamb of God refers to the *tamid* and perhaps again to the new covenant language of Isaiah 27:9 and Jeremiah 31:34, which are the other biblical references to taking away sin.[40] In this way, Jesus, as the lamb, does not *buy* God's presence; instead, he *brings* God's presence.

Jesus, insofar as he is portrayed as a lamb, does not align with sin purgation rituals but instead with rituals of God's presence, favor, and inauguration of a new exodus that reforms God's people with a new covenant in the blood of this lamb.

The Goal: Renewing the Image of God

The ultimate goal of Torah is to fashion a kingdom of priests and holy nation, so that the people will again become the image of God, the renewed children of Abraham who bless and rule the world with God

---

[38] Usage is confined largely to John the Baptist in John's Gospel, 1 Peter, and Revelation.
[39] Jn 1:29, 36.
[40] Rillera, *Lamb of the Free*, 197.

according to his character.⁴¹ This helps us understand how the Old Testament transitions from establishing ritual, sacrifice, and law in the Torah to the indictments of these very things in the Old Testament prophetic writings. Psalm 51; Isaiah 1; and other passages openly acknowledge the limitations of the temple system. David's grievous sins of murder and sexual immorality are impossible to purge through any kind of ritual. This is by design. God does not desire a justificatory mechanism for blatant injustice or "abominations" (*to'ebah*). The existence of an exculpatory mechanism would only encourage injustice. It makes little pedagogical sense to provide rebellious people a means to avoid accountability. This defers responsibility, rather than engendering it. Human life and sexuality cannot be transformed into compensatory damages, to time served. Thus David can do nothing. He's forced to take the only right pedagogical response to such grave injustice: to present himself as a *zevakh*, a freewill offering, in full contrition and acknowledging that God has the right to remove his Spirit. It is the mercy of God alone that can forgive abominations and cleanse the pollution that would destroy his kingdom. Psalm 51 highlights the constraints of ritual or liturgical pedagogy.[42]

Isaiah 1 likewise shows how those who are thoroughly corrupt and unjust cannot use the temple in a performative way, as if God would overlook hypocrites in favor of a humming temple machinery. Good liturgy breaks when struck by a heart of stone. It takes a broken and contrite heart and a right and willing spirit to make effective the presence of God for the formation of the people.[43] So Jesus replaces the machine of the temple to get to the hearts of the people directly.

Jesus recapitulates King David as the second Adam, the one who presents himself as a *zevakh* and *'olah*, a freewill and burnt offering that produces a pleasing aroma.[44] This is the only acceptable form of worship;

---

[41]Ex 19.
[42]Ps 51 also upends the logic of the Oedipus myth and the scapegoat mechanism, by which a sacrificial king is blamed for national calamity and sacrificed for appeasement.
[43]Ps 51:17, 10, 12.
[44]Eph 5:2.

it is the worship that the image of God produces, the gift of oneself, taking full responsibility with a willing heart to be transformed. Jesus, as perfectly obedient, becomes the teacher, the one we must imitate in giving *ourselves* as living sacrifices.[45] To become members of the household of God, it is to Jesus and his cross that we must turn.

Group Discussion Questions

1. How has this chapter suggested that we think of the Old Testament sacrificial system, especially in relation to blood and forgiveness? How is this similar to or different from how you or your community have tended to understand Old Testament sacrifices?

2. What might the implications of this understanding be for how we think about Jesus' death?

---

[45]Rom 12:1.

JUBILEE TIME
The Lord of the Sabbath Arrives

AT THE TIME OF WRITING, my (Gregory's) youngest daughter has just turned one. One of the joys of parenting is seeing how a little human develops quite independently of parental input. My family is not known for dancing or for great musicality. Nevertheless, whenever my daughter hears the beat of any song, she immediately starts dancing, often swinging her hips exactly in time. Dancing is like the external expression of the internal pulsations of a beating heart and flowing blood. What better symbol of abundant and joyous life than a dancing baby who's literally just finding her feet?

Life finds expression throughout creation in dance, song, and blood in the Bible as well. From imagery of waters and trees clapping their hands to mountains and hills bursting into song, biblical authors cast a vision of what creation looks like when subject to God's reign and freed from the time of death.[1] Time has a beat, and the time of Jubilee is a quick tempo, a suitable dancing rhythm. The rhythm of the present evil age, by contrast, is that of a war drum, or the beat directing the rowers on a Mediterranean ship, or the rhythms of heavy labor captured in the working songs of various cultures and enslaved peoples. Time, for us, seems steady, unending, relentless, driving us to work in tune and in time with one another to move the ship of state at the direction of our authorities.

---

[1] Ps 98:8; Is 55:12.

As we travel on our Sabbath journey in the Bible and in life, we will find that time itself is transformed. In this chapter we come to Jesus Christ. We'll consider how Jesus bends time around him, acting like a singularity point of God's gathered Sabbath time that transforms the present evil age around him. Accordingly, rather than simply considering his life in the linear shape of incarnation, crucifixion, and resurrection, we'll instead spend the next three chapters considering three aspects of how Jesus transforms time. In this chapter, we will consider how the presence of the King changes the quality of time itself, bringing *jubilation*—or a time of Jubilee—to the creation.

Creation Liberated

Paul tells us that human rebellion did not only affect humans. It devastated all of creation, and with it the time experienced by the whole creation, which is now vanity "under the sun."[2] Paul writes that creation was "subjected to futility" and to "enslavement to decay" so that "the whole creation [groans] together as it suffers together the pains of labor."[3] But creation is not without hope. Its hope is located in "the revealing of the children of God" and in the "freedom of the glory of the children of God."[4] If all of creation partakes in the household of God, and if humanity was originally charged with taking responsibility for all creation, then its health and well-being are dependent on the whole—even the children of the household. God's economy is not characterized by autonomy or independence but *inter*dependence. For creation to flourish, the children must embrace the maturity and responsibility that was theirs from the beginning.

Creation has been subjected to decay and death. It longs for life—true life. The life we experience now is the half-life that characterizes what Ann Jervis terms "death-time."[5] But even from within this time of death we

---

[2]Eccles 6:12.
[3]Rom 8:20-22.
[4]Rom 8:19, 21.
[5]L. Ann Jervis, *Paul and Time: Life in the Temporality of Christ* (Baker Academic, 2023).

catch glimpses of what true life might be like. The nature of life is difficult to disentangle from the nature of time. In fact, "without life, there is no time."[6] To be dead is to no longer sense the flow of time; conversely, to be alive is to recognize patterns of change and thus of movement.[7] And to be alive—truly alive—is to move. To be alive is to pulse with blood, to be able to keep time, to keep rhythm, even to dance—and be *jubilant*.

The one who brings renewed life to all creation is the one who is the true Jubilee, the Lord of life, whose blood gives life.[8] This one is Jesus, the true image and firstborn Son of the household of God. In this chapter, we will answer the question, Who is Jesus? We'll find that to find who Jesus is, we must also confront and consider who Jesus is *not*—and who he is often mistaken to be.

Who Is Jesus?

The Gospel writers didn't ask "Who is Jesus?" in a vacuum but in the context of Jewish tradition, expectation, and occupation. It was in a time of exile that the Jewish people developed a hope, especially as expressed and refined in the prophet Isaiah, that the royal line of David would be restored within a returned land. A messianic heir would rise who would usher in a new era of peace for the kingdom of Israel. When the Jewish people returned to the land, some of these messianic hopes were projected onto their leaders.[9] A renewed energy to rebuild the temple also emerged. This was the start of the era of Jewish history known as Second Temple Judaism, and it was during this era that Jesus' life and ministry took place.

But the period of Second Temple Judaism left much to be desired. The Persian Empire, which permitted the Jewish people to rebuild their

---

[6]Jervis, *Paul and Time*, 64.
[7]Jervis, *Paul and Time*, 61-62.
[8]For a stimulating theological exploration of blood, see Eugene F. Rogers, *Blood Theology* (Cambridge University Press, 2021).
[9]See, for example, Hag 2 on Zerubbabel, a descendant of the line of David who led a wave of exiles from Babylon to resettle. According to Zech 4:9, he relaid the foundation of the temple. Ironically, his name means "seed of Babylon."

religious institution, was just one in a line of rising and falling empires that held sway over their swath of the Near East. By the time of Jesus, the Roman Empire was the established authority. Even though they had rebuilt and purified their temple, the Jewish people were an occupied people, taxed to the hilt and saddled with a puppet king named Herod occupying the throne of David. They were also plagued by a battle over the legitimacy of the priesthood. Things still weren't as they should be. And in this cauldron of dashed hope and ongoing oppression, Isaiah's original messianic expectation fermented into a desire for a messiah who would put the Roman occupiers in their place with all the retinue of a true King: by sword. Such had happened within relatively recent memory under the Hasmonean dynasty led by the famous Judas Maccabaeus ("the Hammer"), who had defeated the Greeks and cleansed the temple of Jerusalem, giving birth to Hannukah and a tradition of warrior messiahs.

It is in this context that Jesus claims to be the long-awaited Messiah of Jewish hope. Yet even Jesus' own followers indicate that he didn't live up to expectations. John the Baptist, Jesus' cousin and predecessor, after observing the initial work of Jesus' ministry, explicitly asked whether he should have been expecting someone else.[10] Even after Jesus' resurrection, his conversation with two disciples took a whole day's worth of explaining before they realized that he *was* the one who would "redeem Israel."[11] Jesus may have been the answer to the question "Who is the Messiah?" But he broke the mold in such a way as to raise another. If Jesus is the Messiah but not the Messiah we were expecting, then who is Jesus?

The temptation has been to spiritualize Jesus' discussion of the kingdom to justify his failure to fully realize it in the present by transposing it to a hidden realm where success cannot be validated. However, by understanding messianic expectations in terms of Sabbath and Jubilee, we find that Jesus is creating a kingdom made of people who believe and behave differently from within the present world order, empowered by God's own

---

[10] Mt 11:3.
[11] Lk 24:21.

Spirit. They are not violent world-conquerors but a community of ambassadors who create mature people who need no kings. If Sabbath is about the character of God's reign in time, a time characterized by patience, provision, healing, and reconciliation, as well as the suffering required to transition from the immaturity of the world to this kingdom, his messiahship is that of a pioneer who lifts others up rather than a conqueror who tears down the opposition.

Matthew and Luke link Jesus to both David and Abraham through the ancient genre of genealogy in order to establish his legitimacy as king even when his campaign for the throne seemed like an obvious failure. But these genealogies aren't typical for one glaring reason: Jesus isn't necessarily genetically related to the names mentioned, at least not all of them. Jesus is born of a virgin who conceived by the Spirit. The names listed in Matthew and Luke's genealogies are presented as those of Jesus' stepfather, Joseph, not his birth mother, Mary.[12] Jesus is adopted. He has no human father, only a human mother. Jesus is not the result of human sexual reproduction or, in other terms, human effort or intention.[13] And in an ironic twist of the covenantal sign of circumcision, Jesus is not of any seed at all (although he is genetically related to Abraham via Mary). Yet Jesus is the true seed of Abraham who establishes the household promised to Abraham.[14] He is born apart from any (especially male) sexual desire or project of family building or heir making. And Jesus' being begotten by God, not by a human father, at the same time both restores the image of God to humanity and establishes the principle of adoption, even to a royal lineage. In him, all might become children of God who are grafted into the family and made royal heirs not by their effort or their genes but by the work of God.

---

[12]There are discrepancies between these two genealogical lists that have puzzled scholars for centuries. One hypothesis is that some of Mary's ancestors were conflated with Joseph's, a confusion that was likely caused by the fact that Mary's own father was named Joseph. See Barbara Sivertsen, "New Testament Genealogies and the Families of Mary and Joseph," *Biblical Theology Bulletin* 35, no. 2 (2005): 43-50.
[13]Jn 1:12-13.
[14]Gal 3:16, 19.

In other words, Jesus came to "cast fire upon the earth" by combusting the expectations of a human dream house in which God and people cooperate in creating a cosmos by the destruction of the forces of chaos.[15] Those who wanted Jesus to establish Jewish sovereignty, or even a system of predictable divine providence, were disappointed. It is no wonder, then, that even among an oppressed and occupied people Jesus' first message to them is to repent.[16] And as we'll see, God's people have not lost their tendency to project their misguided projects onto God. Repenting from our inclination to contribute to ungodlike plans is still our first step on the path of discipleship too.[17]

The True Image and Son of God

As begotten by God, not man, in a woman, Christ brings God's indwelling presence into creation in bodily, human form. He is the Creator-creature, the Creator who becomes a creation in a bid for reconciliation and unity. Jesus embodies a personal invitation to return to God's Sabbath rest. In Luke's Gospel, Jesus invokes language of Jubilee, as refracted through Isaiah, to establish the terms for his ministry.[18] Jesus ushers in God's presence not only physically but temporally—not just in space but also in time. We might say that Jesus is not just God incarnate but God "intemporaneous." Christ is the invasion of God's seventh-day Sabbath time into the exiled time of creation. Jesus ushers the Sabbath order of God's household into the world *now*.

Jesus does this not just by virtue of his genealogy but by his character. As the Son of God by conception, Jesus is the exact and unique image, the

---

[15] Lk 12:49.
[16] Mt 3:2. This point is made in Miroslav Volf, *Exclusion and Embrace: A Theological Exploration of Identity, Otherness, and Reconciliation* (Abingdon, 1996), 114.
[17] Heb 6:1.
[18] Lk 4:16-21. Although the biblical allusions that link Jesus' proclamation in Lk 4 to the Jubilee commands in Lev 25 by way of Is 61 are more implicit than explicit, they are also fairly assumed. See Christopher R. Bruno, "'Jesus Is Our Jubilee' . . . but How? The OT Background and Lukan Fulfillment of the Ethics of Jubilee," *Journal of the Evangelical Theological Society* 53, no. 1 (2010): 93, 95; John Bergsma, *The Jubilee from Leviticus to Qumran: A History of Interpretation* (Brill, 2006), 12-13; John F. A. Sawyer, *Isaiah Through the Centuries* (Wiley & Sons, 2017), 369-73.

monogenēs of God.[19] But just as Cain and Seth were both sons of Adam, and yet only Seth was the image of Adam, so too Jesus is the image of God by having the character of God.[20] Like Father, like Son.[21] Jesus, as the unique image of God who does the Father's will, represents what it looks like when God is king in his own life. And he insists that the family of God is made up of those who do his will.[22]

At the moment of Jesus' baptism, in the same Jordan River that the freed children of Egyptian slaves had crossed so many years prior, God opens the heavens and declares, "This is my son." As the dual image of God and human, Jesus is appointed as the head of God's people in a new exodus and entry into the kingdom of God, which John preached. The announcement of God's kingdom's immanent arrival coincides with Jesus' taking up the task of recapitulating the story of the people of God as the firstborn son who will bring a host of adopted children into the household of God. If we identify the entry to the Promised Land as entrance into Sabbath rest, as the author of Hebrews does, this is the beginning of the retelling and reliving of the story of God at work in time, of the coming of God's time of rule, the invasion of Sabbath into the present evil age.[23]

After his baptismal debut, Jesus is immediately sent to the wilderness to be tempted. He endures a similar probation to that of Adam and Eve but with raised stakes. Rather than temptation in the garden, he's tempted in the wilderness. Rather than being tempted surrounded by good food with a forbidden fruit, he is tempted in hunger with simple food. Rather than being tempted with godlikeness in judgment, he is tempted with immediate dominion over all the earth. These temptations correspond to the temptations of the people of God against their divine mission.

---

[19]*Monogenēs* has historically been translated as "only begotten" but is probably better rendered "one and only" or "unique."
[20]Athanasius describes the difference between Jesus being the image of God uniquely and humans being made "in" the image or bearing it. For him, this means we are created in Christ as the image, and Adam is not the image in the same way Christ is. See *On the Incarnation*.
[21]Jn 8:39-47.
[22]Mt 12:50; Mk 3:35; Lk 8:21.
[23]Heb 4:8.

The temptation with bread links food and sovereignty. If God is not king, Jesus will not eat, for his life relies on the word and will of God above food. He will not take food at the price of submission to the enemies of God.[24] The temptation to dominate all earthly kingdoms is the temptation to which the people of God succumbed when they demanded a king like the other nations.[25] But this time, Jesus faces the ultimate temptation of every kingship—universal dominion and hegemony. This is a shortcut to the goal of the mission of the Son of Man, to take for himself the dominion otherwise only given by God, the Ancient of Days.[26] Last, Jesus confronts the temptation to throw himself from the heights, to imagine that he is indispensable, that God will move heaven and earth to protect his Son. This is the temptation of God's people to presume on the covenant of God and turn it to their own advantage, as Saul did with the ark of the covenant, as Solomon did with his throne, and as dozens of other biblical figures who used religious power as a weapon of entitlement to wield instead of as a gift to steward.[27] Jesus passes the probation that the people of God regularly failed and so is worthy to "receive power and wealth and wisdom and might and honor and glory and blessing!"[28]

But it is not simply in the temptations that Jesus will prove his right to be king. His life and ultimately his death show how mastery over sin is the expressed human vocation since the time of Cain.[29] Jesus is the firstborn among many children because he fulfills the mission of taking responsibility for others, of bearing others' burdens in order to give rest.[30] This is the mark of true divine kingship. Jesus does not claim authority by exploiting others' labor, or by proudly demanding their submission, or seeking to rise to godlikeness. Jesus proves his membership of the divine

---

[24]Cf. Esau's forfeiting of his inheritance for immediate satisfaction (Gen 25:29-34).
[25]1 Sam 8:5-7.
[26]See Ps 2:7-9; 8:1-6; 110; Dan 7.
[27]1 Sam 4; 14–15; 1 Kings 11.
[28]Rev 5:12.
[29]Gen 4:7.
[30]Gal 6:2.

council and bears the image of the character of God from within the conditions of the sixth day by undergoing the burden of death for others. Paul expresses this understanding in the Christ hymn of Philippians 2. The divine king is a servant to his creation. Servants are typically those who provide rest to their masters. But God is the master who gives rest.[31]

Proclaimer of the Year of Jubilee

It is just on such terms as giving rest and release that Jesus frames the start of his ministry in the Gospel of Luke. In a scene set on the Sabbath day in the synagogue, Jesus selects writings from Isaiah that echo the law of Jubilee from Leviticus.[32] He reads them aloud and then declares them fulfilled. It's worth quoting the verses here directly:

> "The Spirit of the Lord is upon me,
>   because he has anointed me
>   to bring good news to the poor.
> He has sent me to proclaim release to the captives
>   and recovery of sight to the blind,
>   to set free those who are oppressed,
> to proclaim the year of the Lord's favor."
>
> And he rolled up the scroll, gave it back to the attendant, and sat down. The eyes of all in the synagogue were fixed on him. Then he began to say to them, "Today this scripture has been fulfilled in your hearing."[33]

Jesus declares himself Messiah. But he reclaims the term from prevailing messianic expectations. His task is not one of military conquest but of proclamation. What he proclaims is "good news," the gospel, or *euangelion*. In Roman times, a gospel was the declaration a herald would carry to announce the accession of a new Caesar or a great military victory. Jesus invokes sovereignty by the use of the very term "good news." But by announcing it to the poor, he fashions himself as a new kind of sovereign, one quite apart from contemporary kings, who would

---
[31] Lk 12:37.
[32] See note 18 above.
[33] Lk 4:18-21.

claim their ascension to power with a victory parade bringing in spoils of war.[34]

In both Greek and Hebrew, *poor* can refer not just to the economically poor but the spiritually humble.[35] This accords with what we've explored in relation to the dream home. The world is characterized by projects of false rest that enslave and exploit people in body and spirit. Jesus positions *himself* as the point of exit from the dream homes of the world and their tendency to impoverish, imprison, blind, and enslave people according to false logics of value. Jesus the King is ushering in a new order of time and a new calendar. This is the "year" of God's favor, of God's resetting the value systems of the world. This is a new economy, one that provides genuine rest grounded in a divine favor that is *given*, not earned or bought by worldly measures, whether money or merit or sacrifice. Jesus' teachings consistently employ economic terms to demonstrate how his presence in the world ushers in a new order that either subverts or undoes the economics of the world from within. It isn't a coincidence that much of the antagonism Jesus receives from his Jewish contemporaries relates to misunderstandings of the meaning of Sabbath as the grounds of a divine economy set apart from both worldly and religious structures. We'll focus our attention to one representative example in which Jesus ascribes a telling title for himself: Lord of the Sabbath.

Lord of the Sabbath Household

"Lord of the Sabbath" has garnered little attention in biblical and theological scholarship compared to other titles such as "Son of God" or "Son of Man." Although it occurs less frequently in the Gospels, it arguably gives a more concrete assertion of Jesus' identity and self-perception.

Let's explore the context within which Jesus claims this title. In Matthew 12, Jesus and his disciples are walking through fields of grain on the Sabbath. His disciples pluck some grain to eat. The Pharisees see this

---

[34]N. T. Wright has an extended discussion of this in *Paul and the Faithfulness of God* (Fortress, 2013), chap. 5.
[35]Hence the difference in text between Mt 5:3 and Lk 6:20.

and are alarmed that his disciples have worked on the Sabbath. Jesus responds by appealing to a similar situation in the Old Testament, in which David and a retinue of soldiers ate the bread of presence in the temple while they were on a military expedition. By suggesting that Jesus and his disciples are a similar exception, Jesus effectively places himself above David as well as above the priests, who—as Jesus points out—are allowed to work on the Sabbath in the temple. In one fell swoop, Jesus claims to be greater than both the temple and the iconic king. Jesus' disciples are guiltless of breaking the Sabbath because they are doing Sabbath work for a king greater than David, who replaces the temple as the presence of the very household of God in the flesh. Thus, at the end of the exchange, Jesus suggests that he himself is "Lord of the Sabbath."

At face value this pericope presents a petty squabble about Pharisaic legalism. But it cuts to the quick of Jesus' identity and mission. Just prior to this story, Jesus thanks God and claims, "All things have been handed over to me by my Father," which prompts him to preach, "Come to me, all you who are weary and are carrying heavy burdens, and I will give you rest. Take my yoke upon you and learn from me, for I am gentle and humble in heart, and you will find rest for your souls. For my yoke is easy, and my burden is light."[36] The Lord of the Sabbath is the one who, with all authority from God as the united Son/image of God and Son/image of Man, invites his people to lay their burdens on him so they can take up his yoke of Sabbath work. They are invited to exchange their allegiance so that, instead of deriving value and security from the world's economies, they do so from the responsible, mature one who has come to liberate them from captivity.

This invitation to rest is wrapped in a story about food and its source. The basic economic or household need of providing food—the lord as the breadwinner, as we've previously considered—forms the foundation of all human social, political, and physical life. In gathering raw grain, the disciples are making a political claim: It is not from the hands of others

---

[36]Mt 11:27-30.

that Jesus' disciples receive their food. Instead, like the wilderness generation and their provision of manna, they eat wild, straight from the hand of God. The Pharisees may think they are simply raising a concern about obedience to the law. But their question reveals a mistaken assumption about the order of the world. Is it from God that the people will receive their food or from the works of their hands? Shall they dwell in the economies of humanity or in the household of God? Hence, Jesus preaches about God's free provision to those who will but be his children and ask for bread from their Father.[37] In the Father's house is free and abundant provision.[38]

But this story is not about infantilizing dependence. True paternity does not allow children to remain children but educates them to maturity. The purpose of God's provision, of Jesus' easy yoke, is to build the strength needed both to carry the burdens of others and so "fulfill the law of Christ" and to smash the yokes of oppression, "to proclaim release to the captives and recovery of sight to the blind, to set free those who are oppressed."[39] The gifts of God for the people of God are not to be digested in ease, nor to be capitalized on by building a household or economy of their own. Instead, God's people are nourished to propel them on God's mission to bring his Sabbath dominion to the world. This looks like taking responsibility for others: "*You* give them something to eat."[40]

Hence, Matthew continues in Matthew 12 to tell the story of Jesus' healing on the Sabbath. The Lord of the Sabbath's work is to free people to do *good* works. Not only is it lawful to do good works on the Sabbath, but Sabbath sets the conditions for good works. The goodness of work depends not on the work itself but on whose household law/economy it lives out of. This is in part what Paul means by "redeeming the time."[41]

---

[37]Mt 6:25-33; 7:7-11; Lk 12:22-31.
[38]Is 55:1-5.
[39]Gal 6:2; Is 58:6; Lk 4:18.
[40]Mt 14:16; Mk 6:37.
[41]Eph 5:16. Many translations have this as "making the best use of the time" or some variation, but this doesn't seem to do justice to the clear context of the same verse in which Paul describes the days as evil. Time belongs to evil; therefore it must be bought off the marketplace of slavery.

Sabbath is not about rest in abstraction. It is about the character of God's sovereign reign described by a different mode of time. It looks like the free healing and provision that Isaiah 55 prophesizes. This is a household law of grace, not a law of quantified transactions with rigorous bookkeeping expressed through the institution of sacrifice or payment: an all-too-human means of trying to appease the gods by an offering of valuables. Jesus is *better* than the temple, not a perfect fulfillment of the demands of temple logic. The temple institution, originally purposed to symbolize God's household order, had instead become a means of human bids for manipulation and control: a dream home. Jesus both destroys the temple as a dream home and surpasses it as the true representative of God's order and reign.

Altogether, Matthew 11–12 shows that Jesus' appropriation of the title "Lord of the Sabbath" is not simply a claim to declare what is permissible according to God's law. It's a revelation of the kingship, character, and mission of Jesus in bringing the household of God to all the earth. And it's even more than a title of royalty: It's a declaration of divinity. Jesus is not claiming lordship of a weekly religious practice. Jesus is claiming lordship over nothing other than the Sabbath of God's final rest of his people—of created time and the end of history itself.

Thus, previous ritual observances are shown to be a "shadow of what is to come," as Paul explains at the end of Colossians 2. Sabbath, new moon, festival, food, and drink are all dark images without detail whose shadow is cast by the *true* reality, who is Christ.[42] The true philosophy, as it were, is neither Gentile wisdom nor Jewish ritual but the household order of Jesus. Jesus *is* the time of Jubilee, because he ushers in the presence of the reign of God within time. This reign of God in Jesus transforms the nature of time around it, drawing in all rebellious human history. Jesus is a time of celebration, of feasting, and of economic reordering.

Our Sabbath journey has brought us to Jesus as Lord of the Sabbath and of all time as characterized by the free grace of God. But why, then,

---

[42] Col 2:17.

does Jesus die? And how are we to understand Christ's resurrection and ascension in the light of Sabbath? These are questions we'll consider in the next chapter of our journey.

Group Discussion Questions

1. Who is Jesus to you? What words have you used to describe him? How does that compare with his claim to be "Lord of the Sabbath" as explored in this chapter?

2. What might it look like for you or your church community to live into the reality of Jubilee? How might you characterize time itself differently in light of Jubilee?

RECAPITULATED TIME

Blood of the New Covenant

THIS CHAPTER OF OUR JOURNEY heads to the summit. Even if it is one of the shortest chapters of our book, it constitutes the greatest altitude change. In chapter eight, we considered the nature of Jesus' ministry through his title "Lord of the Sabbath." In this chapter, we consider his death, resurrection, and ascension, which together will grant us a far-reaching view of God's work in, through, and *despite* human history.

If you've ever climbed a mountain, chances are you didn't make a beeline to the top. Most mountain paths are staggered to reduce their incline, even if they add more distance to the overall journey. In Colorado we call these switchbacks. Some mountain paths even spiral to the top, easing the overall ascent if at times lending the sense that the journey is headed nowhere in particular.

In a sense, this spiraling motion is just the path Jesus takes as he brings human history to a completion in himself. We have already touched on the theological term *recapitulation*, the notion that Jesus sums up, or brings to a culminating head, all time. This may be difficult for us to grasp. We tend to think of space and time as separate, even if overlapping, domains. However, Abert Einstein's now well-known theory of relativity posits that space and time are actually inextricably linked. According to his theory, toyed with in numerous sci-fi stories since, fast-moving bodies accelerate time. Correspondingly, material bodies—from planets to black holes—warp the fabric of spacetime with their gravitational pull. This cosmological hypothesis can begin to sensitize us to a theological truth that has been championed by the Christian tradition long before Einstein's theory revolutionized the scientific world.

Jesus, in his body, brings the very character of God's household order of Sabbath rest into the time of the household of sin, warping it around him in the process. Jesus mysteriously gathers up all of history to put its rebellious, death-ward trajectory to an end, ironically by allowing it to put him to death. On the cross, Jesus reveals what rebellious human history actually looks like and does. It terminates lives through religious and political dream homes. At the same time, through his life and resurrection, he also sets history back onto its true path of Godward obedience. Jesus is the true image of God, who faithfully fulfills Adam's and Israel's incomplete vocations. Jesus puts rebellious human history to a terminus and end at the same time that he redirects it toward its true purpose and end. As one recent theologian puts it, "History consistently looks like Jesus."[1] Jesus transfigures history from within and beckons us to join him on his trailblazed path of transfiguration. Because of this, history is not straightforwardly linear or progressive. Like a zigzagging mountain path, at times the way to the summit entails what appears to be tracing paths against the same direction on the mountain. Each generation may traverse only one arm of the spiral. But they are no less being transfigured on the Way.

History and Holy Saturday

We began our exploration of Sabbath in medias res, in the middle of things. To consider the meaning of Jesus' death, we're starting not with his crucifixion or with the empty tomb but with his dead and entombed

---

[1]Ephraim Radner, *Time and the Word: Figural Reading of the Christian Scriptures* (Eerdmans, 2021), 34.

corpse. By considering Christ laid to rest on the Sabbath day, we see in an acute way how Jesus gathers up—recapitulates—all time in himself, particularly the history and purpose of the Old Testament people of God. And the crux of that history is on an inconspicuous day when nothing eventful seems to occur.

Holy Saturday gets short shrift in Holy Week celebrations. Between the poignant drama of Maundy Thursday, the painful pathos of Good Friday, and the joyous surprise of Easter Sunday, Holy Saturday falls flat. Maybe it's because nothing seems to, well, *happen*. Jesus does not die and immediately resurrect. There is a day of rest. Perhaps as much as Good Friday and Easter Sunday, Holy Saturday tells us something about the character of God and of the household God is establishing. Jesus is laid to rest just as the Sabbath is approaching. Holy Saturday—the day the crucified body of Jesus rests in a tomb—is a synecdoche for God's patient waiting and suffering of human rebellion across the entirety of human history.[2] From another vantage, it represents the final destination of human history from the direction that humans, left entirely to themselves, were taking it: in the laying to rest of their Creator, in the false hope that they could attain the aseity of divinity without competition, that they could build their dream home without a judge. But as it turns out, the success of humans in putting God to rest is matched and surpassed by the patience of a God who not only endures their wayward history but whose death within its march results only in the resurgence of life. The grace and power of God is that he uses human purposes for his own—love is stronger than death.[3]

According to John's Gospel, Jesus dies with the words "it is finished" on his lips just a few hours before the start of the Sabbath.[4] There is a striking parallel with God's finishing creation and then sanctifying the seventh day of Sabbath.[5] God completes creation on the sixth day, and also on the sixth

---

[2]Synecdoche is a literary device in which a part represents a whole (e.g., "all hands on deck"; "boots on the ground").
[3]Song 8:6.
[4]Jn 19:30.
[5]The Greek translation of the Old Testament uses a Greek verb to describe God's completion of creation in Gen 2:1 that shares the same root with the verb that Jesus cries from the cross.

day of human history, he lets rebellious humans "finish" him on the cross. God declares the sixth day, as with the other days, "good," and in the church's tradition it has also called the Friday on which Jesus died "good."[6] The story of the sixth day is the story of humanity attempting to steal the rest of God. God lets them lay him to rest in time so that he can make a way *through* time into his everlasting rest. The cross displays the logic of creation from inside a rebellious creation. The Creator God—the one who out of abundant life and love fashions an-other apart from himself, endows it with its own volition, and exposes himself to its rejection—also takes on the logical terminus of that rejection in time as its Redeemer while yet overcoming it with life and love: and a patience that still wills for the creation to willfully return. Sabbath, as both the reality of God's reign of rest and the weekly sign from inside a creation of unrest, displays the heart of God. Holy Saturday demonstrates that God does not attempt to establish his household by force. He seeks, rather, to persuade humanity by love expressed through time, by a passionate love that suffers—and waits. Holy Saturday puts on bright display the same truth of the rainbow and the cross: God sets aside his wrath to give humans *time* to return to his rest.

Yet even if he is laid to rest on Holy Saturday, according to the Christian tradition Christ does not simply rest in the grave. In the words of the Apostles' Creed, he "descended to the dead." First Peter 3:19-20 is commonly read as the most explicit biblical reference to Christ's experience on Holy Saturday.[7] It states that Christ preached to those "in prison, who in former times did not obey, when God waited patiently in the days of Noah."[8] Notice that Peter deploys two words to describe God's patience

---

[6]Gen 1:31.

[7]Although early Christian interpreters frequently understood 1 Pet 3:19-20 as a reference to Christ's descent to the realm of the dead between his death and resurrection, more recent commentators read this verse as a postresurrection appearance. E.g., Peter H. Davids, *The First Epistle of Peter* (Eerdmans, 1990), 115. See also Craig S. Keener, *1 Peter: A Commentary* (Baker Academic, 2021), 315-19. On the other hand, Matthew Emerson makes a compelling case that other biblical references support the creedal descent and affirm the traditional patristic interpretation of this verse. Emerson, *He Descended to the Dead: An Evangelical Theology of Holy Saturday* (IVP Academic, 2019), chap. 2.

[8]1 Pet 3:19-20.

in the time of Noah, one noun and one verb. In the quoted translation, God "waited patiently." On Holy Saturday, instead of immediately and righteously vindicating himself against his crucifiers and betrayers, Jesus instead visits those who had themselves died in the flood due to their disobedience. God's patience—which characterizes and permeates all of human history, including the far reaches of cosmic space—is seen in concentrated form on Holy Saturday. God's waiting and resting, even in its active form of Christ's preaching to the dead, gives opportunity for human response. God's waiting, God's *passion*, is an invitation to join his rest—even at the nadir of the relation between God and humanity and of the cosmos. God's patient withholding of judgment, his longsuffering, offers the chance to practice responsibility in the most rudimentary sense: It grants time to *respond*.

Holy Saturday consummates a lesson begun on Good Friday: that God's sovereignty is both demonstrated and veiled by God's patience. God is no less a king on the cross or in the grave, and yet God chooses not to assert his will but to withhold it. Jesus' suffering prayer in Gethsemane is certainly Jesus' submission to the will of God, knowing the cup he must drink. But this is not the cup of God's wrath poured out on Jesus; rather, it is the cup of human wrath poured out on God. Jesus is betrayed "into the hands of sinners."[9] The Lord of the Sabbath, the Son of God's household, is handed over to the household of sin.

Thus, when Jesus prays, "Thy kingdom come," he is at once praying to God the Father and praying *as* God, inviting his followers to pray and to live accordingly. It is a prayer for the church to get busy in answering its own prayer, not because their God is not able to bring about his kingdom without them but because in his patience he wills his people to willingly join him in the work of his reign to bring rest. Holy Saturday *is* God's sovereignty: God rests from his work so humans might work to join in his rest.

It is from the place of God-at-rest in the tomb, encased in stone, darkened in death and shut out from the world of life, that we can now

---

[9] Mt 26:45.

see Holy Saturday as the black-hole singularity around which all human history is gravitationally pulled. And it is where we can see the theme of recapitulation of all history in Jesus. For Jesus is, in himself, living the story of all history, which begins not at the incarnation with his birth but here in the tomb, in the darkness before God spoke. Here is Jesus as the *tohu wabohu* from which new creation will spring with the word of God.[10] Moving backward, Jesus recapitulates or sums up in himself the history of God's people. Moving forward, he creates a people who will renarrate all history as it works to direct that history toward a new end: not the death of God but the life of God's people *with* God.

Jesus' death is necessary not to change the mood of an angry God but to terminate a history whose end was the death not only of God but of all creation. Jesus is not redeeming history by fixing what is broken about it. Jesus finishes it off. Jesus swallows the cup of history in his flesh and dies. But he bursts forth from the tomb as the light of a new dawn, unleashing a new and living way.[11] He reestablishes the people of God to invade the domain of darkness, the reign of death, with the power of resurrected life that journeys *through* death.

The Cross: A Throne of Mocking Mastery

We've surveyed how Jesus recapitulates the whole household order of God outlined in the Old Testament. Now we must see what happens when the obedient Son of the Sabbath house confronts the household of sin at its source, beginning with his trial and execution. Our initial instinct might be to locate the ultimate confrontation between Jesus and the powers of sin at his temptation by the devil or his interaction with demons. But it's

---

[10] Among Pauline scholarship there is something of a spectrum between those who emphasize continuity or renewed creation and those who emphasize discontinuity with a radically new creation. Theologians such as N. T. Wright and Oliver O'Donovan occupy the continuity side, and theologians such as Phil Ziegler and John Barclay emphasize discontinuity. Our understanding of time through the lens of Sabbath suggests that there is radical discontinuity between human history and the sovereignty of God, and that for the sovereignty of God to be expressed requires wide-scale judgment. But the hope is for radical continuity if the ambassadors of reconciliation are successful and judgment is averted.

[11] Jn 1:4-5; Heb 10:20.

at the hand of mere humans conducting the everyday machinery of their human institutions that the power of sin is most manifest in striking the fatal blow against God. For the root of sin resides not in cosmic battles but in distorted human notions of the good, of the dream home's refusal to master sin and resignation to instead be mastered by it.

The Son is delivered to systems of legitimized human authority: the court of law. It is human power that puts Jesus on trial. In a sense, the semblance of justice and order in the dream home foundationally derives from this singular event of submitting God to human justice. The desire for an ordered universe is ultimately expressed by the execution of God in a human court of law. But it is this very moment that also reveals the character of God in human time. In the crucifixion, Jesus shows the character of a God who is love and whose patient faithfulness to his rainbow covenant remains steadfast even at the very point where humans, pulling back the bowstring, release the deadly arrow. God will not repay evil with evil but will overcome evil with his good.[12]

To instead understand Jesus' death as a payment for sin would be to legitimize sin's claims and sin's logic. Victory over sin could never come by beating sin at its own game. Healing could only come by the defeat of the cancer at the source: the desire to fashion a household of our own at the price of commanding the labor of others to realize that dream. But it is in the crucifixion of the Creator that any possible stability or meaning of the dream home is at the same time undermined. Sin cuts off the branch it rests on and guarantees its own ultimate failure.[13] It sows the wind and reaps the whirlwind of its own destruction.[14] The stone the sinful builders rejected has become the cornerstone, and it is also the stumbling block that will break them.[15] Victory and mastery over sin comes through Jesus' becoming the foundation and cornerstone of God's habitation.

---

[12]To take Rom 12:17, 21 somewhat out of context.
[13]Ps 7:14-15.
[14]Hos 8:7.
[15]Ps 118:22 and Is 8:14-15, as quoted in Mt 21:42-43; Mk 12:10-11; Lk 20:17-18; Acts 4:11; 1 Pet 2:7.

On the cross, God does not validate the orders of the world. Instead, he subverts them. Jesus is humiliated and shamed by the manner of his death. The cross was specifically designed to murder in the most public and humiliating way: naked, exposed, elevated for all to see, for days of dying and begging for *release*. Jesus comes to *release* by giving freely, by breaking the whole order of the household law of the rulers and authorities, such as that of Caesar and Mammon. Jesus exposes the law and economy of human empires *to* shame by allowing himself to *be* shamed. In Colossians 2:8-23, Paul explains how God pulls off this great inversion. The God of all creation made his death a mockery of the supposed power of worldly empires and economies to establish their ironclad truths of systems of debt and justice by rising from the dead. Jesus, in his naked crucifixion, exposes human dream-home empires as shameful absurdities. Jesus' triumph is the undermining of the faith structures that keep the slavers in power. In this way the victory of Jesus is a new Jubilee. Slaves are forgiven and debts released because a new economy has come to power that shames the old. The principalities and powers themselves are founded on the honor and faith placed within them so that public shaming is the mechanism of demythologization, of undermining the foundation of credibility. Jesus fulfills Psalm 2, "He who sits in the heavens laughs; the Lord has them in derision."[16]

Jesus is also presented as a king in his death. In being "lifted up" on the cross, Jesus is ironically glorified.[17] Our English word *exalt* derives from the Latin for "lift up." Jesus' crucifixion is his exaltation. His crucifixion is even staged as a satirical coronation. Roman soldiers dress him in mock royal robes and a crown of thorns.[18] But God's power is made complete in his weakness.[19] To save his people, he would die for them and in this way reveal his very character. This is his definition of love: to lay down his life for his people.[20] The king is lifted up by laying down. In becoming

---
[16] Ps 2:4.
[17] Jn 8:21-30.
[18] Mt 27:27-31.
[19] 2 Cor 12:9.
[20] Jn 10.

King, Jesus completes the Sabbath-oriented journey described in Hebrews 4.[21] That is, Jesus becomes king and takes up his victorious throne *of rest* at the flashpoint of human violence. Jesus invokes Psalm 22 to interpret this moment.[22] It's a psalm that begins in an outcry but ends in a vision of the final victory of God. By invoking this psalm, Jesus is ultimately declaring his trust in God and offering us an interpretation of his death: God's victory over his enemies, the rulers, authorities, powers, and, lastly, death.[23]

Powers Dethroned: The Logic of Leviticus

Jesus' death is the victory of God that liberates its captives from the power of sin. He decontaminates the world that had gathered its religious and political forces at his cross, which becomes the throne of God cleansed by the power of Jesus' life poured out in his blood. The blood of Jesus spilled on the ground is unlike the blood of Abel, which is "meaningless" (*hebel*). The blood of Jesus poured onto the earth is what brings new life to the earth. Rather than returning life to God by spilling it on the dirt, the life of God is brought to the dirt, making Golgotha the place where new creation begins. Jesus dealt with the accumulated sins of the world on the cross, not by satisfying God's wrath and paying off an accrued debt but by purging the power of death with the power of his "indestructible life," symbolized in his blood and realized in his resurrection.[24]

In this way, the atoning aspect of Jesus' death is unlimited because it defeats the *power* of sin *by cleansing or decontaminating* God's throne on earth, the center of God's power. All sin is defeated on the cross, according to the logic of Leviticus, because the throne of God himself is decontaminated "once for all," as Hebrews says.[25] Sin can no longer impede the work

---

[21]N. T. Wright explores this notion at length in *Jesus and the Victory of God* (SPCK, 2012) and more popularly in *How God Became King: The Forgotten Story of the Gospels* (HarperOne, 2016).
[22]Mt 27:46.
[23]1 Cor 15:24-26.
[24]Heb 7:16; so 1 Jn 2:2 makes the blood of Jesus decontaminate—not propitiate—the sins of the whole world. Andrew Remington Rillera, *Lamb of the Free: Recovering the Varied Sacrificial Understandings of Jesus's Death* (Cascade Books, 2024), 214.
[25]Heb 10:10.

of God. But this does not mean that the cross removes the *capacity* of people to sin or operate as rebels.[26] Rather, as part of the new covenant promise, as Ezekiel and Jeremiah describe, no one will now be subject to collective punishment for ancestral sin.[27] They are also no longer beholden to the power of sin: It has been crucified in Christ.[28] The powers are dethroned, and we are expected to take up responsibility for our own behavior, a responsibility that, as we saw above, means that God will freely forgive those who repent and do justice. The *power* of sin is broken on the cross, which means we have the power to master sin and to live in the reality of God's household economy, if we present ourselves as living sacrifices.

Resurrecting a New Bloodline

So, if on the cross Jesus is not paying off God's wrath but exposing and dethroning the power of sin, what are we to make of the language of blood that, in both Scripture and popular hymns and songs, is so often attached to Jesus?

Blood is the life of the people of God. From Old Testament rituals to the blood of Jesus, we've seen that, rather than a currency to appease wrath, blood is the gift of life to be freely shared among his people. Jesus' blood leads to life, even though the household of sin has made it into a symbol of death. Blood has been terribly misconstrued by reading it through the lens of the world's economy. It is the world's economy, not God's, that turns blood into money.[29] Instead, blood is the life of the economy of God's people when we rediscover how we come to share in Jesus' blood by participation. We share in the life-giving nature of Jesus' blood when we follow the way Jesus led in giving his own life for others.

At the Last Supper, in the blood of the covenant presided by Jesus in a shared meal with his people, the reality to which the sign of Sabbath pointed has arrived: God dwelling and dining with his people, in their very

---

[26]See L. Ann Jervis, *Paul and Time: Life in the Temporality of Christ* (Baker Academic, 2023), 143.
[27]Jer 31:29-30; Ezek 18.
[28]Gal 2:20.
[29]Mt 27:6.

midst, even in the middle of an ongoing history of rebellion that will lead to his death. Yet Jesus calls his disciples to do something seemingly abominable to Jewish sensibilities: to *drink blood*.[30] Why don't his disciples recoil in horror from what the Torah expressly forbids? For one, his disciples might have been accustomed to this language. They were already shocked in John 6 when Jesus enigmatically told them to eat his flesh and drink his blood. Perhaps at the Last Supper they are already primed to understand that imbibing Jesus' blood means to share in the very same life of Jesus. God's blood circulates in the social body of his people to give them life and to join them to his new family. In Jesus Christ, God's blood becomes our lifeblood.[31] Jesus is the blood transfusion for the body of his people that marks and readies them to be members of his household. Jesus' blood is not the blood of his death but the blood of a life given *unto* death; Jesus' blood is not consumed as by a vampire but received as by a transfusion patient. Jesus' blood doesn't satisfy God's wrath but produces God's righteousness. Jesus' blood doesn't pay; it's not a currency or commodity to be valued independently of the life and relationships it oxygenates. His blood is the food and lifeblood of the new household economy of his people.

Blood continues to renew its meaning when we read in the light of the scene with Nicodemus in John 3. The blood of life is the power of life and is present at birth and in the womb. The notion of being born from above *by water and Spirit* evokes the powerful image in Ezekiel 16 as a contrast. In the first covenant, Israel is a foundling, a newly born infant writhing in its birth blood, whom God raised and married and who became a faithless bride, forsaking the covenant. Now, in John 3, Jesus describes a renewed people who are *born*, not found. Some early Christian interpreters understood the piercing of Jesus' side with a spear at his death, releasing blood and water, as the release of birthing waters that give birth to the church, akin to the formation of Eve from Adam's side.[32] Because

---

[30]Lev 17:10-14; Deut 12:23.

[31]Jn 6:53-56; Heb 2:14

[32]See Ambrose, *Exposition of the Holy Gospel According to Saint Luke: With Fragments on the Prophecy of Isaias*, trans. Theodosia Tomkinson (Center for Traditionalist Orthodox Studies, 1998),

these newly born children will be filled with the blood of Jesus, they share in his "indestructible life," or as John 3:16 has it, they will not perish but have *aionic life*, that is, kingdom life, Sabbath life. The blood of Jesus is thus the power of the time of God, flowing into the present evil age, filling our veins and so securing our life with God. This is how the logic of resurrection works for Paul: "You have died, and your life is hidden with Christ in God. When Christ who is your life is revealed, then you also will be revealed with him in glory."[33] To be born from above is thus to be born by the Spirit, to have Christ as our life.

"The cup of blessing that we bless, is it not a sharing in the blood of Christ?"[34] Indeed, drinking the blood of Jesus commingles his life with ours. This creates a new household, a new people, not a people who supersede the people of Israel or replace them but a people who are given new access to the holy place of God by the very sharing in the life of God through the blood of Jesus. And Jesus' lifeblood enables his people to live in this new life even while still sojourning through the sixth day of history. Like the umbilical cord of a child in utero, the church is connected to the lifeblood of its mother and also to the world it is poised to enter, even as it remains in the darkness of the womb. By sharing in Christ's blood, Christ's time invades and transforms our bodies. The love of Christ, which is expressed in time through the pulsing blood of Christ, is a love stronger than death.[35] The end of human history looks like the death of God; but the death of God is abundant life that kills death.

Ascension: Handing Over Responsibility

Ironically, the end of history doesn't end there. That is, Jesus doesn't resurrect and remain on earth. He leaves. He ascends. And in this, he leaves it to his body politic on earth—his people, the church—to complete the

---

73-74; Bede the Venerable, "Book I of *In Genesis*," in *Genesis 1–3*, ed. Michael Glerup and Robert C. Hill, trans. Carmen S. Hardin, Ancient Christian Texts (IVP Academic, 2010).
[33]Col 3:3-4.
[34]1 Cor 10:16.
[35]Song 8:6.

path of history to its true end as revealed in him. He has blazed the trail to the summit, and they are to follow by the same path: lives of sacrifice oriented to give rest to others in the Spirit of the household of God.[36]

Jesus' ascension in effect makes us responsible. It gives us work to do. Jesus leaves it to us to provide food for one another in our journey out of Egypt as members of his economy: "You give them something to eat."[37] But the work we are to do is not that of construction. God is the one who builds up his household; Jesus leaves that he might prepare a place for us in that household.[38] Like the Israelites in the wilderness, our time on earth is one of preparation; of learning to live like a free, responsible people that we might live as true citizens of our coming home. And through the body of Jesus Christ and through his body the church, we are outfitted with God's very own Spirit in order to shape us into the family resemblance.

Conclusion: A Living Sacrifice

As the true image of God all humans were destined to be, Jesus sums up—or recapitulates—all human history. The mystery of the gospel is this recapitulation, which sees the people of God joining in the kingdom inheritance even from inside the household of sin. Elsewhere Paul makes clear that this means to rule with him and to *become* the image of God in Christ.[39] Paul concludes his Ephesians prologue by showing that the same power or authority that brought life to Jesus' dead flesh and elevated him to the highest authority at God's right hand for all ages made him head (*kephalē*, as above with *recapitulate*) over all things, *for the church*, which is his body, the fullness of him who fills all in all.[40] Thus Jesus, in summing up everything in himself, opens up the future to the people of God to be filled with the Spirit and become the holiness that extends to all space and time *as the body of Christ*.

---

[36] Jn 14:6.
[37] Mk 6:37; Mt 14:6.
[38] Jn 14:3.
[39] Rom 8:29.
[40] Irenaeus is widely known for championing the recapitulation understanding of Christ's work as the second Adam, particularly in his *Against Heresies*.

As Rillera so wonderfully summarizes it, Jesus dies *ahead* of us, not *instead* of us.[41] In his life, death, resurrection, and ascension, Jesus leads humanity toward its final end by opening access to the very life he lived for others. This open access is nothing less than the "narrow gate" Jesus calls people to when he says, "Follow me."[42] Such following entails daily cross bearing, suffering, and obedience so as to offer ourselves as living freewill sacrifices and mobilized signs that invade a dark world with Sabbath by the *Christians* (little Christs) scattered throughout as leaven causes dough to rise.[43]

The Sabbath journey we've been on in this book has been gravitationally drawn to this singular point that contains the origin and the end, the intersection of human history and the Sabbath time of God. Sabbath led us to consider the household character of families as a form of sovereignty that is contested. It led us to see that God's primary mode of operation is resting, patience, and pedagogy, in order that God not judge and destroy but love. All of this is condensed into the blood of Jesus, which, as the life of God, contains within it the whole of the household of God who will be born of him. The Sabbath gospel is one that calls us to join the people of God by participating in the life, death, resurrection, and ascension of Jesus. It invites us to join a new community by forgiveness that comes through this new birth of a new covenant in Jesus' blood, a blood that does not terminate in a payment but generates true and lasting life.

Group Discussion Questions

1. According to this chapter, what does it mean that Jesus recapitulates human history?

2. If Jesus' blood is the life of his people, how does that change our understanding of how he reconciles God and humanity? How might that in turn change our practices?

---

[41]Rillera, *Lamb of the Free*, 7, 174, 229, 240, 242, 274.
[42]Mt 7:13-14; Lk 13:24.
[43]Mt 13:33.

EXODUS TIME
Entering into God's Final Rest

In late August 2005, a tropical storm developing in the Atlantic grew to become the strongest recorded hurricane in the Gulf of Mexico at the time. At the urging of meteorologists and other government officials, New Orleans mayor Ray Nagin ordered a mandatory evacuation of the population of over one million. The gym at my (Amy's) high school in Austin, Texas, served as one of many temporary housing sites to accommodate the sudden influx of fleeing refugees. (A year later, I went with a team from my church youth group to serve in the ongoing cleanup efforts that were still well underway.) But tens of thousands of residents did not leave. Although the strongest parts of the hurricane ended up glancing the city, the subsequent storm surge overwhelmed its levee system. Over three-quarters of New Orleans was submerged underwater. Remaining residents were left battling not only the floodwaters but supply shortages, sanitation issues, and looting. The death toll of well over a thousand included some who, despite surviving the initial flooding, died from heatstroke while trapped in their attics in the ensuing heat.

Hurricane Katrina remains the most expensive natural disaster in US history and the third deadliest hurricane. And as the frequency of natural disasters continues to grow in the ongoing waxing of climate change, so too will deaths of those who refuse to adequately heed and respond to the call to evacuate sites of coming disaster.[1] There are those who would rather cling to the familiar than take the safer risk of exiting crumbling structures for those that are more secure. As we'll consider shortly, the books of Revelation and Hebrews are explicit warnings to us to not be such kinds of people but rather to be those who heed God's call to exit worldly empires and strive to enter his everlasting rest.

In chapter nine, we reexamined the life, death, resurrection, and ascension of Jesus Christ through the lens of Sabbath. Jesus fulfills the story of Israel as the true image and Son of God; he ends rebellious human history on the sixth day from its middle. He is the dawn of reconciliation between the sixth day and God's Sabbath rest. His ascension puts responsibility on God's people to join in the reality of that rest, the way back to which is now open to God's people like a portal in time.

If in the last chapter we reached the highest altitude mark on our journey, in this chapter we begin our descent to our journey's end. From here we take up the task of considering what will change when we return home. In this chapter we explore the final Sabbath rest displayed in Revelation. We'll see how many of the themes we have been tracing culminate in the final book of the Bible. We'll then turn to consider how Hebrews suggests that Sabbath should shape how God's people inhabit the time that remains. Here too we'll see further harmonies with some of the Sabbath threads we have been following throughout.

What we will ultimately conclude is that humans are to serve as ambassadors of a new world order as they take their leave from within the old. This new order is one in which reconciliation between God and humanity removes the need for any attempted mediation through constructions or institutions made by human work. Only through this final reconciliation, secured in Christ, can humans rise to their intended vocation of ruling with God. Meanwhile, in the time that remains, humans

---

[1]Though we note that many who decline to evacuate from large-scale disasters do not necessarily do so out of refusal but from disadvantage.

work for reconciliation in the period of God's patience and prepare to join God in judgment when the final day arrives.

Revelation: The Final Sabbath That Awaits

It's fitting that the book of the Bible itself named Revelation would offer a vision of Sabbath in a kind of concentrated form, even if, as with Psalm 92, Sabbath is not mentioned explicitly. Revelation, in its odd, perplexing, dreamy way, is the dream home of Scripture. But it's the dream home to end all dream homes. Revelation reveals the undoing of human dream homes and their misguided attempts to achieve aseity on human terms. Revelation even has a specialized name for the bids for aseity that have polluted human history: Babylon. Babylon is the acme of human civilization, a city that takes the project of Cain and his lineage to its ultimate conclusion. This is a picture of the household of the world: rich, decadent, sexually free, a land of free trade, built on the souls of slaves.[2] At its end, Revelation envisions the final exodus of God's people from demolished human structures into the eternal rest and reign of God.

The book of Revelation is the denouement of the line of Sabbath signs we have traced throughout Scripture. It is the final end the Sabbath-eyed author of Psalm 92 foresaw, in which God will finally vanquish all enemy threats to his reign, though not before giving them ample opportunity to join his household. It is the establishment of the divine council, within which humans take their place as coregents with God and shoulder responsibility for creation in dialogue with their Father. Revelation describes the climactic end to the tale of two peoples begun in Genesis, where the line of Cain in its manifestation in Babylon is overcome by God's victory on behalf of his people who are the spiritual descendants of Seth. It is the culmination of the unmediated relation between God and his people, who experience true unity in Christ instead of the faked or forced uniformity of dream homes. And it is the foundation of a new household order, a new economy, in which provisions are distributed not

---
[2]Rev 18.

by labor or by merit but by sheer gift and in which responsibility is allotted not by monarchical lineage or democratic popularity but by proven maturity. This is the shape of the Sabbath time that approaches human history from beyond the horizon—except for the preview granted by God's revelation.

John shows how the new creation is characterized by an unending rest in which God is present with his people, now *in* creation as the unified Creator-creature in Jesus Christ. God's Sabbath presence in the incarnation of Jesus Christ culminates in Revelation as the unmediated relation between God and creation. The new creation does not exist in some other, divine realm, some far-off heaven.[3] It is the reunion between exiled wanderers and God's seventh-day Sabbath reign. Revelation proclaims, "The kingdom of the world *has become* the kingdom of our Lord and of his Messiah."[4] The sixth day, characterized by rebellion, is judged and purified. From it are redeemed those creatures God himself created. But the sixth day is not brought into the seventh wholesale. Human history must be a story retold by Christ and the people of God. God frees his creation in a great Jubilee. Relationships are restored. But not all the work of history is redeemed. Indeed, God does not redeem the structures of bondage, the creations of Cain, the pride of human civilization. Babylon is destroyed, not whitewashed or renovated. The work of many will be burned up like straw in a fire, with the people escaping with their lives.[5] But the work of history is not erased. The seventh day redeems the people of the sixth by recapitulation, but this narrative retelling is not without impact to God himself. Jesus retains his scars.[6]

In this final Sabbath rest there are no longer any structures or institutions that must span the gap between God and his people. In Revelation 21:15-21 the luxurious dimensions and decorations of the new city

---

[3] N. T. Wright's work has labored hard to disabuse contemporary Christianity of that notion. See, e.g., Wright, *Surprised by Hope: Rethinking Heaven, the Resurrection, and the Mission of the Church* (HarperOne, 2008).
[4] Rev 11:15.
[5] 1 Cor 3:12-15.
[6] Rev 5:6.

of Jerusalem are reminiscent of that of the holy of holies, the location in the temple building inhabited by God's presence in concentrated form. Revelation then declares that *there is no temple* in the city, "for its temple is the Lord God the Almighty and the Lamb."[7] The dwelling place of God now encompasses the entire earth. The Bible begins in a palace garden, but it ends inside the throne room, where "the home of God is among mortals."[8]

Unlike the false unities of dream-home structures, which either fake unity through a homogenization of diversity or enforce a false unity through their enslavement to symbolic structures, the reconciliation of all things in Christ permits for true unity, which preserves and embraces diversity rather than circumvents or short-circuits it. In Revelation, John witnesses "a great multitude that no one could count, from every nation, from all tribes and peoples and languages, standing before the throne and before the Lamb, robed in white, with palm branches in their hands."[9] The very punishment of diversity by means of linguistic variety, which God inflicted on humans in their false attempt at constructed unity in Babel, is not eliminated.

As much as Revelation is replete with stereotypical scenes of praise and even harps, humans are occupied by more than mere singing.[10] God did not create people to be court musicians who do nothing but assuage the fragile self-image of a ruler. Humans are to reign with God as coregents of his kingdom on earth as members of his divine council. Though the divine council is not referred to explicitly here, as in Genesis we can detect it implicitly. After all, humans are found to be gathered in God's throne room—the divine headquarters, as it were. And the voices of the exotic, celestial creatures John meets in Revelation 5 explicitly sing that the role of the humans Christ has redeemed is to serve God by reigning.[11]

---

[7] Rev 21:22.
[8] Rev 7:17; 21:3.
[9] Rev 7:9.
[10] Rev 15:2. Though we note the moratorium on Babylonian harp playing in Rev 18:22.
[11] Rev 5:10.

Revelation also showcases one final, critical element of the nature of God's final Sabbath rest: the practice of a new economic order.[12] True to the theme of food that intertwines with Sabbath, this new economic order is epitomized by feasting. Recall that Jesus as the *tamid* sacrificial male lamb signified God's presence with his people. This is why the slain lamb is the one worthy to open the scrolls of judgment, and in this role Jesus symbolizes communion between God and his people. It is the wedding supper of Christ, the Lamb of God, that culminates and consummates the history of the world and the story of God's people.[13]

Feasting is, more than anything else, what we can be the most confident we will be doing in the time beyond human history. And it gives the lie to the dream of the dream home, the impulse of which is to eliminate all human needs and dependencies. Even if this feast is what will truly satisfy, it is the opposite of the elusive self-satisfaction, which can never be achieved and the pursuit of which ends only in destruction.[14] Eating and drinking together is the bond of nonaseity. The perpetual sharing of food cements the continual relation of God's people with one another and with God. The image of feasting underscores the interdependency and the circulation of shared gifts that characterize the economy of the kingdom of God. It also signifies a flourishing creation that yields fruit in season.

All of this establishes a new economic order at variance with the economic orders—the Egypts and Babylons—of the world. In the very final verses of Revelation and of the whole biblical canon, the reader is extended an invitation: "Let anyone who wishes take the water of life as a gift."[15] Life in God's time is a gift. It is, in the words of the prophet of Isaiah resonant here, "without price."[16] It cannot be bought or bartered

---

[12]There are rich resonances between Isaiah and Revelation on the theme of feasting. See Rev 21:4; Is 25:8; also Rev 21:6; Is 55:1. In Is 25, God is the one who provisions his people with food, as it was from the beginning. And as his people feast, God swallows not their sacrifices (see Is 1:11) but death (Is 25:8). Note also the Jubilee-like economic terms of Is 55, with its opening invitation to supplies without cost.

[13]Rev 19:7-9.

[14]Is 55:2.

[15]Rev 22:17.

[16]Is 55:1.

for by work, merit, or any other construct of human value or currency, just as all food was originally a gift to humans on their first day of creation. This is an economy grounded in grace. But although nothing is earned, participation in God's Sabbath order is still valued and rewarded.[17] Gift generates responsibility and relationship. This is how goods are circulated in God's household economy. And Revelation makes clear that it will overcome the economies of the world that pursue aseity through self-made values that generate only exploitation, debt, and estrangement.[18]

Revelation's bizarre and complex structure—at least before the climactic calm of its final chapters—reveals the messy confusion that occurs when the world's Babel-esque edifices are overwhelmed and conquered by the kingdom of God. God's people are, after all, still in Babylon, living in the middle, yet being called to "come out of her" in their true and final exodus from exploitative economic systems that God will thankfully destroy.[19] The question Revelation implicitly and explicitly repeats echoes the question of God to his people in Abram, Lot, Moses, and others. Will they come out?[20] Whose side are they on? Of which city are they citizens? A city of self-pursued pleasure that forges an empire of slavery? Or the city of interrelated gift and responsibility grounded by the very presence of God? And what shape should the life of God's people take as they make their exit from the dream homes of the world? The answer to this question for the book of Hebrews is clear: God's people willingly wander to pursue the true rest of God's Sabbath.

Hebrews: Still at Dusk—Faithful Formation in the Time That Remains

From early on, the church had to reconcile itself with the ever elongating passing of time between Christ's ascension and his return. In some ways,

---

[17] Rev 14:13; 19:8; 22:17.
[18] Rev 18.
[19] Rev 18:4.
[20] Rev 22:17.

the question of what to do with time is the question that animates the book of Hebrews. And Hebrews shows that one cannot properly grapple with time unless one begins to imagine the final Sabbath that awaits. Conversely, one can't begin to imagine the final Sabbath that awaits without considering the implications for our present time—our now.

More than any other book in the New Testament, Hebrews considers the cultic life of Israel. Yet after examining the temple, the sacrifices, and the priesthood, Hebrews ultimately appoints Sabbath as the lodestar by which God's people are to navigate their present.

Let's trace Hebrews' development by observing how Hebrews grapples with the nature of time. Five times it repeats the word *today* in extended reflection and direct reference to Psalm 95:7, which is quoted most fully in Hebrews 3:7-9: "Today, if you hear his voice, do not harden your hearts as in the rebellion, as on the day of testing in the wilderness, where your ancestors put me to the test."[21] Through the psalmist, Hebrews considers an incident recorded in Exodus 17:1-7. This incident takes place in the wilderness after the Israelites have escaped from Egypt, immediately after their manna gathering and first Sabbath lesson in Exodus 16. Here the thirsty Israelites quarrel about the lack of water to the point of questioning whether they should have left Egypt at all. Although the desire for hydration seems reasonable enough, the Exodus account indicates that this wasn't an innocent request for a water break: The Israelites were questioning whether God was with them.[22] It was a betrayal of trust in God's sovereign provision and timing, and a failure to comprehend and internalize God's powerful display of rescuing power, which they had only just witnessed. The psalmist diagnoses it as a kind of sclerosis: a hardening of heart. The same Hebrew word is even used to describe the hardening of Pharaoh.[23]

Both the psalmist and the author of Hebrews highlight these quarreling, doubting, freshly freed Israelites as a negative example: "Do not

---

[21]Heb 3:7-9, 13, 15; 4:7 (2×); cf. 2 Cor 6:1-2.
[22]Ex 17:7.
[23]Ex 7:3; 13:15.

Exodus Time

harden your hearts as in the rebellion."[24] In other words, even though they had been dramatically rescued by God, they failed to allow that reality to shape their character and posture. They did not believe.[25] This is the opposite of faith, of trust in God's works and anticipation of the completion of his work in final rest, which is expressed as a commitment through time.[26] The time to express that faith is *today*, which is at once this very moment—now—and something more: It is all of human history, or as we have been identifying it in this book, the sixth day. All of God's people are, in some mysterious way, conjoined with the Israelites out of Egypt. Their today is also our today.[27] All of what we experience as linear, sequential history is equidistant to God's final Sabbath rest. Human history is arrayed on the cusp of the Promised Land. And the Christian's position within this time is just as fragile as that of the wandering Israelites. Christians too could forfeit their freedom if they behave like those Israelites of whom God declared, "They will not enter my rest."[28] God's rescue is a free gift; it is not forced. Yet at the same time, this gifted rescue entails the responsibility of developing the kind of character that can participate in the rest of the household order of God.

Hebrews teaches an important lesson about the relationship between faith and time. Faith is not an atemporal intellectual assent, nor a formless waiting; it takes a shape. In particular, it looks like striving to enter into God's rest—in entering into an economy grounded in his work and sovereignty. For this reason Hebrews exhorts sobriety. God's people are not entitled.[29] Salvation is about entering into God's rest, not resting on one's laurels. Even those who were rescued from Egypt forfeited their entry into the Promised Land. And even those who have tasted the freedom that is found in Christ might yet reject entry into the household of God. How one treats time reveals one's relation to God's Sabbath. Time must be

---

[24] Heb 3:8.
[25] Heb 3:19.
[26] Heb 3:6, 14.
[27] Heb 3:13.
[28] Heb 3:11; cf. Ps 95:11.
[29] See Rom 11:17-21.

taken back from the marketplace of the present evil age, as Paul states.[30] This doesn't mean that God's Sabbath is something that is brought about by human effort. No one can construct God's Sabbath. God's kingdom is not built; it is entered into.[31] The life of the Christian now is a matter of preparing for the final Sabbath, which is not constructed or earned. In this way, Hebrews' exhortation to enter into God's rest is the mirror image of Revelation's call to "come out of" the dream homes of Babylon, issued from the other side of God's Sabbath.[32] On this side of God's final Sabbath, the work of entering begins today.

One way to read the rest of the book of Hebrews is as a catalog of what entering into that rest looks like. The priesthood, the sacrifices, and the holy places are shown to be shadows that should have pointed to the rest brought by Jesus, who is greater than all of these by being their summation.[33] Hebrews stresses three aspects of the present time that should be embraced by those who are striving to enter into God's rest: corporate gathering, worldly exile, and godly discipline. All told, entering into God's rest looks like becoming united as the people of God who are being fashioned as citizens of a different order of time. This formation is energized both by the precariousness of the situation and by the breakdown of institutional religion. After all, Christians are no more guaranteed entry to God's Sabbath rest than the freed Israelites were guaranteed entry into the Promised Land. And the temple is gone. But someone greater than the temple is here.

Corporate gathering. The first aspect of entering into God's rest that the author of Hebrews emphasizes is corporate gathering and dialogue.

---

[30] Eph 5:16.
[31] Heb 10:25; Mk 10:23.
[32] Rev 18:4.
[33] It's not coincidental that, in the reflection on Sabbath through the lens of Ps 95, the author of Hebrews has resorted to reflection on the exodus. Although the remaining chapters of Hebrews are often read as a kind of doubling down on sacrifice, their foregrounding with the exodus narrative suggests that the animating concern is not about Jesus' offering a propitiating sacrifice as much as marking his people for liberation. Consider, e.g., Heb 5:8; 8:12; even Heb 9:14 speaks of Christ's offering of himself as a cleansing rather than a payment. Again in Heb 9:26, 28 Jesus removes and bears sin rather than compensates for it. Heb 10:5-7 makes clear that God does not demand sacrifice but desires maturity. Heb 10:18 says it all: "Where there is forgiveness of these, there is no longer any offering for sin."

Hebrews heavily indicates that faith is not private. By its very nature, faith joins the individual to a body of people who span space and time.[34] To prepare to enter into God's Sabbath means belonging to God's household. It's a family affair. Twice the author of Hebrews presses the importance of corporate gathering and communication in direct reflection on the approaching Sabbath day that God's people are preparing to enter into in the "today" of the sixth day:

> But exhort one another every day, as long as it is called "today," so that none of you may be hardened by the deceitfulness of sin.[35]

> And let us consider how to provoke one another to love and good deeds, not neglecting to meet together, as is the habit of some, but encouraging one another, and all the more as you see the Day approaching.[36]

Sin, as we've discussed in previous chapters, is not primarily lawbreaking. Sin behaves as a "principality and power." Correspondingly, sin cannot be resisted in isolation. Sin must be combated ecclesially, with the whole communion of saints who, by being joined to Christ in the Sabbath household of God, are joined in a time of resistance to the power of sin. The responsibility of Cain to master sin is possible only through shared labor of giving others rest, encouragement, and exhortation to take responsibility for one another's good works and growth.

Exile and wandering. The second theme the author of Hebrews stresses, in concert with Genesis, is wandering. To prepare to enter into God's rest means becoming a sojourner. Insofar as Hebrews frames the life and work of Christ as launching a new exodus, it also blows up institutional stability. Because of this, the Christian life is a journey.[37] From Abraham to John the Baptist, this was the shape of God's people all along. Those who are settled or comfortable are doing something wrong, as the

---

[34] Heb 4:2; 11:40; 12:1.
[35] Heb 3:13.
[36] Heb 10:24-25.
[37] The inherent nature of God's people as wanderers is taken to be the controlling theme of Hebrews in Ernst Käsemann, *The Wandering People of God: An Investigation of the Letter to the Hebrews*, trans. Roy A. Harrisville and Irving L. Sandberg (Augsburg, 1984).

Beatitudes admonish.[38] Those who live in the true Sabbath rest know that their true residence is elsewhere. This transforms one's posture to the current environment. Hebrews 11, the hall of faith, considers in detail how the lives of particular people of God are determined by their postures as sojourners: as people who know that their commitment to God means they can never be at home or expect hospitality from the world.[39] To be a Christian is to accept one's status as the foreign, wandering people of God. Christian faithfulness does not look like building settlements like Cain but in taking next steps in the direction of home.

Discipline. Last, preparing to enter God's Sabbath rest requires discipline. Good parents discipline their children.[40] Discipline, for the author of Hebrews, looks like embracing rather than resisting or resenting the purgative nature of the present time. It's a certain posture to what God permits in his patience. The suffering God permits can either embitter or develop character. It is for this reason that James exhorts his readers to consider trials and testing something to rejoice in because of their ability to spur growth in those who persevere.[41] A mark of a maturing child of God is leaning into challenges as a source of growth. And a healthy kind of fatherhood is revealed in the giving of opportunities to grow through hardships. At no point is the Bible naive about the severity of hardships faced by the people of God. The God who reveals himself to Job is the same Father of Jesus Christ. The trials of "today" shape God's people into those who can inherit in his household.[42]

---

[38] Mt 5:3-12.
[39] Heb 11:13-16.
[40] Heb 12:7.
[41] Jas 1:2-3.
[42] Sittser articulates the posture of a disciple who leans into trials as an opportunity for growth: "My own catastrophic loss thus taught me the incredible power of choice. . . . I wanted to gain as much as I could from the loss without neglecting ordinary responsibilities. I wanted to integrate my pain into my life in order to ease some of its sting. I wanted to learn wisdom and to grow in character. I had had enough of destruction, and I did not want to respond to the tragedy in a way that would exacerbate the evil I had already experienced. I knew that running from the darkness would only lead to greater darkness later on. I also knew that my soul had the capacity to grow—to absorb evil and good, to die and live again, to suffer abandonment and find God. In choosing to face the night, I took my first steps toward the sunrise." Gerald Sittser, *A Grace Disguised: How the Soul Grows Through Loss* (Zondervan, 1995), 40.

But Hebrews also shows that discipline is not just a matter of one's individual attitude to hardship. There is a communal element of discipline as well. Discipline also encompasses pursuing reconciliation and peaceful relations with others.[43] Correlatively, discipline includes exhorting others to align their lives with the gift of God revealed in Jesus Christ.[44] God's people must keep each other accountable to keeping to the Way and heading toward the Sabbath sunrise.

"Today" is in the dusk of the sixth day, before the dawn of God's seventh-day Sabbath rest, which God's people strive to enter as they exit the structures of Babylon. Although God's Sabbath is approaching his people, Hebrews exhorts them to strive to enter it. This is the calling of God to his people to meet in the middle, in medias res. Entering God's rest requires community, wandering, and training. It is ultimately Jesus who leads in this communal and disciplined journey of faith.

The book of Hebrews from the framework of Sabbath is theologizing itself out of a temple logic. The author of Hebrews realizes that Jesus is better than the temple, not some perfect fulfillment of the temple's demands. Jesus is the priest who ends the priesthood. Jesus' death doesn't enact a sacrifice to appease God by death; it is the expression of the will of God to bring people back to him *through* death.[45] In this way, Jesus forges a way back to God's Sabbath rest. Jesus is not so much a priest as a pioneer.[46] Jesus has punched a path from the sixth day to the seventh day of God's rest.[47] He has made a way in time. Jesus has blazed the trail, and his people have prepared the way and made straight the paths in the wilderness. As any backpacker knows, keeping to the path requires others to help provision and provide direction on the way. It requires a spirit of sojourning and the discipline to keep pace even in the face of unexpected trials.

---

[43]Heb 12:14.
[44]Heb 12:15.
[45]Heb 10:1-10.
[46]Heb 12:2.
[47]Heb 12:2.

The Judgment of God

Until now we have only touched here and there on the theme of judgment and wrath in our Sabbath journey. Now is the time to confront it squarely. The boundary between the sixth and seventh day is a hard barrier of conflicting sovereignties. To cross that boundary requires one not only to prove faithful to the king but also to submit to the law of the sovereign by coming clean about past actions of infidelity, seeking forgiveness, and striving for reconciliation. There can be no entry into the Sabbath, into the time of God, unless the will of God is done on earth as in heaven.

Throughout Scripture we are confronted with judgment and wrath. For those who have not suffered grave injustice, God's vengeance can feel awkward at best and offensive at worst. But to those who have suffered or continue to suffer—those in chains, who are trafficked, whose bodies are violated, whose children have been exploited or murdered—the notion of a God who takes evil seriously and responds appropriately is sometimes their only comfort. It is only when we realize that the Bible, and particularly its most prophetic books, such as Revelation, were written by suffering and marginalized minority peoples that we can begin to appreciate the importance and *hope* of the wrath of God, which cannot be bought with blood money. Those who hate God's wrath have not understood the clash of sovereignties dramatized in the Bible. God will ultimately not condone the exploitative dream-home project of the world and of human civilizations but will destroy them. The principalities and powers exploit the blasé attitude of the bourgeois Christian toward God's wrath. We should never minimize the difference between the reign of God and the present evil age. That is not to deny that God's wrath cannot be or has not been appealed to in manipulative and abusive ways that ultimately, and ironically, perpetuate the exploitative nature of the worst of the very human structures God's wrath will one day consume. But this does not mean that God's wrath should be dismissed. Minimizing the wrath of God justifies the world as it is and so renders meaningless the cross of Christ.

Sabbath gives us a renewed perspective on wrath from several vantages. To begin, it is God's wrath that results in the exile of Judah from the Promised Land. And God's wrath on the Southern Kingdom was not simply for their personal moral failures, their ritual impurity, or even their injustice against the weak and poor. It was also because they failed to give the land itself its Sabbath rests as commanded. So God provided to the land what Judah had withheld by expelling them.[48] Judah's behavior expressed a people who did not live with God as their king, who did not reveal God's character, and so who systemically neglected giving rest to the very least of these: the land itself.[49] Judah had tried to build a dream home out of the Promised Land. And so, as with Babel in Genesis 11, God came to them in judgment.

Recall that the sin of Adam and Eve consisted not only in failing to listen to God but in deciding—or judging—for themselves what was good. Their act of insubordination attempted to perform what only God has both the ability and right to do: to judge. Judgment requires supreme wisdom and maturity of character. Judgment comes with the weighty possibility of condemning another. For that reason, a just judge never desires that wrath has the final word. And so it is with our Judge: "The Lord . . . is patient with you, not wanting any to perish but all to come to repentance."[50]

We saw that God's rainbow covenant vowed to take judgment on himself before judging the world. And indeed, Jesus underwent the judgment of rebels. God does not judge Jesus on the cross but bears patiently in his flesh the very sin of the world—that is, the judgment sinners put on him. If God had poured out his wrath on Jesus, then there would be no wrath that remains and therefore no coming day of judgment. But wrath remains because sin remains. The cross eliminates neither God's wrath nor human rebellion. It provides a path away from both and toward God's Sabbath rest by forming a people who give rest to the world by also becoming "living sacrifices." It is only by suffering in this way, by standing

---
[48] 2 Chron 36:21.
[49] 2 Chron 36:21.
[50] 2 Pet 3:9.

on the other side of the rainbow covenant with Jesus to take the arrows of sinners, by "filling up what is lacking in Christ's afflictions," being "crucified with Christ," "tak[ing] up [our] cross," and "becoming like him in his death," that the people of God become what we are predestined to be, "the image of his Son, in order that he might be the firstborn within a large family."[51]

Once the people of God are prepared for this mission by obtaining maturity, they can join with Jesus in judging the world and even the angels.[52] We might suggest that Paul also means that we shall judge the principalities and powers that were shamed on the cross but not eliminated. Thus, judgment rightfully understood is what the mature in Christ take up, together, in Christ's appointed time. This is what being "more than victorious" entails.[53] And because nothing can separate his people from his love—that is, from his household—they join with God in his victory that leads to judgment. Thus, the members of the household of God are to gain skills in practicing judgment through the kind of discipline and discipleship Paul assumes would preclude the need to engage the world's judicial systems.[54] Judgment is the quality of the image of God, par excellence. But it is achieved only through taking up one's cross.

In light of the Sabbath journey, both God's wrath and his restraint of judgment express his *desire* for union with his creation. God is patient and delays wrath because God does not will that he should pour it out on anyone but that all would repent.[55] Yet neither does God force repentance through terror. Rather, God comes inconspicuously to provoke true repentance through experiencing "perfect love" that "casts out fear."[56] This is the commission of Jesus to his representatives: to love others as he loved so we may have boldness on the day of judgment.[57]

---

[51]Col 1:24; Gal 2:20; Mt 16:24; Mk 8:34; Lk 9:23; Phil 3:10; Rom 8:29.
[52]1 Cor 6:2-3.
[53]Rom 8:37.
[54]1 Cor 6.
[55]2 Pet 3:9.
[56]1 Jn 4:18.
[57]Jn 13:34, 15:12-17; 1 Jn 4:12, 17.

God has wrath because God is love. And it is because God is love that God has withdrawn the Sabbath reality of the seventh day from his creation. Yet it is God's love for his whole creation that compels him to wrath. The solution to this conundrum is this: The people of God are to be the love of God to the world, fearlessly calling all to repentance by being the reconciling love of God that calls all to maturity.

But what are we to make of the frightening passages of God's judgment poured out on all the world? First, we should note that the vast majority of imprecations (particularly in the Old Testament and also in Revelation) are reserved for kings, states, and powers, not for common people. The principalities and powers are the power of sin and death. These are what hold people in bondage, and the message of exodus and Sabbath must first involve the judgment of the slavers. This is why salvation, with the Israelites and also with us, starts with the defeat of Pharaoh. This does not mean there is no complicity in or even love of bondage and corruption. This is the problem of the Israelites in the wilderness to which Hebrews draws our attention: They wanted to return to their former slavery. The principalities and powers have power because people love, respect, and fear them.

The judgment of God requires that all dream homes and economies be destroyed. These are rival realms and systems of value. One cannot live by competing systems of value. No one can serve God and money. So, for God to win, money must die. Those who invest their life in a dream house will be left desolate; all the world's hellish structures will be cast into a lake of fire.[58] And yet, while Revelation 21:8 describes evildoers whose "place" (Greek *meros*) is in the lake of fire, Revelation 22:15 describes a list of people who continue to exist *outside* the gates of the heavenly Jerusalem, a city whose gates also remain continuously *open*.[59] The Bible's final

---

[58] 1 Cor 3:15; Rev 20:14.
[59] Rev 21:25. The word *meros* basically refers to one's part in something, and while traditionally this is translated as "portion" or "place," implying these people are sent to eternal conscious torment, it is also possible to see this as their "concerns" or "business" or "those things they were about," or even their "share," such that the lake of fire consumes all that they valued. This

picture of God's enemies comports well with those given most everywhere else: They are exiled. Rebels are kicked out, and God does not renege on the rainbow covenant in the end.

Just as the Bible isn't a book of cosmology or the laws of the universe, so too does it not offer a detailed script of a final end. Revelation and Isaiah are not concerned with exact sequences or dates. They are highly concerned with the finality of God's final victory, that God's character will shine through, that evil will cease, that death will end, and that God will be King with his people ruling alongside as worthy of the role they have been given. To speculate on the nature of hell divests ourselves of responsibility; it betrays us for standing apart from Jesus on the wrong side of the rainbow. To be sure: There are profoundly evil people in the world who do profoundly unspeakable acts. There are those who Jesus claims are better off thrown into the sea with a millstone around their neck and for whom, like Judas, it would have been better if they had never been born.[60] But we should note that Jesus' millstone discourse precedes a teaching on untiring forgiveness; it is also closely followed by an exhortation that addresses us in the second person, not the third. It appears that the wisdom of Scripture is to speak with dual convictions rather than attempt to solve the problem of another's eternal fate: God's wrath is real and serious, but God is patient, generous, merciful, and forgiving beyond our comprehension.[61]

If Sabbath is the seventh day of creation, we might say that judgment is the evening of the sixth day. Our prayer should not be that judgment comes tomorrow but that God would equip us to justify God's continued patience. Our true Sabbath work, ironically, may be to delay the Sabbath. Yet Jesus is coming soon, as Revelation concludes. This exhortation isn't a message of hope in God's wrath to engender passivity or retreat. Instead,

---

would make the inconsistency with Rev 22:15 more sensible if they were destitute beggars whose whole life meaning was thrown with the principalities and powers into a consuming fire.
[60]Mt 18:6 // Mk 9:42 // Lk 17:2; Mt 26:24 // Lk 14:21.
[61]This is a feature that goes back even to the Decalogue, where God claims to punish sin to the third or fourth generation but shows *hesed* to the thousandth generation of those who live by his household rule (Ex 20:5-6).

it's an encouragement for the people of God to get busy with their mission to see that all things may enter into God's rest.

Conclusion: The End of Sabbath

Sabbath ends here in two senses. Revelation gives a glimpse at the final Sabbath, when the line of Cain and its misguided constructions are destroyed and all of history is gathered up into the lasting rest God shares with his people. There is a continuity, not clean break, with the old creation, so even past pains and sorrows are integrated and redeemed. "Where, O death, is your sting?" can be proclaimed by those who have died.[62] Revelation also gives us a peek into the throne room of God, where God's people reign with him in an unmediated rest that reclaims the whole cosmos. This is the Sabbath to which all the Sabbath signs along the way have pointed. This is the light of dawn that rises to cast its shadow over the sixth day of human history, catching its rays on the good works of God's people.

But this chapter also demands the end of Sabbath in another sense. Namely, our reading of Hebrews puts an end to the reductionistic, popularized Sabbath theologies that commodify and personalize Sabbath into an individualized vacation or spiritual discipline, or even try to force Sabbath back into the temple it was designed to surpass and supplant by equating Sabbath with a service of Sunday worship. Instead, Hebrews indicates that a proper Sabbath theology serves to renew and energize God's people as disciples of Jesus Christ. *Sabbath is not an invitation to rest; it is an invitation to strive to enter God's rest.* Sabbath, in the sixth day, doesn't command us not to work as much as it tells us what kind of work we should be busied with.

Hebrews insists that striving to enter God's rest requires community, discipline, and the attitude of a wayfarer. There is a deep irony here to the metaphor of journey that has framed this book: We've finished our biblical journey of Sabbath to find, on our return, that a life lived in the light

---
[62] 1 Cor 15:55.

of Sabbath *is* a journey. To this is added another: The irony of Sabbath is that there is still work to do.[63] Sabbath teaches the nature of its work: to bring people to repentance while the day of the Lord is postponed, while it is still today.[64] God's people are to serve as ambassadors of reconciliation, an embassy not representing the sovereign of another place but the Sovereign of a different order of time.[65] What are the implications for how the church is to be the church today? And what are the implications for our ethics, for how we understand how to obey Scripture's command to do good works from within the value systems of the world?[66]

This chapter brings us to the end of our biblical journey through Sabbath. But we still have two chapters to consider the questions, What do we bring with us from our journey back into the world we left? How can or should our Sabbath journey change us and the way we live in our church communities and in the world? These are the questions that part three will set out to consider.

Group Discussion Questions

1. According to this chapter, in what ways is the life of today's church one of exodus?

2. The end of this chapter suggested three qualities that the book of Hebrews indicates should characterize today's church. How might these characterize your church community?

---

[63] 1 Cor 15:58; Rev 22:12.
[64] 2 Pet 3:9; see also Jonah.
[65] 2 Cor 5:20.
[66] Mt 5:16; 1 Cor 3:13; 2 Cor 9:8; Eph 2:10; 2 Thess 2:17; 1 Tim 5:10; 2 Tim 2:21; Titus 2:14; 3:1; Heb 10:24.

PART 3

Sabbath Now

EMBASSY ECCLESIOLOGY
Ambassadors of Rest

IN CHAPTER ONE, we began our exploration of Sabbath with the mindset of a traveler: off to go somewhere but not entirely sure where our journey would take us. In chapter ten we reached our final stop on our Sabbath pilgrimage. But we haven't yet reached the end of this book. Any trip of significance needs a debriefing session—a chance to reflect on what has been learned from the journey and how it will inform the homecoming. We found that engaging rightly with our work as Christian disciples and ambassadors means taking back on the mindset of a sojourner: those who know they are on their way back home. In other words, it turns out that what our exploration of Sabbath teaches us is that when we return to our earthly home to take up our labors again, we can't stop being on a journey. In these next two chapters, we'll pause to consider what the Sabbath gospel might entail for life together as the church (this chapter), as well as the Christian's work in the economies of the world (chap. 12).

Today the church is held captive to the dream home, to dreams of success by techniques of systems development. Rather than seeing the church as a household that grows people into maturity, much modern Christianity sees the church as an organization that builds the kingdom of God. Yet nowhere does Scripture refer to God's kingdom as something humans build. It is instead something that is to be entered into or waited for, like a growing field or arriving royal. But the church's fixation on building God's kingdom is more than an exegetical error. It risks justifying collaboration with the very forces of sin God is laboring to overcome because it misunderstands that kingdoms are not construction projects; they are loyalty projects. If the church anticipates and represents another kingdom, it needs to reveal its loyalty, not engineer its model of success. In order to resist conformity to the ways of the world, the church must renew its mind.[1] This renewal comes through Sabbath as God's call to a noninstrumental mode of life together in his dwelling presence. The Sabbath gospel at its heart redefines the church as *the people of God's household who are growing up into the image of God and who live as a reconciling sign of God's sovereign order of time by giving rest to the world.*

To be the renewed church of our time, one that renews the tired church we considered in our introductory chapter, requires a *reconstitution*: a renewal of our commitment to be God's people. It is not unlike the moment at the end of the book of Joshua when the Old Testament leader (and Jesus' namesake) invites the rescued and newly settled Israelites to renew their covenant with God and to "choose this day whom you will serve," whether the gods of their former country, the gods of their new home, or Yahweh.[2] In order to be God's people, the church must present a genuine choice between being a minority culture and assimilating with the majority. The authenticity of this choice, and the church's ability to present this choice to the world, rests on the distinctiveness of its shared life as an *alternative* way of life to the life of the world.

To do this, the church needs to act like an embassy, as a delegation of ambassadors. But to act like an embassy, we must think like an embassy. An embassy represents another sovereignty. If the church is to operate as a collection of ambassadors who represent another sovereign who reigns not just over a physical territory, but over a different order of *time*, the

---

[1] Rom 12:2.
[2] Josh 24:15.

church requires a distinct form of belonging, economics, and governance that distinguishes it from the orders of the world.[3] In this chapter, we will explore the implications for reimagining the church along these terms.

Belonging: Sabbath People

The church is a people constituted by Jesus Christ. This notion of a people embraces the whole person's belonging or allegiance. This belonging is not restricted to a spiritual dimension. Let's consider three aspects of belonging in light of our Sabbath gospel journey: purifying holiness, a new *ethnos* (Greek "people") founded on *fides* (Latin "faith" or "trust"), and a people of *agapē* (Greek "love"). As throughout this book, the reach for potentially unfamiliar and foreign biblical words instead of their English counterparts is intentional. The English words have built up an accretion of unhelpful associations and assumptions we intend to shed here. Reaching for biblical words helps us repopulate their meaning and renew our language in a way that will hopefully in turn renew our lives.

A Holy Nation Purifying the Creation

The people of God are created and purified by water. Water is the primordial substance out of which God created all things in Genesis 1:2. It is also the substance that kills all life in the flood.[4] While God's promise to Noah not to flood the creation again displays his patience, it is nevertheless by a symbolic drowning of the old creation that a new creation is formed. We also see this logic in the book of Jonah, where drowning is the moral purgation Jonah requires to bring him to repentance and obedience. The logic of Jonah also underlies the practice of John the Baptist, who calls for repentance signified by ritual drowning as preparation for the coming kingdom of God. However, this baptism of repentance did not convey the forgiveness of sins on its own merit. Rather, the symbolic declaration of dying to one's sinful life demonstrates desire for God's forgiveness, which comes through a renewed covenant.

---

[3] 2 Cor 5:20.
[4] 1 Pet 3:21.

John's baptism also echoes the dual passage through water of the exodus (via the Red Sea) and the entry into the Promised Land (via the Jordan River) as the path to new life for the people of God. Steeped in these biblical allusions, John's baptism invites not simply a personal desire for moral renewal but a shared communal desire for God to liberate the people from bondage to a household of sin. So Jesus describes his own death as a baptism, and Paul sees the baptism of Christians as joining in Christ's death to rise with him in new life.[5] Baptism is a means of recapitulating the life of Christ within the community, even as the life of Christ brings all creation and new creation into himself.

People are not only cleansed with water. They are also sustained by water. Water distributes the most basic means of life. Flowing water is called "living" in the Bible to denote the connection between movement and life. Brackish, still water is deadly, but running water nourishes. Living water also signifies the full-flowing maturity of the people. From Genesis 2:10 to Psalm 1 and Psalm 92, to Revelation 22:1, the river of life flows through Scripture as the source of life, wisdom, and healing. In Genesis 2, the river that flows out of Eden and courses on to water the Fertile Crescent signifies the connection between the throne of God (recall that Eden is a palace garden) and the flourishing of creation. Thus Psalm 1 depicts the maturity nurtured by the pedagogy of Torah as being planted by this living water. Psalm 92, which we discussed in chapter three, shows that these trees are planted in the court of the house of God. And Revelation 22 describes the river of life flowing from the throne, through the city, watering tree(s) of life with diverse fruit whose leaves heal the peoples of the world. Throughout, the trees themselves symbolize the people of God, diverse, healthy, transforming the purifying living water into fruit and leaves that heal and *give rest* to the peoples of the world.[6]

---

[5] Lk 12:50; Rom 6:4; Col 2:12.
[6] E.g., as in Ezek 31. While the leaves might be understood as some kind of natural remedy by touching or consuming, it is also possible to see them as akin to the leaf of the story of Jon 4, which gives him rest.

But beyond water-lined trees, Jesus takes the image further. When he speaks of himself as a fount of living water to the Samaritan woman by the well, he reveals that by drinking himself one becomes a source of living water also.[7] Thus, all the imagery of water as death, new creation, purification, maturation, healing, and life is contained in the Christian who becomes a source of living water as well.

Baptism, then, is far more than a ritual entry into church membership. It marks citizenship to a new sovereign nation whose well-watered citizens give life and rest to the world. Baptism recapitulates Jesus himself, with the attendant movement of liberation, allegiance transferal, forgiveness, development into his image, and purification of the whole creation from the power of death. The Christian life and community is thus summed up in baptism. To fixate on the mechanics of baptism often misses the point, just as fixation on practicing Sabbath can miss Sabbath. Baptism should represent the whole movement of recapitulating the life of Christ just as he recapitulated the life of Israel even in *his* baptism.

New *Ethnos* Founded on *Fides* and Born of the Spirit

From Abraham to Jesus, language of fruitful multiplication through numerous descendants forms the imaginary of the household of God. The New Testament transfigures this language by underlining that the people of God are ultimately defined not by resemblance transferred by biology but by Spirit-oriented character. Ultimately, the life that animates Abraham, characterized as faithfulness, is what distinguishes the family of God.[8] Recall that this is how the image language is characterized in Genesis 5: as a form of paternity that communicates the character of the parent to the child. This is not a spiritualization of seed or blood but a recognition that all life comes from God, so that if Abraham behaves differently, *faithfully*, it is because he is animated by a life(blood) that God himself chose and sanctified for his purpose, which is truly the life(blood)

---

[7] Jn 4:7-15.
[8] So Jn 8:39, "If you are Abraham's children, you would do what Abraham did."

of Jesus.[9] For this reason, when Jesus defines fatherhood in John 8, he describes a whole-bodied orientation of one's life. Jesus envisions a people whose Father is God himself, *born* not by flesh and blood but by the Holy Spirit.[10] This is the second birth, "from above," but it is not thereby bloodless or fleshless.[11] The source or origin of belonging to God's household is not through human paternity or maternity but through the Holy Spirit's adoption. But without the lifeblood of Jesus, this people has no life within it.[12]

This is a new lineage, a new people group or *ethnos* (Greek), *goy* (Hebrew), or *gens* (Latin), founded on that which made Abraham unique: his faith.[13] This word has also been misconstrued. Faith as intellectual assent, or passionate inward feeling of confidence, is ultimately mistaken because it is disembodied. There are no words in the Old Testament for such a kind of faith. Instead, faith is always faithfulness, being true, acting reliably according to one's word. *'Aman* and *'emunah* are the Hebrew words translated "faith." Both refer to a firmness or confidence rooted in the union—not separation—of word and deed, of spirit and body. Abraham's faithfulness was more than trust in God; it was *trust put into action*. The proof lay in his testing at the abortive sacrifice of Isaac whether he would be loyal to God not just in principle but in the arena of actual history. The faith/works divide only bears witness to a false dichotomy of spirit and matter. Faith does not consist of merely intellectual assent or even an internal trusting; faith manifests as actual doing: "Faith by itself, if it has no works, is dead."[14]

---

[9] So in Jn 14:6 Jesus claims to be the only way to the Father because he is the "life." That is, his blood animates all those who are of the household of God.

[10] Jn 1:13.

[11] Jn 3:3. Note that traditional translations such as KJV have "born again," but given the context it is far more likely that Jesus is speaking of the point of origin rather than focusing on going through the process a second time. It may even be that he was speaking Greek to Nicodemus and the ambiguity of the word *anōthen* was what confused Nicodemus into asking about entering again into his mother's womb.

[12] Jn 6:53-54.

[13] Most modern words fail to communicate birthright without superimposing political categories. Tribe, nation, clan, people, race all contain overtones that are hard to avoid. The Greek *ethnos* ("ethnic, ethnicity") is the translation of Hebrew *goy*, for which the Latin is *gens* ("generation, Gentile").

[14] Jas 2:17.

There's nothing profoundly deep or mysterious about this notion of faithfulness, *pistis* (Greek), or *fides* (Latin). It's what one would wish from a family member—loyalty to the household. This is why Gentiles may be counted as children of Abraham: "Those of faith are the children of Abraham."[15] Paul elaborates on this point when he insists that fulfillment of legal demands does not result in righteousness if law keeping does not lead to maturity and wisdom exemplified by faithfulness in realms outside the law.[16] The question for both Jesus and Paul is one of loyalty. The law, as Psalm 119 stresses through its likening of the law to a path, offers simply a means of learning loyalty. Law is mistaken as its own end instead of as a pedagogue. It has no power to justify.

All people are welcomed into this family of faith-in-action through election, or God's choice.[17] This household is not a metaphor for an institution. Humans are by nature familial animals, not social, political, corporate, or technological animals. Thus, when the gospel is told in terms of a family or household, it speaks to the very heart of human identity prior to any social constructs that reorganize natural links into artificial ones imposed by larger-scale groupings. For Jesus, there's nothing fictive about this kinship network. Instead, by identifying God as the only source of life, Jesus also identifies God as the only true Father or life giver.

The kingdom of God thus derives its reality solely from the body of the king as it intersects the body politic of faithful subjects. This union means that no amount of human institutional structuring or planning can build the kingdom. For this reason, no institution can claim to embody the body politic of Jesus without simplifying the kingdom or usurping Christ's role. The people of God are united, then, not by human allegiances, nor by shared ideology or faith, nor by race, ethnicity, gender, social class, or any other mode of human union. Only Jesus can be the source of unity, *and only union with Jesus unites us to the people of God.*[18] The people of

---

[15]Gal 3:7, our translation.
[16]Gal 3:11.
[17]Eph 1:4-5.
[18]Gal 3:26-29.

God are thus joined into a new lineage or *ethnos*, a new paternity. This is a ruling family destined to inherit the sovereignty of all things, which is the age of Sabbath. Put another way, the Sabbath is the time when all God's people have entered into the rest of their inheritance and rule with God as members of the divine council, not like angels but as children.

A People of Agapē

Paternity and *fides* do not exhaustively account for what it means to belong to this family. For that, Jesus—and especially the Johannine literature—also refer to love, or *agapē*. The Christian community is revealed by relationships with others mediated through whole-life loyalty to Jesus. And in this way they are constituted primarily by *love*. The church is thus Christ's love manifest among living people far more than it is about institutional form. The quality of agapeic love between Christians reveals a tear in the fabric of the spacetime reality of the present evil age. Time is about quality or character, not simply measurement of change. And so the church is a revelation whenever two or three gather in Jesus' name.[19]

This love is also one that disciplines, insofar as it belongs to a family built on provoking one another to maturity manifested in good deeds.[20] The Lord disciplines those he loves, and so should this discipline be regularly exercised through the meeting of God's people together locally.[21] A proper biblical ecclesiology is expressed through consistent practice of embodied agapeic love, not in questions of delegated authority or instrumental methods of attaining goals and visions. Which structural configurations best facilitate this will inevitably vary by context but must not detract from the fostering of loving relationships between real people in real time.

The church thus functions as a formational community in which all people by "speaking the truth in love . . . grow up in every way into him

---

[19] Mt 18:20.
[20] See Rom 8:29; Heb 10:24; Eph 2:10.
[21] Heb 10:25; 12:6; Rev 3:19.

who is the head, into Christ."²² All are to recapitulate Jesus, to become like the head, the one who reheads all things in himself.²³ The church is the body of Christ that itself continues his work of summing all things up, putting an end to the history of rebellion through its own shared life. In this way the church is a people on a journey toward Christ, a spiraling journey that follows the pattern of enslavement, liberation, formation and forgiveness, pedagogy and discipleship, celebrating the common life, becoming a holy people, and thus ending as the image of God. The very presence of this image in the world, though imperfect now, rips open the present evil age by simply living out together the very life of Christ. Sabbath sensitizes us to the invasive nature of God's time to apprehend how active Christian discipleship spirals in on Jesus. This pattern of movement of the history of Israel and the church summarized in Christ occurs when Sabbath time intersects the present evil age. It is thus by the imitation of Christ that the individual disciple and the living community spiral in toward the singularity where all time is gathered in Jesus.

This does not efface individuality or destroy cultural diversities. Instead, it is the only guarantee of their ongoing value. By being gathered in Christ, his people are liberated from the inevitable simplifications of other projects for human unity, such as the ongoing massification of society and cultural appropriation of globalism, which ultimately expresses the devaluation of relational value for instrumental value that fuels the development of the dream home. The image of God is not monolithic but multifaceted. Union with Christ is freedom from making bricks for Babel or Egypt. It is in union with Christ that individuals can truly be individuated—not because they are controlled, compelled, or conformed through pressure but because *they are loved*. It is in Jesus that individuals come to completion as individuals. It is in agapeic love that people are loved as others, not tolerated or normed but matured. After all, Jesus is the most patient one, the one who would suffer fools for millennia before judging

---

²²Eph 4:15.
²³Eph 1:10.

and condemning the innocent or those who might be rescued. Jesus does not judge but desires mature people to judge with him on the day of judgment, when God's patience is satisfied that none have been forsaken and that all things can be reconciled through such a judgment.

Thus the church is the living sign of Christ, of freedom, of a community of Jubilee. It is the embodiment of the image of God. The church is the living evidence that God and his sovereignty are defined as love in action far above conversations about aseity or sovereign decrees. The church is the antidote to the dream home precisely to the degree that it reveals the sovereignty of the love of God.

Economics: Sabbath Sustenance

Belonging to the people of God consists of purifying holiness, a new *ethnos* of *fides*, and a people of *agapē*. What does the order of this household look like, then?

In Christ, God is reconciling all things to himself.[24] This reconciliation defines the life of the community and ought to remind us of Jubilee-inspired language. A reconciliation does not have to mean that debts are paid and all accounts balanced. It means that relationships are healed by ending the reign of false value and that freedom is restored for people to make a living without being subjected, employed, or otherwise instrumentalized. The Sabbath economy is the reconciliation of value and values, of work and works, of material and spiritual. It is a reconciliation of all creation to God by destroying the mythical foundation of the dream home. In this we see the *logic* (logos) or word of God, which is love. *Agapē* is the foundation stone, the stumbling block, and the cornerstone that crushes the builders of the dream home.[25]

The Word of God *is* Christ, who is the foundation and the logic of the household of God. The Word became flesh, and so too must the logic of Christ be made flesh. The economy of Sabbath cannot be immaterial.

---

[24] Col 1:20.
[25] 1 Pet 2:4-8, quoting Is 28:16; Ps 118:22; Is 8:14-15.

Rather, this Word is the fundamental logic of the Creator who became flesh, who united word and deed, and who in this way is the righteousness and faithfulness of God. Jesus is not righteous *instead* of us. Nor did he come in the flesh in order to save our souls alone. The Word became flesh to redeem *even* the flesh. Such redemption entails the whole world of what we normally call economics—work, provision, shelter, security, and more. Thus the economy of God's household is expressed in symbolic actions that unite word and deed. Historically these have been called sacraments, institutions, or ordinances. And because material reality has been relegated to a secular sphere, the sacraments have lost much of their content, ossifying into dead rituals that gain meaning only when they inspire religious feeling. Without a shared material reality, the sacraments often point as much to the structures of the dream home as anything else. From disposable plastic communion cups to individuals receiving numerous baptisms as forms of affirmations of personal choice, the signs have lost their referent.

Our aim here is to reclaim the sacraments as living signs expressed in physical form to integrate the people of God into the economy of the household of God. At its most simple, baptism—as we just considered—is simply about entry into the household through something like a citizenship ceremony. The Lord's Supper is a feast that indexes the economic produce of the community with the life of Jesus that his people must recapitulate in themselves. In this way questions of their efficacy must be attached to the continued formation of the community of the church and its members rather than the application of disembodied divine power to individuals through the church.

An Internal Economy: The Lord's Supper

Bread and body. Throughout this book we've spoken of Sabbath as the sovereign reign of God over time. This is a whole order of time that invades the present evil age, most pointedly in the life, death, resurrection, and ascension of Jesus. But at the heart of Sabbath, and indeed at its first delivery as a command, is the question of food and sustenance.[26] Sabbath is first commanded in relation to God's provision of manna in the wilderness. This is in contrast with the grain of Pharaoh, for which the Hebrew people's lives were exchanged in slavery. At the Last Supper Jesus attaches his flesh to unleavened bread—the underprepared bread of liberation. While we don't have space to consider the significance of yeast in Jesus' thinking, we note here that the bread of the first Passover in Egypt was made with the last of Egyptian grain. So too does Jesus' body break the sovereignty of the order of time in which we reside, replacing it with his own broken body, distributed among his people. The bread of Passover is replaced by the manna in the wilderness or "the bread of angels."[27] The Passover lamb breaks the dominion of the bread of Egypt, replacing it with God-sourced bread: Jesus himself.[28]

Jesus' flesh as food is a difficult concept for contemporaries to digest. Attempts have been made to translate this into philosophical categories of, for example, Aristotle through the Roman Catholic theology of transubstantiation. Other people have been comforted by an allegorization of these claims, arguing that Jesus deploys rhetoric of hyperbole and concrete imagery to explain spiritual realities by means of material signs. But it seems that Jesus was highly insistent that his body was indeed food to be consumed.[29]

A number of threads traced throughout this book converge here. Eating Jesus' body is the reconciliation of Sabbath time with the people of God. In the wilderness, the people ate bread from heaven. God fed them. God provided the basic economic value with minimal labor, with no exchange, no specialization, no transportation, processing, marketing, preparation, or cooking. In other words, God forms his household and establishes its value on himself and *not on adding value through human labor*. Jesus consistently performed miracles of food multiplication and abundant provision without human work.

---

[26] Ex 16.
[27] Ps 78:25.
[28] Jn 6:32-33, 35.
[29] Jn 6.

Eating Jesus' body must mean that the people of God support the basic needs of their own people and are not dependent on the market or economy of the world, which grounds value in labor specialization. This may not seem miraculous if by that we understand the miraculous as defying laws of physics. But it *is* miraculous if by that we mean it reconciles physics with God. Human labor must still be involved with food production. But it is a miracle when food production is not a means of slavery and exploitation but instead a means of "giv[ing] life to the world."[30] Exploitation is inherent in the production of food from the first turn to settled agriculture until today. The only method of producing a surplus of food by the few for the thousands is by valuing the labor of farmers and food producers less than the labor of other specialists. Low wages are necessary if the world aims to produce a dream home where most people do not touch the soil. It is in rejecting the discipline of God in Genesis 3:19 by inducing others to sweat on our behalf that all of human civilization is possible. This is the dream of aseity, of attaining rest by benefiting from the work of others, preferably anonymous, hidden others laboring in far-off places—in middle-of-nowhere rural locations or on the other side of the globe.[31]

What Sabbath proposes, and Jesus confirms in claiming to be bread from heaven, is that God demands a different order of civilization based on a revolutionary economy, one grounded on gift rather than earnings, one that rewards the maturity of those who give themselves away instead of those who develop themselves by using other people, products, and things. Aseity is the false dream of the immature mind, imagining that suffering can be avoided or escaped by passing it off to others.

"Whoever comes to me will never be hungry" indicates that Jesus imagines food security as an ingredient in the agapeic relationships of the church and in a way that defies the structures of the world's economy.[32]

---

[30] Jn 6:33.
[31] Note how even human topographic imagination is defined by an urban "developed" perspective, such that value comes to a place only by transforming it through construction.
[32] Jn 6:35.

The mature mind of Christ makes itself nothing, becomes a servant, and gives its life for others. This is the kingdom of God contained in the flesh of Christ, for this is the body politic of Christ. Those who embody Christ's sovereignty have the same mind as Christ, and thus a collection of such people must create a different way of living, an economy.[33] To eat the flesh of Jesus is to embody the mind of Christ in material community. It does not mean there can be no specialization, which Paul clearly describes in Ephesians 4:28. It does not even mean every individual must grow their own food, though that would do much to transform the world. It means every Christian accepts the discipline of God and sweats for others out of love.

When we pray, "Thy kingdom come. Thy will be done on earth as it is in heaven. Give us this day our daily bread" in the Lord's Prayer, we are inducing ourselves to live the kingdom on earth as in heaven by providing daily bread to the people of God. This is not generic thankfulness for food. To thank God for our daily meals without recognizing the innumerable lives of the poor implicated in our abundant and globally sourced foodstuffs is to attribute to God's sovereignty the oppression of the poor. Gratitude to God—a true Eucharist (Greek "thanksgiving")—should come with thankfulness for the hands that produced and prepared. That thanks reaches its zenith if those hands are known and loved. Thus the body of Christ is true food. We must eat the church, for this is how the church reveals the kingdom of God.

At the same time, we must note that in his temptation to make bread out of stones, Jesus counters Satan by quoting Deuteronomy 8:3, that "one does not live by bread alone, but by every word that comes from the mouth of God."[34] The material economy cannot be divorced from its foundation in the Word of God. As the body of Christ, the church

---

[33] For a biblical, and especially Deuteronomistic and Jubilee-focused, account of what a food-based ecclesial economy might entail for today, see Michael Rhodes, Robby Holt, and Brian Fikkert, *Practicing the Jesus Economy: Learning Disciplines for How You Work, Earn, Spend, Save, and Give* (Baker Books, 2018).

[34] Mt 4:4; Lk 4:4.

reconciles spirit and flesh. We should not dismiss the church of its material obligation to provide bread for the household of God by implying that the Word can replace bread. Rather, it is the Word that establishes and transforms the economy that produces the bread, making it the bread of life rather than the bread of slavery.

Wine and blood. We saw previously how blood in God's household is not symbolic of death but of life. The wine shared at the Last Supper Passover meal, alluding to the blood of the Passover lamb, wards off the power of death by the force of Jesus' "indestructible life."[35] As the blood of the covenant, the wine celebrates union between God and his people, which signifies the forgiveness of sins.

Extending from this, we have proposed that the lifeblood of Jesus is distributed to his people through their ingestion of it. In perhaps one of Jesus' most shocking statements, he commands his people to drink his blood; this idea is anathema to Leviticus and even the Council of Jerusalem in Acts 15. But drinking the blood of Jesus is not subject to the same prohibition because the logic of Leviticus holds that blood is where life is and that all life belongs to God. In this command to drink Jesus' blood, God gives *his* life to his people. We have suggested thinking of this like a blood transfusion. We do not live because Jesus died. We live because Jesus *lives*, and his distributed blood enables his people to be vivified by the very life of God. Thus there is no life for those who do not drink the blood of Jesus because they will not be vivified and resurrected by the power of his indestructible life.[36] Jesus is the tree of life, and his lifeblood the firstfruit we consume to bear the same fruit for the life of the world.

The life of the church is thus contained in the very flesh of its people. The only way for the blood of Christ to be distributed to his people is through the Holy Spirit in the life of the community. While there remains merit in rituals of Communion or the Eucharist, the rituals have also

---

[35] Heb 7:16.
[36] Jn 6:53.

inverted the true sacramental logic. It is not the institution that brings Christ to the people; it is Christ in the people who bring life to one another and thus to the institutions we create to facilitate that life together.

Ambassadors: Living Signs That Give Rest

Ambassadors are elder statespeople sent to represent the interests and values of one nation to another. Paul uses this language in 2 Corinthians 5:20 to describe the function of the people of God in light of the gospel of reconciliation. While this is not the only image used in the Bible to describe the people of God, it is particularly fitting given that "ambassador," *presbytes*, is semantically related to *presbyteros*, or "elder." Mature members of the household of God are expected to represent it. The goal of maturity in becoming the image of Christ is not simply about personal character development as its own end but in order to bear this character, the image of God, *to the world*.

In chapter six we reviewed the covenants of the Old Testament to underscore the mission of God's people to bear signs of God's sovereignty to the world. The purpose of the Old Testament covenant signs is lived forward through Christ into the church. The Old Testament signs are transformed, not abandoned. With the rainbow covenant God opens history to the realm of his patience, stepping back from a sovereignty of direct intervention for the sake of creating space for the pedagogy of his image-bearing people to do their reconciling work. Even if his death is the release of the bowstring of humanity against God, attempting to end God and thus threatening to end his patience, Jesus inaugurates a renewed age of God's patience, proclaiming that he did not come to judge but to bring rest.

Jesus fulfills the sign of circumcision. The circumcision of the heart was the reality to which the physical act always pointed, which Jesus demonstrates by opening the promises of God to the Gentiles, who no longer require the circumcision of the flesh, provided their hearts are transformed to be fruitful and multiply disciples not through biological offspring but through baptism and training in obedience to Christ.[37] The fruit of Jesus is a lineage, a people, who have his law as a pedagogue. Jesus, the Lord of the Sabbath, commissions his people to bear the ultimate sign of Sabbath to the world. This is not an empty or ossified sign related to observance of specific days of the week or debates about what kinds of activity are permissible but the transformation of a world built on *toil* by a people who are designed to *give rest*.

Sabbath, and the people of God's household, do not *take* rest; they give it. "Bear one another's burdens, and in this way you will fulfill the law of Christ," as Paul puts it.[38] This burden bearing might encompass spiritual burdens as well as psychological and emotional burdens but remains perfunctory if it means doing little about the material cause of these weights. As Paul says earlier in Galatians, "In Christ Jesus neither circumcision nor uncircumcision counts for anything; the only thing that counts is faith working through love."[39] Faith is made effective through concrete acts of love. If we read with an Old Testament background, Paul's exhortation here cannot be restricted to mere affection but extends to the actual faithfulness to family obligations, such as the redemption of family members from bondage as stipulated in the Levitical laws of Jubilee. "How does God's love abide in anyone who has the world's goods and sees a brother or sister in need and yet refuses help?"[40] We should caution, though, that this does not mean Paul imagines the end goal here as a church full of independent, autonomous, self-sufficient individuals, as the prevailing dream home of the Western world falsely imagines human maturity. If anything, Paul is inviting the kind of burden bearing that demands a continual interdependence between members of the family of God in a manner that marks their departure from the ways of the world.

---

[37] Deut 10:16; 30:6; Jer 4:4; Mt 28:19-20.
[38] Gal 6:2.
[39] Gal 5:6.
[40] 1 Jn 3:17.

Governance: Sabbath Service

In most published theology, what falls under the heading of ecclesiology generally discusses institutional models of governance. This is symptomatic of prevailing assumptions that reduce the church to matters of institutional organization. One aim of this book is to turn this assumption on its head. We began our journey in medias res. Beginning in the middle also put us not in the clouds of abstraction or as surveyors of a map of a territory but on the ground. With this came a focus on quality of time and relationship rather than structure. To begin the journey toward God's Sabbath rest means starting from one's current situation, in real time, with real people, in real places.

Ecclesiology isn't about institutional models or systems of governance, whether the more contemporary and trendy corporate models that sport executive pastors and managerial staff, with theater-like facilities, or the residual medieval model, with its priestly caste and temple structures that fixate on certain liturgical forms. There is sufficient historical evidence that the institutional imagination of the church is highly conditioned by prevailing cultural understandings of how institutional authority structures work at any given point in its history. (So the Catholic church structure takes on the monarchic governance of the Middle Ages, the Reformation spawned more republican or democratic ecclesial governance, and more recent nondenominational churches take their cues from contemporary corporate models.) Breaking our imaginations free from these imaginative strongholds, whether old or new, means reclaiming the church not as a static institution but as the wandering people of God sojourning toward God's Sabbath rest.[41] This may mean first breaking free of the roles that tend to divide God's people along the very institutional lines that restrict them, whether along the more traditional clergy/laity divide or what is developing into a staff/attendee or even service provider/service consumer divide.

---

[41]To borrow the title of Ernst Käsemann, *The Wandering People of God: An Investigation of the Letter to the Hebrews*, trans. Roy A. Harrisville and Irving L. Sandberg (Augsburg, 1984).

Raising Elders

The Sabbath gospel transforms our conception of the church away from one focused on institutional structure—with common questions of unity, authority, offices, and functions—to one of pedagogical relationships. The church is the people of God who must become the image of God in Christ and so be ambassadors of reconciliation to the world. The church is primarily about nurturing people in Christlike maturity. Jesus recapitulates all of God's people in himself so that we can live the timeline of the people of God. This means that participation with Christ is the only means of becoming like Christ. There are no methods that produce the result of becoming like Jesus apart from the sheer cumulative force of actions that aim for imitation and intimacy. This might simply be called discipleship, though that term is in grave danger of overuse. The point is that to be the church we must *be* the church. The methods we use will produce results consistent with them. And that leads to one of the great initial challenges in being the church. We need imitable elders who are genuinely mature and who are skilled at communicating their maturity to new generations.

This is what a household does: raises new generations. Eldership is not an office but the culmination of a lifetime of wisdom gained by living in Sabbath time, being planted in the courts of God's house.

This also means that those who currently identify as leaders—pastors, priests, or whatever other title they may take—bear a responsibility, even a call, to be people worthy of imitation in all areas of life. They are defined less by what tasks they *do* and functions they serve as much as by who they *are*. They are those who can say with Paul, "Be imitators of me, as I am of Christ."[42] The revolving door of news headlines regarding ecclesial leadership failures and destroyed ministries makes it sadly difficult to imagine that there are many—ourselves included—who could legitimately claim to be worthy of imitation.

To address such a major demand for imitable leaders focused on pedagogical growth of individuals through agapeic love is not easy, even if it

---

[42] 1 Cor 11:1.

is quite simple. We need a vanguard of people to commit to being the body politic of Christ, who "eat the church" and who open their lives to the scrutiny of one another. We need leaders who never consider that their calling is other than "[presenting] everyone mature in Christ."[43] And in fact, it is the remit of *all* members of Christ's body to pursue the health and ultimately the maturity of others to whom they belong.[44] *This Sabbath work is frustratingly inefficient*, and all the more so if we continue with paradigms that raise up specialists as leaders and imagine that scaling our efforts by distributing responsibility to experts is the measure of success. Pedagogy, especially of the kind that attends to a whole person, requires patience. It demands the patience of a parent, not the mentality of a manager. It requires dwelling time and dwelling space. It requires what the early church called *catechesis*.[45] As one early church leader quipped, "Christians are made, not born," and the early church made Christians by a process of formation that was willing to take *time*.[46]

Conclusion: Converting to Patient Pedagogy

How do we reclaim the "patient ferment" that labors to form mature members of the household of God at the pace of God's time? Pastors and others in professional ministry might feel as though their hands are tied by institutional structures, by existing expectations and demands, by the ruts of traditions and precedents that a wise leader knows cannot be quickly discarded or dismissed, by paychecks that are enough to live off but not enough to finance future security to make radical change. Thus the challenge is often attempted to be met from within existing frameworks through processes of slow change. In my (Gregory's) experience in denominational leadership and transitional pastoring, I have not witnessed effective means of cultivating change for a variety of reasons. Most

---

[43] Col 1:28-29; see also Gal 4:19.
[44] 1 Cor 12:7.
[45] For more on the early church catechesis and how it might inform contemporary formation, see Gerald Sittser, "The Catechumenate and the Rise of Christianity," *Journal of Spiritual Formation & Soul Care* 6, no. 2 (2013): 179-203.
[46] Alan Kreider, *The Patient Ferment of the Early Church* (Baker Academic, 2016), 134.

notably, the world's culture imposes rapid adaptations that often take precedent over and even undermine well-considered long-term strategies. Paradoxically, it is difficult to slowly shift a culture of efficient results to a culture of patient formation. Perhaps there is no such thing as slow change to the Sabbath gospel's measured pace. There is only conversion.

This is because the methods produce the results coded into the methods; the nature of the tree determines the nature of its fruit.[47] Religious products produce religious transactions; events produce attendees; marketing produces customers; but only discipling—and disciplining—produces disciples.[48] There must be a clean liberation from Egypt. There must be a transition from slavery bread or a grain dole to manna and the body of Christ. There must be a blood transfusion. We must stop making bricks for Pharaoh and start giving one another rest.

But while institutions themselves may only rarely execute a slow change transformation, the development of a robust community inevitably takes the time that relationships themselves take to develop. It's a matter of getting started with a starter dough. But to develop a core group of people committed to a clean break demands intentional planning, significant trust (*fides*), and wisdom working itself out in love, as well as shared space and, of course, *time*. As right as much of the missional movement has been in its focus on sending and outreach, there is a time to scatter stones and also a time to *gather* them.[49] The signs of the times suggest now is the time to gather together living stones who can form a foundation.[50]

If the purpose of history is for humanity to grow up, and if God has been patient enough to give the world time to live at its own death-spiral pace as well as gracious enough to perturb that time through his people, then integral to the process is for us to grow up and figure it out: "*You* give

---

[47] Mt 7:15-20.
[48] For an excellent theological critique of popular church marketing practices, see Emily Beth Hill, *Marketing and Christian Proclamation in Theological Perspective* (Lexington Books, 2021).
[49] Eccles 3:5.
[50] Lk 12:56.

them something to eat."[51] The very process and struggle is the pedagogy. The call on all is to become mature elders, *ambassadors*, living signs. Do you provide meat for the household—or are you still drinking milk?[52]

Group Discussion Questions

1. This chapter suggested there are three ways that the Sabbath gospel might shape the life of the church in terms of belonging, economics, and governance. Which do you find the most compelling? The most challenging?

2. What concrete steps might your church community take to better operate as a community of ambassadors of God's rest within your context?

---

[51] Mk 6:37.
[52] 1 Cor 3:2.

ESTABLISH THE WORK OF OUR HANDS

W HEN I (AMY) WAS PREPARING to move from the United States to Australia to take up the role I now hold, my visa was significantly delayed. Eventually I began my employment while still in the States. Until my visa approval came through, a year after I had received the job, I remained unsure of when (if ever, it seemed), I would finally relocate to my new home. But although I continued to live in the United States, my world orbited around Australia. Instead of the typical nine-to-five, I worked from 2 p.m. to 10 p.m. to overlap some of my working hours with the waking ones down under. And out of not just mere curiosity but a desire to accustom myself to my new homeland, I drank up its news headlines, studied its geography and history and literature and slang, and eagerly researched activities and communities I could engage as soon as I arrived. I grinned when a friend in California snapped a photo for me of native Australian trees she spotted on a local stroll. By all external appearances, I was living and working in the United States. But in my mind and even in my heart, I was in Australia—despite having never visited and possessing little assurance or control over when I would finally arrive on its shores. I was experiencing, in a palpable and often trying way, a metaphor of the Christian life. We are forced to live according to worldly expectations and conventions to a degree at the same time that we are getting ready for life in another country. And all while the time of our final arrival remains out of our hands.

In this final chapter, we want to explore what the implications of the Sabbath gospel are for Christian work and action in the world. If the Sabbath gospel is going to have a bearing on our lives, it has to be here. If Christian ethics is ultimately about how Christians are to be salt and light, then their very nature as salt and light—by which they act as preservatives and illuminators in a bland and dark world—is dependent on the degree to which they are shaped and, indeed, flavored and enlightened by the nature of the household of rest to which they belong.[1] This should affect how they comport themselves within the world of work (or any ordinary labor or activity, paid or unpaid). Our worry, though, is that some of the contemporary discourse about the nature of work, while well intended, unwittingly does the opposite: Instead of orienting us to the world for which we wait, it exhorts us to be conditioned by the structures of the world, which in turn compromises our ability to season and brighten them. To get at how to be Christians who do good *works*, we need to unmask some mistaken assumptions about the nature of *work*.

Defining Work

In a book about Sabbath, work must be defined carefully. The Sabbath command in the Decalogue indicates that six days are for labor and the seventh is for rest. The Decalogue refers to the basic economic functions of a household and by extension a society. It stipulates that both on the Sabbath day and on the Sabbath year preparations are to be made within the six days or years of labor to prepare for the seventh. These basic economic functions foundationally revolve around food. Food, of course, symbolizes sovereignty. So, the command not to work is foundationally a command not to contribute to the economy.

---

[1] Mt 5:13-16.

This isn't to distinguish work for one's own household and the house of God. The notion of going to church on Sunday as the inverse of economic production is inherently faulty, given that the household economy of God should be lived out by his people who provide daily bread. In many ways, the storage of this food for the seventh day is a weekly festival that celebrates the communion of the people with God, enjoying the fruit of labor in peace. We might say that all work for the household of God is Sabbath shaped and aimed. Conversely, all work that contributes to the dream home, and even rest taken from this work, is not Sabbath shaped or Sabbath aimed. From a Sabbath gospel point of view, work is defined by the master, not the laborer, nor even the work itself. The master will determine the character of the working conditions, the desired outcomes, and the shaping of the worker in the process. This accounts for Jesus' Sabbath-breaking episodes. Instead of defining work as any kind of physical exertion, Jesus saw that Sabbath was expressed in exertions that aid—or bring rest—to others and in so doing participate in the household of the kingdom of God. Sabbath work is formative into the image of God in Christ and aimed at his sovereignty, which reconciles all creation. All other work is aimed at other ends and forms people in other ways. The caveat is that we must not confuse work for church institutions as inherently for God or Sabbath shaped, given that institutions can themselves be deformed or subject to false masters. Yet neither should we automatically justify "worldly" work as kingdom labor.

Demythologizing Work

The myth of work in the "secular" world. "So now tell us, what do *you* do?" You could be almost anywhere: at a party a friend is hosting, at a dinner table meeting a partner's family for the first time, at an opening Bible study gathering. Society stakes a large share of a person's identity in their paid work. In one sense, this is nothing new. A last name may be the vestigial remnant of a family trade long ceded to history but whose identity-shaping power is still impressed: Brewer, Butler, Carver, Cook,

Fisher, Hunter, Mason, Potter, Tanner, Wagenfuhr (German for "wagon driver"). The trades they encode may have long departed in one sense, and yet the economies of the past haunt us still. Even if we have not christened ourselves with new monikers such as Coder, Manager, Pilot, or Engineer, we still seek a name for ourselves—a brand, even—through our occupations and titles.[2] And no wonder. The paradox of work is that we are caught between the necessity, or so it seems, to support ourselves on the one hand and the deep desire for meaning to contribute to something with lasting permanence on the other. We have eternity in our hearts, as Ecclesiastes puts it, and we channel this impulse into our working life. Yet so often labor instead generates some combination of boredom, disillusionment, alienation, or injustice.[3]

Perhaps this tension is perennial for humans (the beginning of Ecclesiastes suggests as much). But it may also be heightened today. There is reason to believe that moderns place an even larger share of identity in work than in the past. Even in the secular world work is cast in religious vocabulary. We may no longer name ourselves by our occupations, but we do describe them as a calling or even a vocation—something that summons and names us.[4] And it is not just individual jobs that are glorified and sanctified. The economy itself is spoken of in deified terms. During Covid-19, it was described as an entity of its own that demanded sacrifice on the one hand and saving on the other. But there are even deeper theological roots to the prevailing contemporary conception that renders the economy into its own corporate person such that it is a kind of secularized church.[5] We propose that this emerged during the Reformation, and what's more that popular contemporary Christian discourse about work shares both the roots and

---

[2] Gen 11:4 should haunt us here.
[3] Eccles 3:11.
[4] That one recent *New York Times* article decries this nomenclature for setting the conditions for exploitation only underscores its entrenchment. It bemoans, "The perceived righteousness of honorable industries covered up poor conditions like frosting on a burned cake." Simone Stolzoff, "Please Don't Call My Job a Calling," *New York Times*, June 5, 2023, www.nytimes.com/2023/06/05/opinion/employment-exploitation-unions.html.
[5] For more here, see G. P. Wagenfuhr, *Plundering Egypt: A Subversive Christian Ethic of Economy* (Cascade Books, 2016).

questionable fruit of this theology. This discourse is variously named "work and faith" or, as we'll identify it, "work and worship."[6]

Let's briefly outline some of the main claims of this contemporary discourse. Then we'll suggest a story of how it came about.

The following bullet points will necessarily be simplified and not exhaustive but together bring a fairly representative collection of assertions that tend to animate the work-and-worship discourse:

- God is a Creator God, and humans image him insofar as they also operate as creators; they are even designated as cocreators.
- Work is inherently and intrinsically good (sin and the fall may be mentioned, but sin overall is not "load bearing," as W. David Buschart and Ryan Tafilowski rightly point out).[7]
- Your work in the world is the means by which God does his work in the world and even brings about his kingdom. When you do your work in the world, you are doing the work of God.

It's not difficult to detect a premature triumphalism regarding human work in the world that tends to characterize this literature. It tells the contemporary worker that their labor in the world's economy is ordained by God and services God's work in the world. Consider a few representative comments that sacralize work:

> [One] of the hopes for our unraveling society is the recovery of the idea that all human work is not merely a job but a *calling*.[8]

---

[6]"Work and faith" is the designation used by W. David Buschart and Ryan Tafilowski, *Worth Doing: Fallenness, Finitude, and Work in the Real World* (IVP Academic, 2025). Among other things, the phrase "work and worship" highlights more clearly the perceived dichotomy the literature seeks to address (and which we will detail later in this chapter). There is also a book title with this very name, although it presents a more chastened view of the literature in which it sits: "In our experience, discussions of faith and work tend to be overly cheery and positive." Matthew Kaemingk and Cory B. Willson, *Work and Worship: Reconnecting Our Labor and Liturgy* (Baker Academic, 2020), 12. Kara Martin has coined a phrase and titular book from the mash-up term *workship*. Martin, *Workship: How to Use Your Work to Worship God* (Graceworks Private, 2017). For a more fulsome list of titles that constitute this literature, see *Worth Doing*, 124-25.

[7]Buschart and Tafilowski, *Worth Doing*.

[8]Timothy Keller and Katherine Leary Alsdorf, *Every Good Endeavor: Connecting Your Work to God's Work* (Penguin Books, 2016), 2.

> We are meant to participate in God's grand mission of redemption by living life with God for the life of the world through our work. God does his work of reconciling all things, all five of the key relationships, to himself through our work!⁹
>
> Your work is a core part of your humanness. You are made in the image of a *working* God.¹⁰

This theology lands squarely within the critique of Karl Marx leveled at the Christianity of industrial exploitation: that it is an opium that inures people to their exploitation and misery with promises of divine blessings unrealized in this life.¹¹ The sociological problems are compounded from Martin Luther's time to our own. Marx's notion of *alienation* shows how in previous eras workers produced their own product and so could potentially see themselves as legitimate creators. Assembly-line workers and corporate team members are alienated from the final product and are no longer creators but cogs, human resources consumed as a capital investment in the wealth of the owner.¹² The logic of *homo faber* ("man the maker") as the image of God is ever more problematic in highly advanced economies because God is no longer the carpenter but the entrepreneur whose goal is mathematical growth, not producing objects of use-value.

David Graeber has more recently shown through anthropological research that this problem of job alienation has reached extreme levels in which few people find meaning in their work due to the nature of what he calls "bullshit jobs."¹³ These are jobs that are obviously meaningless to the workers who, even if well-paid, find themselves disaffected by knowing they contribute nothing. Graeber also identifies a significant sexist attitude that privileges work that is creative when the vast majority of

---

⁹Ross Chapman and Ryan Tafilowski, *Faithful Work: In the Daily Grind with God and for Others* (InterVarsity Press, 2024), 27-28.

¹⁰John Mark Comer, *Garden City: Work, Rest, and the Art of Being Human* (Zondervan, 2015), 47.

¹¹Karl Marx, "Introduction: A Contribution to the Critique of Hegel's Philosophy of Right," February 7, 1844, www.marxists.org/archive/marx/works/1843/critique-hpr/intro.htm.

¹²Karl Marx, *Capital: A Critique of Political Economy*, ed. Frederick Engels, trans. Samuel Moore and Edward Aveling (1887), 1:401, www.marxists.org/archive/marx/works/download/pdf/Capital-Volume-I.pdf.

¹³David Graeber, *Bullshit Jobs* (Simon & Schuster Paperbacks, 2019).

workers, especially female, are engaged in service and care. Maintenance is never as glamorous as creation, and *Homo praesto* ("man the waiter") as the image of God would be too stigmatized to inspire.

Yet this is precisely the image of God we are given through the true image of God, the Lord of the Sabbath, when he dons a towel and stoops to wash his disciples' feet on the eve of his execution by an assortment of religious leaders, politicians, and soldiers going about their daily labor.[14] The tasks Jesus applauds are tasks of service that have no everlasting permanence in a material sense apart from their rendering care to mortal bodies that will one day resurrect.[15] We wonder whether the root desire for a lasting impact is more akin to the myth of eternity that underlies the dream home than the self-emptying actions that characterize conformity, and indeed *cruciformity*, to members of the household of Jesus Christ. Put differently, we wonder whether some forms of work—or more accurately, some *attitudes* to work—represent a misguided attempt to engineer a self-achieved immortality instead of humbly depending on God's resurrection.

Ecclesiastes, as previously noted, appears to challenge this desire for eternity and to rest instead on the unavoidable ephemerality of human labor that resigns itself mostly to chores of maintenance in season. Indeed, the work of the gospel is primarily the formation of a community and of people who bear the family resemblance. The works it commends are largely maternal ones—works not of domination and expansion but of raising new generations, works not of systems or processes but of relationships, works not of creation, but of care: of feeding the hungry, clothing the bare, tending the sick, and visiting the institutionalized.[16]

Yet these works are at odds with the kinds of work that are often affirmed by the work-and-worship literature, which pines for a permanency to human creations. This is not to say that certain kinds of crafts and art will not find their place in the new creation. But they must find

---

[14] Col 1:15; Jn 13:1-5.
[15] Mt 25:31.
[16] Mt 25:34-36. In this, the gospel should resist managerialism, which maintains human structures and systems, as well as stewardship, as a smokescreen for exploitative and expansionist efforts.

their proper place. What a conception of Sabbath does is disabuse us of the masculine fantasy of being fathers and creators; after all, our Sabbath Lord tells us to call no one Father.[17] The truest works are not those that endure of their own but those that yield their energies to other forms of life.

The work-and-worship literature means well; its authors rightly wish to equip Christians to integrate their faith into all of life. This is a cause we share. Neither are we discrediting every aspect of these writings. But we are concerned with the overarching theological foundation and rationale. We're concerned that there exist both mistaken theological premises and unintended consequences of this discourse.

One problem, among others, is that this literature's core claim that all human work is of God is simply not true to the state of affairs, especially for those workers whose jobs are downright exploitative, unjust, or undignifying. As human workers, we may find ourselves victims of our work or even perpetrators of injustice through our work—sometimes in ways that extend beyond our awareness and control.[18] It's highly unlikely that anyone reading these words has *not* engaged with material products—either as consumers or as employees—that have been made under conditions of exploitation. None of our projects, plans, efforts, or jobs—including paid ministry vocations—operate untouched by the sometimes covert and sometimes overt reach of sin.

The economy of the world is defined by adaptation to innumerable determinants of various kinds. All the forces beyond the individual's control, from genetics, to birth location, to educational opportunities, even to the type of food available in a grocery store, impose unchosen structures of "necessity."[19] It is necessity, not freedom, that defines the

---

[17]Mt 23:9.

[18]Buschart and Tafilowski coin a helpful taxonomy that seeks to draw attention to how different forms of work may manifest in a world marred by sin, and in which humans participate on a continuum of more active and passive registers: enmity, absurdity, and tragedy.

[19]Ellul goes so far as to say that all human morality is defined by the conditions of necessity, which are the conditions of enslavement. Most virtue-based ethics is a kind of accommodation to social conditions; even to the extent to which ethics is an attempt to resist these conditions, they are still determined by them insofar as they are a reaction to them. Humanity "never manages

conditions of our life and especially our work. One cannot participate in the world without adapting to these forces of necessity, be they automobiles, the internet, smartphones, or even social taboos. The same conditions that may seem empowering or freeing—the ability to relocate at ease at great distances, to contact individuals instantly from afar by spoken or written word, to exchange measures of value for the purchase of goods, or to prompt various services—are great powers. Yet the returns they demand in the architecture of the social world are also great, if sometimes invisible. The globalized world is struggling to disentangle itself from dependency on cars and the ecological destruction they wreak, an extended internet outage would be catastrophic, and it is nearly impossible to imagine a life removed from the act of purchasing. They are a nested tangle of necessities that exert their force on us in ways that we remain both ignorant of and wholly conditioned to. We often misidentify freedom as adaptation because success and power are often only secured by forms of adaptation. The conditions of work often demand the highest degree of integration to the features of the dream home. To mislabel these conditions as divinely sanctioned is to make a gross error—confusing Egyptian slavery for the exodus. We should not bless that from which God is setting us free.

To understand the freedom of the Sabbath gospel, work must be demythologized. But conceiving obedience to the Sabbath command as taking rest from worldly labor only renews a false dichotomy between material and spiritual. So to demythologize work, we turn next not to Sabbath practices as such (which we'll get to in due course) but to something more foundational. We start by addressing the theological misstep made by Protestantism from its outset, which the work-and-worship conversation recommits. This entails repristinating its doctrine of divine providence.

Revising providence. We'll cut to the chase: The root theological problem the work-and-worship discourse commits is that it mistakes the

---

to formulate a good in itself, escaping these concrete conditions." Jacques Ellul, *To Will and to Do: An Introduction to Christian Ethics*, trans. Jacob Marques Rollison, vol. 1 (Cascade Books, 2020), chap. 4.

world as the household of God. It does this particularly through a doctrine of providence that emphasizes God's ongoing governance and direction of the structures of creation. Formulations of the doctrine of providence are many and nuanced, and not all commit the error we are identifying here. But what some have done, whether in fact or in their misapplication, is mistake God's creation and God's providence over history as a single act. What this falsely implies is that, just as creation is the expression of God's will in space, providence is its expression in history.

We are not denying that God is all-powerful. Nor are we denying that God does intervene in and indeed provide for the world; its existence remains dependent on his power and mercy. What we are questioning is the perception that has sometimes emerged from misinterpretations of the doctrine of providence that *all* acts and events of world history are expressions of God's active will. If this were the case, why does Jesus command his disciples to pray, "Thy will be done"? The mystery that is God's work in human history is that it is primarily the *relinquishment* of God's will, the patience of God that grants humans time to return—if also to rebel. It is the rainbow in the sky that turns away God's wrath for a span of time. It is Jesus' bloody and sweaty prayer that gives his will back to the Father in a garden. It is Jesus' final cry that relinquishes his spirit on the cross. And it is Jesus' being laid to rest for a day in a tomb.

History is not the realm of God's providence; it is the arena of God's patience.[20]

God's providence is not primarily over *history* but over his people. This is why history is the story of a divided household, a tale of two peoples. To mistake all humanity as the household of God is an error that emerges from a Christendom mindset, which conflates the state (and states) of the world with the institution of the church. God's providence is not synonymous with history; rather, it is hidden in history. God's will is in many ways absent

---

[20] William H. Vanstone, *The Stature of Waiting* (Darton, Longman & Todd, 1984), is a compelling reflection on God's status as patient during Christ's crucifixion. At one point Vanstone wonders whether modern capitalism is supported by an anthropology of agency and production that has theological roots in a misguided *imago Dei* that imagines God as pure agency (63).

because history is the space that God grants for human wills to reign; it is where he has relinquished his sovereignty. It is not history that is continuous with God's act of creation but rather the cross. The cross reveals the character of the same Creator who relinquishes his will for the existence of another and who encounters this rebellious creation in time, determining not to destroy them but to win them back with his life-giving love.

To critique the reductionistic doctrine of providence that mistakes history for God's will is not to deny that God does provide for his people in the desert of his unexecuted will. In fact, we wonder whether the doctrine of providence as conceived of as overlaid onto and continuous with all human history cheapens the unique way in which God promises to provide himself as nourishment and sustenance in and through the body of his people, especially at the point of their eucharistic sharing—which is also the very point of their sharing with one another the product of earthly labor. In other words, the doctrine of providence might ironically obscure the reality of God's provision in fulfillment of Christ's promise: "The bread that I will give for the life of the world is my flesh."[21] This is nourishment that God provides to his people not so that they may remain in the exploitative structures of the world but so that they may exit them. Christ is the Passover lamb, the very symbol of liberation from Egypt.

In short, the work-and-worship literature mistakes history and the world as God's household order as opposed to the household order of the evil one that is under invasion and from which God is leading a great exodus of his people. The Christian life does not hinge on the question of whether one's worldly efforts matter. *The Christian life hinges on the*

---

[21]Jn 6:51. There is an interesting word choice that Paul deploys in Rom 8:28. The Greek word *prothesis*, which is often translated "purpose," can also denote the showbread that was presented weekly in the temple on the Sabbath and that exists, among a panoply of biblical images, to figure Christ as the bread from heaven who feeds his people (Mt 12:4; Mk 2:26; Lk 6:4; see also Heb 9:2). The word means literally "that which is set forth," and hence it denotes the showbread placed before God's presence in the temple, as well as an express purpose. For a more detailed account of the showbread in connection to the Eucharist, see Brant James Pitre, *Jesus and the Jewish Roots of the Eucharist: Unlocking the Secrets of the Last Supper* (Doubleday, 2011), chap. 5. Feeding on Christ through their economic sharing, his people become the concrete and material manifestation of God's goodwill in a world gone wrong.

question, What household does one belong to: the household of the world or the household of God? How the Christian acts in the world will ultimately be determined by that question. Again, the question, Does my work matter? is the wrong one. The real question is, Whose household do I show myself as belonging to? Asking this question will inevitably shape the way one approaches one's work, whatever the context, even if only to energize one's homesickness for one's true home.

One can only ask that question, though, if, with the Sabbath psalmist who penned Psalm 92, one can see God's enemies properly and acknowledge their existence without overstating their threat. The world is populated by active resistance to God's rule at every level of existence—the personal, the spiritual, the social, and the institutional. The world as we know it is deformed by this resistance, often in ways to which we remain blind. God does not justify participation in the world's economies any more than God justified the Egyptian brick-making quotas, the civilian appropriation policy of Babylon, or Roman crucifixion policy. To claim otherwise is a dangerous mistruth that at worst risks relabeling service to Satan as service to God and at best weakens the good news of the Sabbath gospel. Jesus has come to free captives and nurture them to prepare the way for the great Sabbath that brings the rest of God's sovereign reign to a world of toil. This Sabbath gospel helps us to see the dream homes we inevitably participate in and get our hands dirtied by, and for which we rely on the cleansing power of Christ's lifeblood. It draws attention to our reliance on the nourishing bread he supplies as we sojourn out of the world's dark structures and into his marvelous light.

In the final section, we will elaborate on how the Sabbath gospel might rehabilitate and reintegrate both our *works* and our *work*: the deeds that are valuable in God's sight as genuine fruit of his household and our inevitable livelihood in worldly economic structures. But first, we pause here to consider: How does the popularized literature around Sabbath relate to the discourse on work? And second, where does the Sabbath gospel leave us with regard to weekly practice of Sabbath? What we'll find is that, at the same time that the Sabbath gospel demythologizes work, it also demythologizes the practice of Sabbath.

Demythologizing Sabbath. The surge in literature around work and worship is paralleled by another trend in evangelical Christian literature: Sabbath.[22] At first blush these two strands of literature may appear at odds, but under closer scrutiny they are complementary. With some exceptions, contemporary Sabbath literature conceives the practice of Sabbath as primarily a privatized, personalized day of rest that palliates the frenzied and hurried pace of the world.[23] In counterpart to the work-and-worship emphasis on work, rest can only be self-care, and in a manner that perpetuates blindness to the level at which the enemies of God's household operate in determining and distorting the very conditions of both our work and our rest.

In other words, Sabbath practices sometimes operate as concessions to the state of the world, especially if defined in reaction to conditions assumed to be necessary. They then reinforce the core logic of the reason for restlessness. Sabbath practice as resting from regular labor serves to

---

[22] Abraham Joshua Heschel, *The Sabbath: Its Meaning for Modern Man* (Farrar, Straus & Giroux, 1951), is a seminal Jewish point of reference for Christian discourse. Popular texts include Walter Brueggemann, *Sabbath as Resistance: Saying No to the Culture of Now* (John Knox, 2014); A. J. Swoboda, *Subversive Sabbath: The Surprising Power of Rest in a Nonstop World* (Brazos, 2018); Dan B. Allender, *Sabbath* (Thomas Nelson, 2009); Marva J. Dawn, *Keeping the Sabbath Wholly: Ceasing, Resting, Embracing, Feasting* (Eerdmans, 2000); Ruth H. Barton, *Embracing Rhythms of Work and Rest: From Sabbath to Sabbatical and Back Again* (InterVarsity Press, 2022). Although not overtly about Sabbath, John Mark Comer, *The Ruthless Elimination of Hurry: How to Stay Emotionally Healthy and Spiritually Alive in the Chaos of the Modern World* (Hodder & Stoughton, 2019), distills many of the sentiments of more popular Sabbath literature, particularly in its impetus in exhorting personalized rhythms of rest as an antidote to a culture of hurry.

[23] Exceptions include Brueggemann. *Sabbath as Resistance* is a more biblically grounded exception, but its stress on resistance mostly conceives Sabbath practice as set against worldly structures rather than constituting its own definition; Swoboda, *Subversive Sabbath*, does devote a chapter to the justice implications of Sabbath practice, but it is still ultimately grounded individually (or familially) rather than ecclesiologically. David Lilley, in a valuable contribution to Sabbath that gathers and probes insights from Barth, notes that in contemporary Sabbath literature "the dominant focus [is] on Sabbath as either artefact or measure of individual utility." Lilley, "At the Invitation of the God Who Rests: The Fidelity-Producing Sabbath Ethic of Karl Barth's Doctrine of Creation" (PhD diss., University of Aberdeen, 2018), 20. That is, Sabbath either forms a distinct religious community separate from the world, shapes a community to become a healing source of engagement with the world, or illuminates the nature of created reality. Lilley locates Barth in the latter camp, and his work goes on to identify freedom, contentment, and joy as characteristic of the covenant relation that constitutes God and his creatures.

make regular labor more efficient, becoming, in effect, *recreation* that gives the illusion of freedom.[24] Sabbath practices, insofar as they mirror other forms of recreational spirituality derived from other traditions—for example, mindfulness, yoga, meditation—actually reinforce the logic of the household of sin by the very structure of their apparent resistance. Put another way, much of what modern Sabbath literature extols is not a discovery of Sabbath but a reinterpretation of modern recreational and therapeutic forms of rest with biblical language. Forced and unjust labor is still rampant, even in the developed world.[25] However laudable, if practices such as fasting from social media and smartphone use are simply means of ameliorating the most egregious problems of integrating into the world, they end up acting like a recharge cycle.[26] This is Sabbath as recreation, flowering our chains, to use Marx's imagery. The Sabbath of the Bible is neither recreation nor piety; it is about creating mature people who can help realize conditions in which rest can be *given* rather than *taken*. Sabbath is the advance of ambassadors of rest, not the practice of retreat for recuperation.

So where does that leave an actual practice of Sabbath as a weekly cessation from paid work and other projects? Sabbath practice in the Bible is never conceived of as an individual practice. It is not a spiritual discipline but a community discipline motivated by the Spirit. "Divide and conquer" is certainly nowhere truer than in the household of sin. Where our Sabbath is personalized or individualized, there is every likelihood that it serves to integrate people into the higher power of the dream house

---

[24]Religion as play or recreation is a thesis I have developed over many years and am planning further work on in the future. Gregory Wagenfuhr, "Religion as Play: The Situation in the 21st Century," *Comment Peut-on (Encore) Être Ellulian Au XXIe Sièecle?: Actes Du Colloque Des 7,8 et 9 Juin 2012*, January 1, 2014, www.academia.edu/10025558/Religion_as_Play_The_Situation_in _the_21st_Century. See also Jacques Ellul, *The Technological System*, trans. Joachim Neugroschel (Continuum, 1980), 250.

[25]Migrant farm labor, for example, is among the most dangerous work and earns around 60 percent of the income of other fields. Abuses seem common, and prosecutions describe modern slavery conditions on certain farms. See Brandon Drenon and Bernd Debusmann Jr., "Migrant Farm Worker Deaths Show Cost of the 'American Dream,'" *BBC*, September 2, 2024, www.bbc.com/news/articles/c4nn1wl69kno.

[26]Barton, *Embracing Rhythms of Work*, chap. 5.

rather than mobilizing resistance to it. True Sabbath practice in the world is not taking a break. It is going on strike.

That said, a weekly practice of Sabbath, rightly conceived, might serve as a helpful tool that throws a wrench in the works of worldly metrics that constantly vie for our souls. True Sabbath practice is exercising the freedom to say no to the world and its forces of necessity while accepting the responsibility and consequences that come with this. Refusing to allow oneself to get ahead in a career or domestic life or social-media influence might be a helpful step in discipleship to Jesus that cracks one's energies and eyes open to God's invitation to simply join his presence with others. What's more, laying down one's labors may be the first condition to give rest to others. But until Sabbath is practiced in a community that can support one another through lean times, the consequences of saying no to the world may prove either too difficult or too ineffectual. More important, perhaps, than the things we choose to do or not do are the kinds of relationships and interdependencies we cultivate with one another.

A weekly Sabbath may be practiced by a group of people and by a collection other than a nuclear family. Coordinating their weekly practice may force them to consider what rest might mean and look like for them if certain members of the group, because of the unjust and uneven economic structures of the world, find it difficult to commit to a shared Sabbath practice. Can the single mom who is working multiple part-time jobs in a bid to support her kids and without the luxury of taking off a twenty-four-hour stretch of potential shifts join in a gathering's Sabbath rest? Perhaps this group's truest Sabbath practice is finding ways to give her rest. The contemporary church must imagine what *these* kinds of Sabbath practices might look like. A church community's true Sabbath practice must be grounded not by answering the question, What day should we take off? and What things should we not do on that day? but, How can we give rest to one another and to our neighbor?[27]

---

[27]For a resource that seeks to help church communities be shaped by the economic implications of Sabbath, see the Christian nonprofit Manna Gum, www.mannagum.org.au/.

Whatever their form, Sabbath practices shouldn't operate as an anesthetic so we can make more bricks for Pharaoh's storehouses while congratulating ourselves for doing God's work.[28] Instead, Sabbath practices should help fashion us into an alternative economy of God's body politic that is taking its leave from the enslaving logics of the world. But for that to happen, we need to let Sabbath do more than just reorganize our schedules; we need it to renew our minds.

Rehabilitating Works

Sabbath is not ultimately about not working. Jesus reveals this when he offends the Pharisees by working on the Sabbath. Instead, Sabbath asks, *Who are we working for?* Whose household do our works reveal that we belong to? What family resemblance do they bear? Whose rest are we ultimately striving for? Or in other words, whose disciples are we? Christian discipleship entails doing good works that show where we are headed.[29] God's gracious rescue ultimately displaces people. On the cross and from the tomb, Jesus both endures and dismantles the death-dealing measures and evaluations of the dream houses of the world—religious and political—that would leave us where we are. Through his lived and living life, he empowers those who would follow him out of the enslaving economies of the world by feeding them with his very life through the body of his people, the church. Jesus doesn't justify us and then leave us as we are.[30] He gives us endurance for the journey he has trailblazed. The

---

[28] For an analogous critique that the sedative spiritual practice of mindfulness is but conformity to capitalist structures, see Ronald E. Purser, *McMindfulness: How Mindfulness Became the New Capitalist Spirituality* (Repeater, 2019).

[29] Eph 2:10; note that the final verb often translated "to do" is the Greek "to walk" (as in the ESV).

[30] The work of Douglas Campbell takes aim at the overdetermination of justification in the reception of Paul in Protestant theology. See his hefty *The Deliverance of God: An Apocalyptic Rereading of Justification in Paul* (Eerdmans, 2009). More accessible is Douglas A. Campbell, Jon DePue, and Brian Zahnd, *Beyond Justification: Liberating Paul's Gospel* (Cascade Books, 2024). Our own theology here is also decentering justification, but—contra Campbell—in order to focus on maturity and pedagogy, and without dismissing the coming reality of God's judgment. For John Barclay's critical assessment of Campbell, see *Paul and the Gift* (Eerdmans, 2015), 77-78, 171-73. For a compelling account that begins with the doctrine of justification but develops an account that mature Christian living is a matter of achieving appropriate orientation to the *when* of the Christian's life now between the ultimate of God's eschaton and the penultimate

steps by which we follow him to a place of rest are good works, works prepared for us beforehand.[31]

The previous sections of this chapter have demythologized mistaken conceptions of both work and Sabbath that would sacralize the economic structures of the world and have us in effect stay encamped in Egypt instead of following Jesus to and through Golgotha to Jordan. Instead of conformity to the current age, how do we be transformed by the renewal of our mind so that we can align our will with the head of our household?[32] It's by reorientation to the rest that characterizes the household of God that we might also renew our participation in the work of God from within the economic structures of the world. This requires a three-step approach: liberation, formation, and invasion.

Liberation: Romans 8 and Colossians 3 (God's Coworkers)

Consider a well-worn verse that is often enlisted to support the prevailing notion of God's providence as the execution of his will through the events of world history. A common translation of Romans 8:28 reads, "We know that all things work together for good *for* those who love God, who are called according to his purpose." The italicized preposition *for* translates what is in the Greek text the dative case but can also be rendered by other prepositions. N. T. Wright's recent translation and commentary defends this alternative translation: "We know, in fact, that God works all things together for good *with* those who love him, who are called according to his purpose."[33]

Wright notes how the preceding and commonplace translation of this verse suggests that, as Haley Goranson Jacob puts it, "the multiple

---

of our present life, see Dietrich Bonhoeffer, "Ultimate and Penultimate Things," in *Ethics*, ed. Ilse Todt et al., trans. Reinhard Krauss, Charles C. West, and Douglas Wayne Stott, Dietrich Bonhoeffer Works 6 (Fortress, 2005), 149-70.
[31]Eph 2:10.
[32]Rom 12:2.
[33]N. T. Wright, *Into the Heart of Romans: A Deep Dive into Paul's Greatest Letter* (Zondervan Academic, 2023), 154. For a more detailed analysis on Rom 8:23, see also Haley Goranson Jacob, *Conformed to the Image of His Son: Reconsidering Paul's Theology of Glory in Romans* (IVP Academic, 2018), 229-34.

disparate elements of life would sort themselves out, under God's benevolent guiding, like a sort of automatic jigsaw puzzle. It might look chaotic, but a happy picture would emerge from it all."[34] Wright clarifies that, although God's providence does assure us that God will prevail victorious over the powers of evil, the classic interpretation does not bear up under closer scrutiny. First, note that in Wright's translation, God not "all things," is the subject of "work." "All things" of the world are not automatically aligned with God's purpose. But God nevertheless manages to work through them. The prophet Isaiah puts this on bright display: That God chooses to use the mighty and terrifying Assyrians to discipline his people doesn't thereby align the Assyrian nation and its culture and politics with God.[35]

Second, God's people are not just the passive recipients of God's work but are active collaborators, coworkers, *synergistically*. This synergism is also invoked in the context of 2 Corinthians 6:1, which immediately follows Paul's declaration that God's mission is the reconciliation of all things through ambassadors.[36] But this is not the cocreative laboring envisioned by the work-and-worship movement. Note that what constitutes their collaboration with God is not their employed labor in worldly economic structures. Instead, it is their reconciling work that challenges the powers and attracts persecutions and sufferings in a world that is in bondage to decay.[37] Thus, *the formative work of the Christian is to endure with fidelity and patience that inevitable friction caused between the household of God and the household of the world*.[38] Such friction is both the necessary immune response of a threatened world order and the

---

[34]Wright, *Into the Heart of Romans*, 158; Goranson Jacob, *Conformed to the Image of His Son*, 154.
[35]Is 10:5-19.
[36]Synergism is correctly understood as a heretical idea if we apply it to salvation. God's victory over sin is monergistic, the work of God alone. However, the error of much traditional theology is to see soteriology as the goal rather than a means to the goal of universal reconciliation or recapitulation through the creation of mature humans. See also Wright, *Into the Heart of Romans*, 158.
[37]Rom 8:18-20.
[38]This is often referred to in the New Testament with the Greek word *thlipsis*. See, e.g., Jn 16:33; Acts 14:22; Rom 5:3; 8:35; 2 Cor 4:17.

necessary formation of those headed toward resurrection in Christ. It is the character forged through trial and the works produced by such character that will last, not any product or artifact.[39] The true Christian work is our role as ambassador from one household to another. This relies less on what we do or produce than who—and whose—we are. Such collaboration with God does not achieve salvation; salvation has already been secured through Christ.[40] This ambassadorial vocation is instead the organic expression of the reality of salvation from within the disorder of the world as it labors as an agent of reconciliation.[41]

This means that our work in the world does not automatically glorify God or contribute to his creation and kingdom. Rather, the resistance we experience from within a world in bondage is a means by which we are joined into God's work to usher that world out of bondage and into his freedom and light. This resistance and suffering may be experienced most viscerally by none other than those who, for whatever reason, are disenfranchised or unemployed by the world's economic structures. Not coincidentally, Paul's assurance in Romans comes right on the heels of Paul's account of prayer, in which the believer is caught up into the very dialogue and prayer of a triune God, true to form as those being conformed into the image of his Son to become mature members of his divine council.[42] Thus God's work through his people manifests as "God's sovereign action *taking up within itself* the active groaning of his image-bearing people."[43] *This*—to act with a character of patient and intercessory hope against the affliction of the world—is the foundational work of God's people as they are formed into elder-ambassadors colaboring with God in his reconciling work.

---

[39]See 1 Cor 3:10-15 and Rom 5:4, the latter of which uses the Greek *dokimē*, a mark of genuineness.
[40]Wright, *Into the Heart of Romans*, 160.
[41]Wright, *Into the Heart of Romans*, 162.
[42]Rom 8:26-27. For a compelling assertion that connects the trinitarian shape of Paul's account of prayer with a distinctively Jewish yet potentially proto-trinitarian approach to prayer, see Sarah Coakley, *The Broken Body: Israel, Christ, and Fragmentation* (Wiley Blackwell, 2024), 89-111.
[43]Wright, *Into the Heart of Romans*, 162.

So the question of Sabbath shouldn't be, What's the meaning of my work *in itself*? The real question is, *Who am I actually working for?*[44] Whose household stands to benefit? Consider again the nature of a sign explored in chapter six. What makes a sign *sig*nificant is the harmony between its physical nature and context and that to which it points. The location of a sign—where we work—also matters, but work in the kingdom of God is the formation of mature disciples in a mutually edifying primary community that serves as a sign pointing to the kingdom.[45] The work of the Christian is always and everywhere the same in nature—to be conformed to the image of Christ. And it is from the formation of a mature disciple that one can be an ambassador, a sign dislocated from—but oriented to—that to which it points.

While on the one hand this means that all kinds of labor are at the disposal of Christians, it also means that certain kinds of labor are ruled out if they preclude proper orientation. For this reason early Christians were right to exclude Christian novitiates from certain kinds of work.[46] If a form of employment inherently deforms or disorients a Christian from operating as a sign, then such employment must be left behind as soon as possible and with ample support from the church community. But there are many kinds of labors, even absurd or tragic ones, that might be taken up by Christians in an ambassadorial function. In the hands of mature Christians, such labors—even from within structures of unjust servitude that are out of their control—may constitute an offering to God.[47]

Paul's injunctions that slaves remain with their masters and that all workers labor as for Christ makes sense within this framework.[48] But that is not because Paul envisions worldly work as its own end. Instead, worldly occupations might still serve as a site at which we perform our true work of pointing others to, preparing for, and entering into God's reign of rest.

---

[44] Col 3:23.
[45] Eph 4.
[46] See Alan Kreider, *The Patient Ferment of the Early Church* (Baker Academic, 2016), 151.
[47] Col 3:23-24.
[48] Col 3:23-24.

Again, our work does not complete, finish, or contribute to God's creation or his coming kingdom. Creation is complete; God declared it finished at the seventh day and again from a cross. Our works don't achieve anything in themselves; they are meaningful only to the extent to which they are oriented to God's works. As we considered above, from within the sixth day and the household of sin this may be most clearly manifest precisely at the point at which we experience suffering, frustration, and ineffectiveness or failure by worldly terms or measures.

If we mistakenly think that worldly vocations or roles are their own end, this may also prevent us from discerning when God may grant us the opportunity or invitation to evacuate certain kinds of occupations in order to better direct our energies and resources toward his purposes. This is not to say that we should idolize or idealize paid or ordained ministry, which is just as susceptible—perhaps even more susceptible—to enlisting our energies into the dream homes of the world. (Pulpit dynasties and priestly abuse rings put this into a particularly glaring display, but there are more subtle and sinister ways that confusion between the household order of God and of the world can occur). Both of these conceits—that either certain forms of worldly work or paid ordained positions are automatically the work of God's kingdom—are obscured and baptized by a popular and dangerous word: vocation. For the Christian, there is no other vocation than taking up the call of bearing our cross as a disciple of Jesus Christ, serving as an ambassador of his reconciliation, and equipping all the saints to become matured in his image.[49] The real question of our work is to what extent we—both individually and as an ecclesial community—are being faithful to this occupation either in the context of, within, or despite any paid labor we might be engaging or providing. Once we are liberated from our misplaced notions of vocation and work, we are better positioned to be formed into the very kind of laborers who contribute to God's household.

---

[49]For a more robust theological account here, see Amy J. Erickson, "Figuring One's Calling: A Lukan Passion Theology of Vocation in Dialogue with Karl Barth," *Journal of Theological Interpretation* 17, no. 1 (2023): 92-108, https://doi.org/10.5325/jtheointe.17.1.0092.

Formation: 2 Corinthians (Liturgy)

The first step in the renewal of our mind is our liberation from mistaking the world for the household of God. But as we have already begun to stress, liberation doesn't automatically make one act freely. Formation is required for that. Consider the word *liturgy*. *Liturgy* literally means "people work." It's come to mean the pattern of worship and prayer that a local church community engages in. The original Greek word was used in Greco-Roman times to refer to public service rendered to the gods, which occasionally also coincided with the distribution of benefactory gifts from the wealthy to the common people.[50] Variants of the word crop up throughout the New Testament, most generally to describe a kind of service. One particular use by Paul is telling when it comes to the question of how to regard our work in the world as itinerant ambassadors.

In the middle of his second letter to the church in Corinth, Paul makes an appeal asking them to make a generous contribution to support Christians in need. Paul calls their potential gift a liturgy.[51] Although he does not explicitly mention work in the world as such, his reasoning a few verses prior is telling: "He who supplies seed to the sower and bread for food will supply and multiply your seed for sowing and increase the harvest of your righteousness."[52] The same God who supplies the very material—and indeed, capital—that through human labor becomes wealth (and, specifically here, food) is the same God who, through that materiality and wealth generation, produces spiritually good work as "righteousness."[53] What's more, the generous sharing of material blessing secured through human labor redounds in the form of thankful (2 Cor 9:11) and intercessory (2 Cor 9:14) prayer from the recipients.[54] The material sharing of wealth and food secured through human labor, combined with the receipt of thankful prayer but also conjoined with

---

[50]R. Meyer, "Λειτουργέω, Λειτουργία, Λειτουργός, Λειτουργικός," in *Theological Dictionary of the New Testament*, ed. Gerhard Kittel, trans. Geoffrey W. Bromiley (Eerdmans, 1967), 215-17.
[51]2 Cor 9:12.
[52]2 Cor 9:10.
[53]2 Cor 9:8.
[54]2 Cor 9:12.

loving and longing intercessory prayer given by the recipient on behalf of the giver, is rounded out by Paul's final exclamation of, "Thanks be to God for his indescribable gift!"[55] By the end, it's not quite clear where the gift started and ended. Is this the ultimate gift of grace through Jesus Christ? The generous donation by the Corinthians? The gift of obedience expressed through giving? The gift of prayer? We think the answer is all the above. God's gracious gift to humanity, in both creation and new creation, in Jesus Christ is made tangible—by his grace—through the material sharing and the loving, thankful, and concerned prayer that characterizes the relations among the mature members of his household.

What does this have to do with formation? It might be that, even if one must work for an enemy under onerous labor conditions, one can still send money home to the family.[56] God can feed his people even through such labor. Note that the gift Paul refers to is not the support for paid ministry positions or the administrative functions of an ecclesial organization; it is direct support for members of the household of God who are not able, for whatever reason, to provide for themselves. But note also that the liturgical work here also applies to the recipients, who both are given cause for thanks and respond in the labor of prayer for their benefactors. For those who are unable—including for reasons of economic and structural injustice—to secure support from worldly labor and find themselves relying on the support of their family of faith: their work of grateful prayer is no less a gift and work from God.

For both the giver and the receiver in this economy of gift sharing among God's people who are, through either their employment or unemployment, disenfranchised by the world's economic structures, it is acceptable—even to be expected and encouraged—to experience homesickness, to long for one's true home, especially while laboring in

---

[55] 2 Cor 9:15.
[56] We are not here endorsing a utilitarian logic that encourages making as much money as possible in order to give as much as possible; this in itself is still captive to a worldly logic. Paul's injunction about generosity is about the posture of the heart toward one's fellow siblings in Christ that manifests as generosity with what one possesses but isn't overly concerned about quantity as such. This is a logic with which Jesus accords (Mt 26:6-11).

the fields of the world while on the journey home.[57] The Jesus-follower is not ultimately either a cog or an outlier in the machinery of the world's misguided bids for a self-fashioned rest. The Christian is a sign of the coming rest and reign of God. And it may be the most scandalous and sacrificial signposting to give up the fruit of one's labor in the world for the nourishment of the people of God, or to prayerfully and gratefully receive from the labor of others.[58] All of this is to suggest that formation occurs at a level other than that of ritual performance or private spiritual discipline; formation also occurs at the sites of both sacrificial giving and grateful receipt, which itself also constitutes the form of a community in its shared economic and, indeed, eucharistic life.

Invasion: Philemon (Subversion)

We've considered how rehabilitating work in the world begins with liberation followed by formation. Formation results in the third step: invasion. The small New Testament epistle of Philemon serves as a case study. Paul's letter to Philemon was written while he was in prison. This much we can gather from context: Philemon was a Christian in an early church somewhere in Asia Minor (now Turkey) who had a slave named Onesimus. Under unclear conditions, Paul met and mentored Onesimus. At the time of the writing of the letter, Paul is sending him back, possibly even as the letter's courier. Details beyond that are left to speculation. Some scholars believe that Onesimus had run away from Philemon and therefore may have been subject to Philemon's wrath.[59] Others think that Philemon may have sent Onesimus on his own volition in order to assist Paul and that Paul was simply returning Onesimus back home.[60] Whatever the situation, it is clear from the rhetoric that Paul is trying to coax Philemon into treating Onesimus no longer

---

[57]Homesickness is one way to understand the Beatitudes of Mt 5.
[58]Lk 7:36-50; 21:1-4.
[59]Joseph A. Fitzmyer, *Letter to Philemon: A New Translation with Introduction and Commentary* (Yale University Press, 2000), 28.
[60]For an overview of these different perspectives, including one that suggests Onesimus actually was Philemon's brother, see Fitzmyer, *Letter to Philemon*, 17-18.

as a mere slave but as a brother in Christ. In other words, Paul is asking Philemon to reevaluate his economic position as a master in light of the gospel.

What's especially interesting is that Paul doesn't ask Philemon to set Onesimus free. At least, not outright.[61] But Paul *is* asking Philemon to eschew the economic logic of his Roman world and to free himself from the mindset of a master. We should note the rhetoric by which it occurs. Paul does not write a manifesto declaring a great revolutionary overthrow of Greco-Roman master-slave relations that all Christians must champion in a great cause of social justice. It is not a lofty treatise about freedom. Nor is it an authoritarian demand to set Onesimus free. Instead it is a letter, directly written to one member of the church community but in earshot of them all. It is an exhortation to the community of faith that directly appeals to their relation to effect nothing more than reconciling grace and equality between two members.

In this regard, Philemon is quite simple. It is a family letter written to remind the family to act like family. But in its simplicity lies its power. The letter abounds in familial and collegial language—not the language of hierarchy and subjugation (Paul even makes a rhetorically dramatic point about not invoking his own gospel-underwritten authority over Philemon).[62] Not only does Paul urge Philemon to treat Onesimus as a brother, but Paul offers a reminder that others in the community are also siblings and coworkers in the same household project. Some of those mentioned (and many not mentioned) would have been present when the letter was read aloud to the church gathering; we can imagine Philemon's church serving not only as witnesses to Paul's exhortations but also as accountability to Philemon's response. They would be watching: Would Philemon follow through on Paul's exhortation to treat Onesimus as not

---

[61] Philem 16. There is some scholarly disagreement here as to whether Paul is indeed asking Philemon to set Onesimus free. For a recent case for the manumission interpretation that also surveys the relevant discourse, see Devin Arinder, "Beyond a Slave: Support for the Manumission of Onesimus from Discourse Analysis," *Journal for the Study of the New Testament* 47, no. 2 (2024), https://doi.org/10.1177/0142064X241268659.

[62] Philem 8, 19.

an economical slave but a Christian brother—or not? And as a brother, would not his duty be to redeem a kinsman from bondage?

And although the world as such is not mentioned, nor any nonbelievers, we can read the letter as itself an invasion of the logic and reality of God's household from inside the logic of the household of the world. Though Colossians 3 makes concessions to slaves with worldly masters, exhorting them not to resist their condition but to populate it with a renewed attitude, the letter to Philemon makes no such allowance within the family of faith.[63] Family relations not only trump worldly orders; they corrode them from the inside. It is within the family of faith, and based on the very quality of their relations as family, that the invasion of God's household begins and radiates outward. Here in Philemon we witness the first chink in the armor of exploitation that would destroy the formalized slave trade in the Western world. Not coincidentally, Paul makes this appeal while identifying himself as an ambassador.[64] Implicitly, Paul also invites Philemon to operate as an ambassador from within his worldly position of economic privilege. Will he continue to oblige the working conditions of the world and its scripts for masters and slaves, or will he demonstrate through his actions to which paterfamilias he ultimately belongs? And will we follow suit?

Conclusion

This chapter has sought to bridge the felt disconnect between worldly work and ethical works. We've contended that a good work—or good works—are good only if they emerge from the faithfulness of disciples formed in God's household. And to be formed in God's household is to also be discipled into a certain kind of time. The Lord of the Sabbath bids us to be transformed by our anticipation: We show whose we are when we showcase in what—or in whom—we await our final rest. Such rest is achieved ultimately and only by God. True Sabbath work, then, is those

---

[63]Col 3:22-23.
[64]Philem 9; Paul uses the Greek *presbyteros*.

actions that organically emerge from children of God who bear the family resemblance by seeking to give rest to others and who through this resemblance operate as signs that point to God's Sabbath rest. These actions may emerge from the context of and coincide with worldly work, but they are not synonymous with worldly work and its worldly measures. Productivity is not the same thing as fruitfulness. As Paul reminds us in 1 Corinthians 13, even our most pious and ethical of actions are worthless if they are not driven by love. And it is only love, not any other kind of accolade or accomplishment, that will endure the vicissitudes of time. Earlier in the letter, Paul indicates that our works will be revealed by the light of the final Sabbath day and purified through fire; he even suggests that for many the only thing that will survive is their character.[65]

In many ways this is freeing, if sobering, news. There is no escaping doing work *in the world*; all our energies are exerted in the time of the sixth day. No paid pastor or employed church staff can escape the conditions of necessity imposed by the world. And although the church community may be responsible to provide economic alternatives or support for those whose potential occupations threaten to deform their character or jeopardize their survival, in many ways our actual jobs are irrelevant to our capacity to mature as members of God's household.[66] None of our labor is in vain if it allows us to express how we are being formed into the image of Christ. And perhaps it is our grieving our inevitable complicity in the household of sin and longing to escape that is indicative of a character that will last beyond the dawn of the approaching Sabbath day.

We began our biblical journey of Sabbath with Psalm 92, the only psalm in the Psalter dedicated to the Sabbath. A preceding psalm shows how a certain relation to time, and conception of God as the ultimate home of his people, also resituates their relation to work. Psalm 90 is a

---

[65] 1 Cor 3:13-15.
[66] This makes a similar point on an economic level that Ephraim Radner makes on a political level in *Mortal Goods: Reimagining Christian Political Duty* (Baker Academic, 2024). Radner insists that the only thing that makes our efforts last is not their effectiveness or achievements but their being positioned as a eucharistic offering to God.

soulful meditation on the nature of mortal life as a generational journey through time. Some scholars propose that Psalms 90–92 are a related set, with Psalm 90 lamenting the mortal condition of humans, Psalm 91 receiving the promise of life and salvation, and Psalm 92 responding in thanks.[67] Psalm 90 is steeped in awareness of human transitoriness and frailty and implicitly that of all human efforts and institutions. Against the backdrop of the ebb and flow of human life is the surety of a God whose work precedes the mountains and whose wrath rightly overshadows and thwarts the rebellious efforts of human history.

The psalm closes by asking God, twice over, to "establish the work of our hands."[68] But it only does so after first asking to "teach us to number our days, that we may gain a heart of wisdom."[69] The psalmist knows that our efforts—whether paid or unpaid—in a world that is passing away are dependent solely on the mercy of a God who alone provides everlasting refuge. It is a gift and work of God to permit our efforts in some way to figure and participate in his work to establish a household of creation that will last. Our works are true and lasting only to the extent to which they reflect and make way for the work that God has already done, in sober awareness that we are taking leave from frail human structures that are passing away. It is a gift and grace of God that our works might participate in his work to bring about life from the midst of death. At least, so we may pray.

For this reason, the mindset of a sojourner keeps us from getting caught up in and trapped by the conditions of the world through which we travel. What's more, the nature of the rest of the land to which we are headed gives us resilience. The good news of the Sabbath gospel is that our value and our worth are not ultimately determined by worldly metrics and measures—by things such as our economic productivity or salary or

---

[67] See Erich Zenger and Frank-Lothar Hossfeld, *Psalms 2: A Commentary on Psalms 51–100*, ed. Klaus Baltzer, trans. Linda M. Maloney, Hermeneia (Fortress, 2005), 424. There are even verbal resonances between the two, e.g., Ps 90:14 and Ps 92:3, 5; Ps 90:16 and Ps 92:5; and Ps 90:17 and Ps 92:5.

[68] Ps 90:17 NIV.

[69] Ps 90:12 NIV.

career progression. The good news is that we have been set free from regimes of value that both enslave and sully us. Christ has taken care of them on the cross and at the empty tomb. This sets us free to go about our true work of serving as signs of God's household, of nurturing fellow family members, and of bearing the burdens of others on our joint journey to our true home.

Group Discussion Questions

1. What are ways you or your community may have become enlisted in structures of sin? What might confronting this look like?

2. What are ways you or your community may have sought to justify your work in the world through a theology of vocation? What might confronting this look like?

Conclusion

A CALL TO RENEWAL

W E'VE COME TO THE END OF the journey of this book. It's possible you are disappointed. Not because the journey has ended but because of the ground that wasn't traversed. We haven't explored quick fixes or ready-made spiritual practices; we haven't told you to develop a rule of life to build a private, personal, spiritual dream home within an exhausting world. We haven't given your church a three-step plan to instant renewal or revitalization. What we've aimed to do instead may seem at once wildly ambitious and woefully ineffective. We've sought to give a renewed language for the gospel through Sabbath. We hope that this book helps generate a fresh telling and hearing of the *narrative* of the gospel. People evaluate time and fashion their identity through the stories they tell. And it is primarily the stories that we tell that dictate the paths we take.

Consider this statement, which may have been nearly nonsensical at the start of our journey but may make more sense now at its close: God is destroying the dream homes of the world in order to fashion a people of a renewed bloodline who inhabit a different economy, a household order of mature children ready to sit on his divine council and rule the world with him by giving rest rather than taking it. That is one of many ways we could restate the Sabbath gospel. There are others. And if that story is true, there are implications for the energies you bring to, the postures you take, and the choices you make in your daily endeavors within your church community and the world.

Amy: A New Language

We began this book with the institutional and spiritual exhaustion of the contemporary church. There's a small book in the Old Testament that diagnoses God's people in a similar condition.[1] Although it is perhaps most famous for the prophet commanded to marry a prostitute, most of the book of Hosea details the fragmentation of Israel's institutions, both of its monarchy and temple. But it's not only the institutions of Israel that are falling apart in the book of Hosea. The very language of the book seems to break down before the eyes of the reader. Apart from the book of Job, Hosea contains some of the most challenging and garbled Hebrew in the Old Testament. It's at times ungrammatical, or at least nonsensical; some verses could be translated in a dozen ways. Although a host of English translations present a clean and sanitized text, the strained language—which itself is symptomatic of the strained relation between Israel and God—still leaks through on occasion. "My God, we—Israel—know you," Israel at one point sputters.[2] "How can I give you up, Ephraim? How can I hand you over, O Israel?"[3] God achingly sighs in response several chapters later. The language of Hosea registers a low point in God's relation with his people. And it is of little surprise that on the way to the cross, at one of the lowest moments of all human history, Jesus reaches for the words of Hosea in some of his last spoken words before his death.[4]

We've suggested that, like the ancient Israelite monarchy and temple of Hosea's time, the institutions of the Western, post-Christendom church are also pulling apart at the seams. As with preexilic Israel, they aren't

---

[1] For more on Hosea and the contemporary church in dialogue with a contemporary theologian, see Amy J. Erickson, *Ephraim Radner, Hosean Wilderness, and the Church in the Post-Christendom West* (Brill, 2020).
[2] Hos 8:2 ESV.
[3] Hos 11:8.
[4] Lk 23:30; Hos 10:8.

facilitating the encounter between God and his people as they perhaps once did. They are breaking down. And alongside the fragmentation of these institutions is the fragmentation of religious language. *Atonement. Salvation. Providence. Gospel. Evangelical.* These words and others have become at best hollowed out and at worse subject to polarization and division. Their very meaning is unassured.

We shouldn't be surprised if our health as God's people can be diagnosed through language. The same tower of Babel that is one of the Bible's most vivid portraits of the dream home is also synonymous with the distortion of language. William Stringfellow, the American lawyer so attuned to the corporate and collective dimensions of sin, rightly insists that Babel "means the inversion of language, verbal inflation, libel, rumor, euphemism and coded phrases, rhetorical wantonness, redundancy, hyperbole, such profusion in speech and sound that comprehension is impaired, nonsense, sophistry, jargon, noise, incoherence, a chaos of voices and tongues, falsehood, blasphemy. And, in all of this, babel means violence."[5] Babel, of course, was constructed by a universal, homogenized language that God disrupted through the diversification of tongues, which is not overcome but transfigured at Pentecost by the work of the Spirit. It is Babel that makes language standardized and commodified, if also ultimately divisive and violent; it is Christ who permits the true poetry and creativity of speech that seeks genuine communion of diversities rather than civilized control.

In its own, if oblique, concern for the state of language, the book of Hosea has a timely word for us today. The close of the book of Hosea calls not for the rebuilding of the monarchy or a temple but for the renewal of language. It invites the people of God to return to God and bring with them not sacrifices or a new candidate for the throne or a ten-year strategy or a revitalization program but simply *words*.[6] Renewal starts with the renewal of the ultimate signs that humans handle and deploy: their words.

---

[5] William Stringfellow, *An Ethic for Christians and Other Aliens in a Strange Land* (Word, 1973), 106.
[6] Hos 14:2.

One of the ways Sabbath helps us to renew our language through the renewal of our lives is—paradoxically—by orienting us to our true work. As we've seen on our journey, Sabbath isn't about not working. Sabbath instead shows us the work we should be about. Sabbath is the meaning of our present work as we strive to enter God's rest. Sabbath tells us that our true work is to become mature, responsible members of God's household. This entails not taking a rest for ourselves but providing rest for others by sharing their burdens. What's more, Sabbath is not about justifying our labor within the exploitative economic orders and value system of the world. Instead, it's about preparing to take our leave of them and setting up signs for others to follow on their own exodus into the freedom of Christ.[7] The implication for this is that the Sabbath gospel does not—and in some ways cannot—generate a single formula, to-do list, or even rule of life. Instead, it aims to develop a maturity by which disciples might discern wisely and even creatively in their context how to live as ambassadors of their Sovereign and speak the tongue of their true home even while conversing in a foreign land.

But ultimately, to renew our language demands the renewal of ourselves, for it is "out of the abundance of the heart that the mouth speaks."[8]

Gregory: A New Heart

As I (Gregory) write this, I have just been to visit my grandmother the last time before her death at ninety-two. While her passing may seem uneventful and timely, it has given me and my family the occasion to consider the influence she has had on our lives . . . and it's complicated. We wrote this book through the framing of a journey. That's not just a literary convention or trope we used. Rather, this has been, at least for me, something of a documentation of my own journey in wrestling with a complicated family legacy deeply enmeshed with vocational identity. I have lived with an angelic demon on my shoulder judging every moment of inaction

---
[7]Hos 14:9.
[8]Lk 6:45.

as laziness. I have lived to please others by aiming at acquiring accolades. In this, I was living my family's legacy. But we're at the end of a lineage. My grandparents have no name heirs; no Caines will follow (they had three daughters). Likewise, many expressions of Christianity are coming to the end of their lineage.

For my grandmother, the basic civilizational narrative worked well. Hard work, grit, determination, and discipline of family for career paid off. My grandmother achieved much, and her ability to chase the next success—born during the Great Depression, going from daughter of an early service-station owner in a small Colorado town to principal of a major high school in a big city, receiving a fellowship in arts and design in New York City in the 1950s, even to a year stint on Capitol Hill as a senator's aide—was a realization of building her dream house, something she also literally did as the designer of the house for which my grandfather was the builder. She modeled the myth of aseity in herself, wanting to do all things for herself and wanting to ensure none surpassed her. And this myth works, provided there is progress. "Progress is the most important product," as my grandfather used to say. The myth worked for Christianity too, provided Western civilization was allied and expanding.

But the myth failed me. I have my achievements, but they don't pay off in career and financial advancement among a collapsing empire. Now, as we put final edits on this book, I am newly unemployed, laid off for financial reasons. In a space where pay is declining, jobs are vanishing, schools and churches are closing, job satisfaction is abysmal, "winning" looks like losing. And it also means that for those who currently hold power, position, and pay, the incentives are to protect a scarce resource. Rather than seeking to empower a new generation to thrive, toxic leadership feels more the norm than the exception. The church is an even more fraught space, because on top of these all-too-human relational dynamics is a dual theology of providence and vocation that makes this myth of the dream home a divine calling. According to such accounts, God is calling us to colabor with him in defeating the chaos of underdevelopment, and those who are lazy, who fall behind, must be the reprobate. The future is not with them but in lasting structures, institutions—a constructed eternal utopia.

Saying no to this myth rationally is not overly challenging. In theory many Christians would react against it. But it's in the very air we breathe, deeply embedded in liturgy, architecture, church employment practices, leadership books, time- and pitch-perfect worship services. This has become a power, a real demon, and I feel possessed. I do the things I do not want to do. I want to believe in the Sabbath gospel, but it feels utterly impossible when the fear of financial insolvency overrides the freedom to make intentional choices for a better future. Maybe slow change can bring it about? No. I used to believe in this pastoral leadership trope. Time is expiring for the church to make slow changes. The problem is that there is no slow change from the God of the personal dream home—the God of vocation—to the God of Sabbath. The two are opposed.

There is no slow change from one to the other. There is no future for a vocational Christianity in a time that has pushed it into the civilizational scrap heap of history. Change from here has to happen now by an intentional paradigm shift we might call repentance.[9]

I personally want to change, to cast out the demon of work and productivity, of achievement and "success." I can't do it alone. I need a community, a church, a body of Christ with the lifeblood of Jesus pumping through its veins. I need a blood transfusion.

Christianity must change at its heart. It must begin anew, from the middle, from now. The Sabbath gospel is not something to believe in word alone but to express in real, economic deeds by rest-giving love and burden bearing. The Sabbath gospel must convert our hearts of stone, inclined to construct bricks for Pharaoh, to hearts of flesh that do works of service that seem to do anything but last.

---

[9]Recent works have highlighted this theme, such as Alan Hirsch and Rob Kelly, *Metanoia: How God Radically Transforms People, Churches, and Organizations From the Inside Out* (100 Movements, 2023).

A New Moses, a New Peter

Previously we saw that Jesus does not portray himself as a new Moses, even if the book of Hebrews does so. While his Sermon on the Mount does parallel the law giving at Sinai, in recapitulating Passover and the exodus Jesus ultimately portrays himself as the lamb, the bread, and the blood of a new covenant rather than the leader who would take his people from Egypt. Jesus initiates an exodus he expects his followers to take up and continue, offering his own body and blood as sustenance for the journey. Today we need new Moseses, Aarons, and Miriams, those who will galvanize a colonized people, instill in them courage, sing their story, and lead them out of the dream homes of Western civilization that Christianity itself even helped to underwrite. We need a new Moses who can unite us, form us, transform us into a people once again.

The great challenge of the church today is its division. Resources still abound, but various dynamics—from puffed-up conceptions of leadership, to fixation on salvation-through-right-doctrine, to the offering of mostly recreational services—have kept the church from uniting and mobilizing. Hence, a renewed gospel vocabulary is necessary, one that is robustly biblical and yet not aligned to any one tradition even if it has affinities with many.

When Jesus commissioned Peter he was not creating a pope, father, or vicar. "Call no one your father on earth, for you have one Father," Jesus said.[10] Rather, Jesus commissioned Peter to feed his sheep, to be a household manager, economist, shepherd. Jesus commissioned Peter to express the sovereignty of the kingdom of God by providing daily bread, to organize his people.[11] And in the other famous commissioning of Peter, Jesus explains that the gates of Hades shall not prevail against the

---

[10] Mt 23:9.
[11] If this seems dubitable, consider that one of the first tasks to be delegated in Acts is the distribution of food in Acts 6, given to the seven, who, in spite of the fact that they were mainly tasked with food distribution, also end up being evangelists or ambassadors: Stephen, who gives the first and most deadly sermon in Acts 7, and Philip, who gains the ear of a royal ambassador of Ethiopia in Acts 8.

church.[12] This is a clarion call to advance, not retreat. Perhaps again Tolkien perceived the moment clearly in his depiction of King Theoden of Rohan, put under the spell of aged tiredness, with the lies of false council in his ear. The time has come for the church to stand on its own feet and take the kingly responsibility of creating and maintaining a true community that is able to give rest and reveal Sabbath to the world. The false council of fools, of the paranoid and the collaborator, must be expelled so right reasoning and solid strategy may come forward, that we might take up Christ's yoke by obeying his command, "Feed my sheep."[13]

---

[12] Mt 16:18.
[13] Jn 21:17.

ACKNOWLEDGMENTS

It takes a village to raise a book. I (Amy) am grateful for the support of my parents and siblings in Colorado Springs, my brothers and sisters at St John's Canberra, and my friends and colleagues at St Mark's National Theological Centre over the years this book was in gestation. Bill and Tracey Sutherland generously hosted (and nutritiously fed!) me for a week in Dulwich Hills, Sydney, during an initial drafting of chapter twelve (and not a few footnotes), as did Anna and Gavin Krebs for a stretch in Goulburn during the final stage of revisions. A St Mark's postgraduate seminar offered critical input on an early version of what later became chapters eight and nine, and the second session of my 2024 Being the Church class offered supportive suggestions for the introduction and chapter eleven.

An army of people read and commented on one or several chapter drafts along the way: David Adams, Sophie Ballard, Judith Bartholomeusz, Linda Devereux, Jan DeVos, Evan Durrant, Winifred Lamb, Dave McLennan, Marilyn Pietsch, Jacqui Service, Charles Vandepeer, Sarah Wadley, and Jennay Wilson. Special thanks goes to those who met in a series of pre-reader discussions in Canberra in May and September 2024: Matt Andrews, Josh Axtens, Kai Boylan, Luke Keenan, Michael McAlister, Laura Rademaker, Fiona Reid, Estelle Stambolie, Cecelia Symonds, Jacob Traeger, and Russ and Ros Tunks. Their feedback and engagement were invaluable, incisive, and heartening. This text is a much better one as a result.

And I'm also profoundly grateful for Gregory's invitation to join in this meaningful collaborative project. I continue to count him and his wife, Ainhoa, even from the other side of the world, as coworkers in the gospel (Rom 16:3).

I (Gregory) am grateful to my students at the Flourish Institute of Theology who have wrestled with and tested these ideas, working out how the Sabbath gospel might be lived out in real ministry contexts. Additional prereading thanks goes to Rogelio and Paula Prieto.

Also I want to especially thank Amy, friend and godmother to my eldest, collaborator on many projects and visions, and now esteemed coauthor. While I've managed many collaborative writing projects, coauthoring on this level was new and life giving. I'm confident that the end result is better than what I would have written alone.

Our gratitude too goes to the team of saints who met in person and virtually across the United States from 2020–2022 to respond to an invitation by the Evangelical Covenant Order of Presbyterians to write a new theological document to cast a vision for the future of the church: Heather Bauman, Tom Boone, Clay Brown, Mark Patterson, and Trevor Smith. It was in conversation with that team that the untapped power, beauty, and significance of Sabbath initially dawned on all of us, and which continued to develop over deep writing, thinking, discussion, and—indeed—debate. This book is a direct output of that work.

We're grateful to the team at IVP Academic for affirming and investing in the initial vision of this book, and for the labor of Rachel Hastings and Noel Forlini Burt to corral it into its final form.

Soli Deo gloria.

SELECTED BIBLIOGRAPHY

Augustine. *Confessions*. Translated by Henry Chadwick. Oxford World's Classics. Oxford University Press, 2008.

Bauckham, Richard. *Bible and Ecology: Rediscovering the Community of Creation*. Baylor University Press, 2010.

Bauman, Heather, Tom Boone, Clay Brown, Amy J. Erickson, Mark Patterson, Trevor Smith, and G. P. Wagenfuhr. "Lord of Time: Living in the Rest and Reign of God." ECO: A Covenant Order of Evangelical Presbyterians, 2023. www.academia.edu/98351142/Lord_of_Time_Living_in_the_Rest_and_Reign_of_God.

Bonhoeffer, Dietrich. *Creation and Fall: A Theological Exposition of Genesis 1–3*. Edited by John W. de Gruchy. Vol. 3. Dietrich Bonhoeffer Works. Fortress, 2004.

Brock, Brian. *Joining Creation's Praise: A Theological Ethic of Creatureliness*. Baker Academic, 2025.

Brueggemann, Walter. *Sabbath as Resistance: Saying No to the Culture of Now*. John Knox, 2014.

Bruno, Christopher R. "'Jesus Is Our Jubilee' . . . But How? The OT Background and Lukan Fulfillment of the Ethics of Jubilee." *Journal of the Evangelical Theological Society* 53, no. 1 (2010): 81-101.

Buschart, W. David, and Ryan Tafilowski. *Worth Doing: Fallenness, Finitude, and Work in the Real World*. IVP Academic, 2025.

Dawn, Marva Jenine Sandberg. "The Concept of the 'Principalities and Powers' in the Works of Jacques Ellul." PhD diss., University of Notre Dame, 1992.

Ellul, Jacques. *The Ethics of Freedom*. Translated by Geoffrey W. Bromiley. Eerdmans, 1976.

Ellul, Jacques. *Living Faith: Belief and Doubt in a Perilous World*. Translated by Peter Heinegg. Harper & Row, 1980.

Ellul, Jacques. *The New Demons*. Translated by C. Edward Hopkin. Seabury, 1975.

Ellul, Jacques. *The Technological System*. Translated by Joachim Neugroschel. Continuum, 1980.

Ellul, Jacques. *To Will and to Do: An Introduction to Christian Ethics*. Translated by Jacob Marques Rollison. Vol. 1. Cascade Books, 2020. Kindle.

Ellul, Jacques. *What I Believe*. Translated by Geoffrey W. Bromiley. Eerdmans, 1989.

Emerson, Matthew. *He Descended to the Dead: An Evangelical Theology of Holy Saturday*. IVP Academic, 2019.

Erickson, Amy J. *Ephraim Radner, Hosean Wilderness, and the Church in the Post-Christendom West*. Brill, 2020.

Erickson, Amy J. "Figuring One's Calling: A Lukan Passion Theology of Vocation in Dialogue with Karl Barth." *Journal of Theological Interpretation* 17, no. 1 (2023): 92-108. https://doi.org/10.5325/jtheointe.17.1.0092.

Girard, René. *Things Hidden Since the Foundation of the World*. Translated by Stephen Bann and Michael Metteer. Stanford University Press, 1987.

Heiser, Michael S. *The Unseen Realm: Recovering the Supernatural Worldview of the Bible*. Lexham, 2015.

Heschel, Abraham Joshua. *The Sabbath: Its Meaning for Modern Man*. Farrar, Straus & Giroux, 1951.

Hill, Emily Beth. *Marketing and Christian Proclamation in Theological Perspective*. Lexington Books, 2021.

Jervis, L. Ann. *Paul and Time: Life in the Temporality of Christ*. Baker Academic, 2023.

Käsemann, Ernst. *The Wandering People of God: An Investigation of the Letter to the Hebrews*. Translated by Roy A. Harrisville and Irving L. Sandberg. Augsburg, 1984.

Kreider, Alan. *The Patient Ferment of the Early Church*. Baker Academic, 2016.

Lilley, David. "At the Invitation of the God Who Rests: The Fidelity-Producing Sabbath Ethic of Karl Barth's Doctrine of Creation." PhD diss., University of Aberdeen, 2018.

Marx, Karl. *Capital: A Critique of Political Economy*. Edited by Frederick Engels. Translated by Samuel Moore and Edward Aveling. Vol. 1. 1887. www.marxists.org/archive/marx/works/download/pdf/Capital-Volume-I.pdf.

Mathews, Jeanette. "Difficult Texts: 'I Have Set My Bow in the Clouds' (Genesis 9.13)." *Theology* 122, no. 1 (2019): 38-42.

Meyers, Ched. *The Biblical Vision of Sabbath Economics*. Tell the Word, 2001.

Mullen, E. Theodore. *The Assembly of the Gods: The Divine Council in Canaanite and Early Hebrew Literature*. Scholars Press, 1980.

Peeler, Amy L. B. *Women and the Gender of God*. Eerdmans, 2022.

Pitre, Brant James. *Jesus and the Jewish Roots of the Eucharist: Unlocking the Secrets of the Last Supper*. Doubleday, 2011.

Proudhon, Pierre. "The Celebration of Sunday." 1839. www.marxists.org/reference/subject/economics/proudhon/1839/celebration-of-sunday.html.

Radner, Ephraim. *Mortal Goods: Reimagining Christian Political Duty*. Baker Academic, 2024.

Radner, Ephraim. *Time and the Word: Figural Reading of the Christian Scriptures*. Eerdmans, 2021.

Rhodes, Michael, Robby Holt, and Brian Fikkert. *Practicing the Jesus Economy: Learning Disciplines for How You Work, Earn, Spend, Save, and Give*. Baker Books, 2018.

Rillera, Andrew Remington. *Lamb of the Free: Recovering the Varied Sacrificial Understandings of Jesus's Death*. Cascade Books, 2024.

Rogers, Eugene F. *Blood Theology*. Cambridge University Press, 2021.

Rosa, Hartmut. *The Uncontrollability of the World*. Polity, 2020.

Scott, James C. *Seeing Like a State: How Certain Schemes to Improve the Human Condition Have Failed*. Yale University Press, 2020.

Sittser, Gerald. "The Catechumenate and the Rise of Christianity." *Journal of Spiritual Formation & Soul Care* 6, no. 2 (2013): 179-203.

Smith, Mark S. *The Origins of Biblical Monotheism: Israel's Polytheistic Background and the Ugaritic Texts*. Oxford University Press, 2001.

Ticciati, Susannah. *A New Apophaticism: Augustine and the Redemption of Signs*. Brill, 2013.

Vanstone, William H. *The Stature of Waiting*. Darton, Longman & Todd, 1984.

Wagenfuhr, G. P. *Plundering Eden: A Subversive Christian Theology of Creation and Ecology*. Cascade Books, 2020.

Wagenfuhr, G. P. *Plundering Egypt: A Subversive Christian Ethic of Economy*. Cascade Books, 2016.

Wagenfuhr, G. P. *Unfortunate Words of the Bible: A Biblical Theology of Misunderstandings*. Cascade Books, 2019.

Wright, N. T. *How God Became King: The Forgotten Story of the Gospels*. HarperOne, 2016.

Wright, N. T. *Into the Heart of Romans: A Deep Dive into Paul's Greatest Letter*. Zondervan Academic, 2023.

Wright, N. T. *Jesus and the Victory of God*. SPCK, 2012.

Wright, N. T. *Paul and the Faithfulness of God*. Fortress, 2013.

Wright, N. T. *Surprised by Hope: Rethinking Heaven, the Resurrection, and the Mission of the Church*. HarperOne, 2008.

Zuboff, Shoshana. *The Age of Surveillance Capitalism: The Fight for a Human Future at the New Frontier of Power*. Profile Trade, 2019.

GENERAL INDEX

Abel, 54, 74, 78, 80, 163
Abraham, 26, 54, 87, 96, 103-4, 106-7, 115, 138, 145, 179, 195-97
Adam, 60, 66-72, 77, 80-82, 85, 88, 90, 94, 101, 106, 120, 147, 183
    second, 139, 167
agapē, 121, 193, 198, 200
ambassador(s), 5, 120, 145, 160, 170, 188, 191-92, 206, 209, 212, 226, 230-34, 238, 241, 246, 249
ascension, 9-10, 86, 130, 150, 154-55, 166-68, 170, 175, 201
aseity, 17-21, 25-27, 29, 31-32, 36, 44, 47, 50, 61, 66, 76, 79, 86, 88, 119, 157, 171, 175, 200, 203, 247
    nonaseity, 174
Athanasius, 79, 147
atonement, 131, 132, 137, 245
    Day of Atonement, 115, 135
    See also Yom Kippur
Augustine, 5, 34, 51, 79, 89, 97
Babel, 8, 22, 29, 35-36, 83-89, 105, 119, 143, 173, 175, 183, 199, 245
    See also Babylon
Babylon, 8, 23, 45, 47, 87, 122, 143, 171-72, 174-75, 178, 181, 224
baptism, 107, 135, 138, 193-95, 201, 207
    Jesus', 147
Barth, Karl, 28, 225
blood, 120-29, 132-38, 140-41, 143, 164-65, 195-96, 205
    of Abel, 163
    of Abraham, 106
    bloodline, 164, 243
    of Jesus, 126, 128, 134, 163-66, 168, 196, 205, 249
    money, 182
    of the new covenant, 120, 127, 129, 135, 164, 205, 249
    of the Passover Lamb, 109, 124, 205
    transfusion, 165, 205, 211, 248
    See also lifeblood
Bonhoeffer, Dietrich, 30, 70, 229
bread, 110, 148, 152, 201-5, 223-24, 234, 249
    bread-keeper, 93
    daily, 93, 101, 107-8, 110, 204, 215, 249
    of Egypt/Pharaoh, 107, 109, 202
    of presence, 151
    of slavery, 205, 211
    unleavened, 109, 125, 202
    See also manna
bricks, 4, 13, 35, 85, 87, 113, 119, 199, 211, 228, 248
Brueggemann, Walter, 31, 108, 225
Cain, 46, 54, 73-74, 76-78, 80-83, 85, 88-89, 91-94, 147-48, 171-72, 179-80, 187
calling, 210, 216-17, 233, 247
    See also vocation
chaos, 16-17, 21, 23, 43, 45-50, 58, 64, 72-73, 101-2, 105, 146, 245, 248
Chaoskampf, 45-47, 49
church, 87, 98, 109, 125, 137, 159, 166-68, 175, 191-93, 195, 198-201, 203-212, 215-16, 222, 228, 232, 234, 237, 239, 243-44, 248, 250
    birth of, 165
    in Corinth, 125, 234
    discipline of, 69
    early, 86-87, 236
    purpose of, 79
    renewal of, 11, 192, 250
    of today, 3-7, 10, 24, 118, 188, 191, 227, 244, 247-49
    work of, 4
    See also Christ: body of; ecclesiology

General Index

circumcision, 98, 103-7, 109, 112, 115-16, 118,145, 206-7
city of God/*City of God*, 5, 34, 51, 79
communion, 205
   between God and people, 137, 174, 215
   cups, 201
   of diversities, 245
   of saints, 179
   See also Eucharist; Lord's Supper
community, 5, 6, 11, 24-25, 31, 39-40, 51, 63-64, 69-70, 91, 94, 108, 110-12, 114-15, 123, 125, 130, 137, 140, 145, 154, 168, 181, 187-88, 194-95, 198-201, 204-5, 211, 212, 219, 226-27, 232-34, 236-37, 239, 241, 244, 248, 250
coronation, 60, 162
   See also enthronement
covenant, 96-99, 122, 126-29, 148, 192-93
   with Abraham, 87, 116
   ark of, 148
   blood of the, 120, 127, 129, 135, 164, 205
   first, 165
   of Jesus, 120
   new, 127-28, 138, 164, 168, 249
   people, 9
   rainbow, 161, 183-84, 186, 206
   sign(s) of, 100, 103-6, 109, 112, 125-26, 206
   of Sinai, 112, 127
creation, 6, 8-10, 22-23, 25-28, 30-31, 34-35, 37-40, 43-53, 55, 58-63, 65-68, 72, 74, 76-78, 80, 84, 88-89, 91, 93-95, 100-102, 105, 107, 112, 116, 141-43, 146, 149, 157-58, 162, 171-72, 174, 184-85, 187, 193-95, 200, 215, 222-23, 231, 233, 235
   first account of, 44, 59-61, 65-66, 93
   household of, 58, 61, 65, 93, 95, 113, 240
   as a human work, 4, 219
   of humans, 175
   new, 160, 163, 172, 193-95, 219, 235
   recreation, 105
   second account of, 44, 62, 66
   seventh day of, 6, 61, 186
   sixth day of, 61, 89
cross, 49, 118, 120, 140, 156-160, 162-164, 182-84, 222-23, 228, 233, 241, 244
   bearing of/taking up one's, 168, 184, 233
David, 33, 62, 76, 117, 139, 143-45, 151
Dawn, Marva, 75-76
death, 8-9, 36, 69-71, 82, 85, 87-90, 120-25, 129, 132-34, 142, 149, 156-57, 160, 163-64, 166, 169, 174, 181, 185-87, 195, 205, 211, 228, 240, 246
   of Jesus, 9, 118, 120-21, 125-26, 129-31, 135-36, 140, 148, 155-57, 159-63, 165-66, 168, 170, 181, 184, 194, 201, 206, 244

debt, 132, 162-63, 175
desire, 8, 15-22, 25, 33, 57, 67, 71, 73-74, 76, 139, 144-45, 161, 176, 184, 193-94, 216, 219
detergent, 132, 134, 137
devil, 54, 124, 160
   See also Satan
disciple(s), 5, 28, 119, 126-27, 144, 150-52, 165, 187, 191, 199, 206, 211, 219, 222, 228, 232-33, 238, 246
discipleship, 59, 90, 146, 184, 199, 209, 227-28
discipline, 72-74, 85, 90-91, 102, 178, 180-81, 184, 187, 198, 226, 230
   of Adam and Eve, 67
   of Babel, 85
   church, 69
   of God, 66, 69, 74, 81-82, 203-4
   of homelessness, 81
   spiritual, 187, 226, 236
diversity, 22, 25, 84-87, 173
divine council, 51, 54-58, 63-69, 82, 85, 93-94, 171, 173, 198, 231, 243
dream home, 8, 13-25, 28-29, 35-36, 39, 43, 47-48, 51, 63, 70, 76, 84, 86, 88-89, 113, 119, 150, 153, 157, 161-62, 171, 173-74, 182-83, 191, 199-201, 203, 207, 215, 219, 221, 243, 245, 247-48
ecclesiology, 79, 198, 208
   See also church
ecology, 94
   ecological, 9, 95-96, 113, 221
economy, 8, 68, 76, 87, 92, 94-95, 98, 108, 115, 122, 152, 164, 203, 205, 214, 216-17, 220
   biblical, 120
   of God 10, 78, 80, 88, 92, 94, 97-98, 110, 126, 129, 135, 142, 150, 162, 164-65, 167, 171, 174-75, 177, 200-201, 203-4, 215, 228, 235, 243
Eden, 9, 30-31, 37, 39, 44, 56-57, 62, 66, 69-70, 74, 78, 80-81, 106-7, 115, 194
Egypt, 4, 8, 23, 26, 38, 87, 107-9, 116, 122, 124-27, 129, 167, 176-77, 199, 202, 211, 223, 229, 249
elder(s), 206, 209, 212, 231
   See also presbyteros
Ellul, Jacques, 28, 60-61, 75, 78, 84, 220-21, 226
embassy, 188, 192
   See also ambassador(s)
enemy/enemies, 29, 31-40, 57, 63, 73, 82, 85-86, 148, 163, 186, 171, 224-25, 235
Enoch, 81-82
enthronement, 33, 55, 60-62
   See also coronation; throne
eschatology, 10

eternity, 7, 20-21, 27, 88-89, 216, 219
Eucharist, 77, 204-5, 223
   See also communion; Lord's Supper
Eve, 60, 66-73, 77, 80-81, 85, 88, 106, 120, 126, 147, 165, 183
exile, 51, 62, 66, 69-71, 83, 116-17, 121-22, 125, 143, 178-79, 183
exodus, 4, 10, 22, 48, 50, 107-8, 123, 125, 138, 147, 171, 175, 178-79, 185, 188, 194, 221, 223, 246, 249
faith, 34-35, 80, 87, 102, 128, 135, 162, 177, 179-81, 193, 196-97, 207, 217, 220
   See also fides
faithfulness, 23, 26-28, 66-67, 102-3, 128, 138, 161, 180, 195-97, 201, 207, 238
fides, 193, 197-98, 200, 211
food, 60, 67-68, 74, 78, 93, 109-11, 137, 147-48, 151-53, 165, 167, 174-75, 202-4, 214-15, 220, 234, 249
   and sovereignty, 60, 78, 93, 99, 108, 148
forgiveness, 82, 126-29, 131, 134, 136, 140, 168, 178, 182, 186, 193, 195, 199, 205
formation, 9, 43, 63, 73, 80-82, 105, 106-7, 110-11, 115, 125-26, 139, 165, 178, 199, 201, 210-11, 219, 229, 231-32, 234-36
freedom, 22, 44, 60-61, 67, 78, 119, 124, 142, 177, 199-200, 220-21, 225-27, 231, 237, 246, 248
   See also liberation
garden, 23, 31, 37, 39, 56, 66-67, 80, 147, 173, 194, 222
   See also Eden
Girard, René, 129
gospel, 6, 8, 11, 21-22, 39-40, 64, 86, 98, 118, 135, 149, 167, 197, 206, 212, 219, 237, 243, 245, 249
   false, 8, 21
   See also Sabbath: gospel
Hagar, 103
Heschel, Abraham, 225
hesed, 26, 28, 85, 186
history, 5, 9-10, 27-30, 35, 40, 46-47, 61-62, 66-67, 70, 79, 83, 86-89, 101-2, 114, 116, 121-22, 143, 153, 155-60, 165-72, 174, 177, 187, 196, 199, 206, 208, 211, 215, 222-23, 229, 240, 244, 248
holy, 53, 112, 126, 130-31, 134, 138
   holiness, 130, 136, 138, 167, 193, 200
Holy Saturday, 157-60
Holy Spirit, 86-87, 196, 205
household, 6-8, 10-11, 37, 43, 47, 51, 53-54, 57-59, 61-63, 65-66, 70, 74-80, 84, 86-88, 91, 93-98, 102-26, 129-30, 135-38, 140, 142-43, 145-47, 151-53, 156-62, 164-68, 171, 175, 177, 179-80, 184, 191-92, 194-97, 200-202, 205-7,

209-10, 212, 214-15, 219, 222-26, 228-35, 237-41, 243, 246, 249
identity, 20, 43-44, 84-85, 97, 109-10, 112, 124-25, 129, 136, 197, 215-16, 243, 246
   of Jesus, 150-51
   Jewish, 103
image of God, 52-54, 57-60, 63-64, 67-68, 93-94, 97, 99, 106, 116, 138, 140, 145, 147, 151, 156, 167, 184, 192, 199-200, 206, 209, 215, 218-19
in medias res, 29-30, 63, 67, 109, 156, 181, 208
incarnation, 27, 63, 79, 142, 160, 172
institution(s), 3-4, 6, 9-10, 39, 53, 56, 58-59, 75, 77, 80-81, 83, 94-96, 98, 108, 112, 144, 153, 161, 170, 172, 197, 201, 206, 208, 211, 215, 222, 240, 244-45, 248
Irenaeus, 167
Jesus (Christ), 9-10, 11, 13, 26-28, 53-56, 58-60, 63, 66-67, 79, 85, 87, 90, 98, 102, 107-8, 112, 115, 118, 125, 128-30, 133, 136-40, 142-74, 177-84, 186-87, 192-93, 194-207, 209-10, 215, 219, 222-24, 227-29, 231-32, 235-37, 239, 241, 244, 245-46, 248-49
   ascension of, 167
   blood of, 126-28, 134, 136, 164-66, 168, 205
   body of, 167, 199, 204, 210-11, 248
   crucifixion of, 162
   death of, 121, 125-26, 130-31, 135-36, 140, 160-61, 163, 168, 181, 194, 205
   disciple(s) of, 5, 233
   resurrection of, 144
   See also messiah
Job, 34, 46-47, 55, 180
John the Baptist, 92, 138, 144, 179, 193
journey, 4-7, 9-13, 23, 25, 28-30, 40, 63, 65, 70, 92-93, 98, 107, 120, 126, 142, 153-55, 163, 167-68, 170, 179, 181-82, 184, 187-88, 191, 193, 199, 208, 228, 236, 239-241, 243, 246
Jubilee, 9, 98, 113-16, 126, 128, 141-47, 149, 153-54, 162, 172, 174, 200, 204, 207
judgment, 36, 57, 74, 84-86, 90, 95, 101-2, 120, 125, 135, 147, 159-60, 171, 174, 182-86, 200
Käsemann, Ernst, 179, 208
king, 6, 27-28, 33, 37, 56, 60-61, 63, 79, 85, 93, 105, 117, 139, 142, 144-45, 147-51, 159, 162-63, 182-83, 186, 197, 250
kingdom, 9, 22, 27-28, 39, 66, 80, 85, 87, 90, 107, 118, 129, 138-39, 143-45, 147, 159, 166-67, 172-75, 178, 183, 191-93, 197, 204, 215, 217, 231-33, 249
kipper, 131-32, 134-35, 137
language, 10, 40, 84, 86, 98, 193, 243-46
   gendered, 43

General Index

liberation, 88, 109, 123-26, 129, 178, 195, 199, 202, 211, 223, 229, 234, 236
  See also freedom
lifeblood, 120, 134-35, 165-66, 196, 205, 224, 248
liturgy, 139, 234, 248
Lord's Prayer, 129, 204
  See also prayer
Lord's Supper, 93, 108, 129, 201
  See also communion; Eucharist
love, 9, 26, 28, 44, 47, 49-50, 71, 79, 85-87, 92, 95-96, 119, 122, 129, 157-58, 161-62, 166, 168, 179, 184-85, 193, 198-200, 204, 207, 209, 211, 223, 229, 239, 248
management, 19, 22, 115, 129
manna, 93, 109-11, 113, 126, 152, 176, 202, 211, 227
marriage, 71, 97, 104-5, 128
Marx, Karl, 218
Mary, 43, 145
maturity, 22-23, 25, 54, 57, 65, 67-70, 74, 76, 82, 85, 92, 97, 102, 126, 130, 142, 152, 172, 178, 183-85, 191, 194, 197-98, 203, 206-7, 209-10, 246
messiah/Messiah, 37, 144, 149, 172
metaphysics, 25-26
Moses, 108, 126, 175, 249
myth, 45, 49, 83-84, 139, 215, 219, 247-48
  demythologize, 221
Noah, 36, 65, 100-103, 158-59, 193
palace, 56-57, 173, 194
Passover, 48, 108-9, 124-27, 129, 136-37, 202, 205, 249
  lamb, 124-26, 202, 205, 223
patience, 88, 99, 107, 126, 145, 157-59, 168, 171, 180, 186, 193, 200, 206, 210, 222, 230
Paul, 71, 73, 79, 97, 125, 130, 142, 149, 152-53, 162, 166-67, 178, 184, 194, 197, 204, 206-7, 209, 223, 228, 232, 234-39
pedagogy, 97, 107, 116, 126, 128-29, 139, 168, 194, 199, 206, 210, 212, 228
Pentecost, 86-87, 245
Peter, 158, 249
Pharaoh, 4, 108-9, 123-24, 126, 176, 185, 202, 211, 248
prayer, 19, 58, 129, 159, 186, 222, 231, 234-35
  See also Lord's Prayer
presbyteros, 206, 238
  See also elder(s)
principalities and powers, 75, 162, 182, 184-86
Promised Land, 34, 101, 113, 147, 177-78, 183, 194
providence, 73, 146, 221-23, 229-30, 245, 247
purification, 130, 133-35, 137, 195
Radner, Ephraim, 156, 239, 244

rainbow, 98-100, 102-3, 107, 109, 115, 118, 158, 161, 183-84, 186, 206, 222
ransom, 123
recapitulation, 59, 155, 160, 167, 172, 230
reconciliation, 5, 23, 47, 72, 80, 100-103, 105-7, 115-16, 131, 145-46, 160, 170-71, 173, 181-82, 188, 200, 202, 206, 209, 230-31, 233
redemption, 102, 123, 126, 201, 207, 218
rest, 4, 6-18, 20-23, 25, 28-34, 36-37, 40, 45, 49, 51, 60-63, 65-66, 73, 78-79, 81-82, 86, 88, 92, 101-2, 107-8, 110-13, 116-17, 119, 130, 146-51, 153, 156-59, 163, 167, 170-72, 174-75, 177-81, 183, 187, 192, 194-95, 198, 203, 206-8, 211-12, 214-15, 218-19, 221-22, 224-29, 232, 236, 238-40, 243, 246, 248, 250
resurrection, 9-10, 118, 130, 135, 142, 144, 154-56, 158, 163, 166, 168, 170, 201, 219, 231
Roman Empire, 86, 144
Rome, 8, 79, 86-87, 122
Sabbath
  command(ment) of, 106, 111, 130, 214, 221
  day, 55, 130, 149, 157, 179, 214, 239
  gospel, 13, 22-23, 25, 29-30, 32, 40, 43, 47, 87, 168, 191-93, 209, 212, 214-15, 221, 224-25, 240, 243, 246, 248, 252
  journey, 12, 23, 29, 92, 142, 153, 168, 182, 184, 188, 193
  practice of, 4, 6, 8-9, 31, 93, 98, 113, 116, 195, 221, 224-28
  sign of, 6, 9, 92, 98, 107-8, 112, 117, 164, 171, 187, 239
  work, 59, 151, 186, 210, 215, 238
  year, 113, 214
sacrifice(s), 56, 58, 80, 83, 118, 120-21, 123-24, 128, 131-32, 134-40, 150, 153, 164, 167-68, 174, 176, 178, 181, 183, 196, 216, 245
Satan, 204, 224
  See also devil
Seth, 46, 54, 73, 77, 80-82, 90, 94, 147, 171
sex, 46, 104-6
sign(s), 6-7, 9, 37-38, 71, 87, 92, 96-113, 115-20, 124-27, 145, 158, 164, 168, 171, 187, 192, 200-202, 206-7, 211-12, 232, 236, 239, 241, 245-46
sin, 9, 21, 23, 66, 73-78, 83, 87-91, 99, 102, 120-26, 128-29, 132-36, 138, 148, 156, 159-161, 163-64, 167, 178-79, 183, 185-86, 192, 194, 217, 220, 226, 230, 233, 239, 241, 245
Sinai, 44, 112, 117, 127, 249
sixth day, 61, 88-89, 110-11, 149, 157-58, 166, 170, 172, 177, 179, 181, 186-87, 233, 239
slave(s), 4, 53, 73, 103, 109-11, 123, 126, 147, 162, 171, 232, 236-38

slavery, 85, 87, 107, 109-10, 121-22, 126, 129, 152, 175, 185, 202-3, 205, 211, 221
Smith, Adam, 73
Solomon, 33, 59, 117, 148
sovereignty, 7-9, 16, 27-28, 31, 33, 35-36, 39, 43-44, 47, 50, 56, 59-63, 65, 67, 71, 74, 76, 78-79, 83, 85, 87-88, 90, 93, 96-97, 99, 101, 108-10, 115-16, 122, 146, 148-49, 159-60, 168, 177, 192, 198, 200, 202, 204, 206, 214-15, 223, 249
technology, 17, 75, 83-84, 110
temple, 9, 34, 37, 39, 51, 53, 56-58, 95, 112, 117-18, 122, 125, 131, 135-37, 139, 143-44, 151, 153, 173, 176, 178, 181, 187, 208, 223, 244-45
throne, 34, 38, 60, 90, 130, 144-45, 148, 160, 163, 173, 194, 245
   room, 61, 173, 187
   See also enthronement
time, 5-7, 9, 21, 26-30, 36, 39-40, 44, 50, 62, 66, 70-71, 73-74, 85-86, 88-90, 97, 107, 109-10, 119, 124, 126, 128, 139, 141-43, 145-47, 150, 152-60, 167, 170, 174-81, 184, 188, 192, 198-99, 201-2, 208, 210-11, 222-23, 238-40, 243
   God's, 7, 9, 28, 34, 38, 43, 89, 120, 147, 166, 174, 182
   human, 28, 40, 61, 70, 89-90, 161
   management, 19
   Sabbath, 7, 62, 70, 88-90, 117, 142, 146, 168, 172, 198-99, 202, 209

tohu, 45, 48, 50, 160
Tolkien, J. R. R., 5, 11, 91, 250
Torah, 110, 112-13, 117, 130, 138-39, 165, 194
tov, 50-51
tree(s), 36-40, 44, 67, 82, 103-4, 141, 194-95, 211, 213
   of knowledge, 67-69, 77-78
   of life, 67, 69, 205
vocation, 64, 138, 148, 170, 216, 231, 233, 247-48
wandering, 81, 89, 177, 179-81, 208
wilderness, 23, 45, 49, 56, 109, 111, 113, 126, 135-36, 147, 152, 167, 176, 181, 185, 202
wisdom, 5, 35, 57, 66-68, 76, 78, 91, 148, 153, 180, 183, 186, 194, 197, 209, 211, 240
work, 4-5, 7, 36, 49, 70, 72, 81, 98, 102, 108, 111, 152, 159, 167, 172, 175, 178, 187-88, 191, 200-201, 214-41, 246-48
   of Christ, 10, 63, 136, 144, 167, 179, 199
   of the church, 4, 59, 102, 187, 206
   of God, 5, 32, 36, 38-39, 100, 102, 109, 112, 145, 155, 164-65, 177, 222, 231, 240
   human, 10, 63, 99, 101-2, 105, 112, 170, 202, 217
   Sabbath, 59, 151-52, 186, 188, 210, 215
wrath, 100, 120, 158-59, 163-65, 182-86, 222, 236, 240
Wright, N. T., 27, 58, 150, 160, 163, 172, 229-31
Yom Kippur, 135-36, 138

SCRIPTURE INDEX

OLD TESTAMENT

Genesis
1, *44, 45, 48, 50, 57, 62, 107*
1–3, *30, 166*
1–11, *52, 83, 84*
1:1–2:3, *65*
1:2, *48, 50, 193*
1:4, *51*
1:6-8, *51*
1:26-27, *52*
1:26-29, *58*
1:29-30, *59, 93*
1:31, *158*
2, *56, 67, 194*
2–3, *62, 66*
2–11, *65*
2:1, *157*
2:2, *60*
2:4, *44, 65*
2:5–3:24, *58*
2:8, *62, 80*
2:9, *67*
2:10, *194*
2:15, *62, 81, 106*
2:16-17, *67*
2:17, *69*
3, *65, 66, 68, 69, 74, 77*
3–10, *89*
3:1, *69*
3:3, *69*
3:6, *68*
3:15, *71*
3:16, *71*
3:19, *203*

3:21, *74*
3:23, *80*
3:24, *30*
4, *33, 54, 74, 75, 76, 80*
4–11, *46, 66*
4:1-2, *80*
4:6-7, *80*
4:7, *74, 148*
4:9, *80*
4:12, *81*
4:16, *81*
4:17, *81*
4:26, *81*
5, *78, 195*
5:1-3, *54*
5:3, *80*
5:13, *54*
5:29, *101*
6:2-4, *55*
9, *54, 100*
9:12, *100*
9:13, *100*
9:20, *101*
10, *83*
10:4, *85*
10:7, *85*
11, *36, 65, 183*
11:3, *4*
11:4, *84, 216*
12:2, *96*
12:2-3, *103*
15:2-5, *103*
17:9-10, *106*
17:12-14, *106*
22, *138*
25:29-34, *148*

Exodus
1:11, *108*
1:13, *108*
1:14, *4*
3:6, *26*
3:14, *26*
5, *85*
5:18, *108*
6:5, *108*
7:3, *176*
12–13, *108*
12:13, *109, 125*
12:48-49, *109*
13:9, *109*
13:15, *176*
15, *34*
15:13, *26*
16, *108, 110, 176, 202*
16:4, *110*
16:29, *110*
16:31, *111*
17:1-7, *176*
17:7, *176*
19, *139*
20, *6*
20:2, *26*
20:5, *54*
20:5-6, *186*
20:8, *111, 130*
20:8-11, *61*
20:11, *60*
23:12, *111*
24, *127*
24:9-11, *127*
31:13, *112*
31:16, *112*

31:17, *112*
34:7, *26*

Leviticus
1–16, *133*
5:14–6:7, *132*
6:26-30, *134*
8, *133*
11:44, *130*
14, *133*
14:21-32, *132*
16, *135*
17:10-14, *165*
17:11, *135*
17:14, *122*
18:28, *122, 133*
19:23-25, *104*
20:22, *133*
23–27, *48, 121*
23:23-25, *48*
25, *113, 146*
25:1-7, *113*
25:8, *114*
25:23, *114*
25:30, *114*
25:43, *58*
26:12, *27*

Numbers
11, *126*
21:6, *69*
21:8, *69*
33, *4*

Deuteronomy
5, *6*

5:14, *111*
6, *97*
8:3, *204*
10:16, *207*
11:10-11, *101*
12:10, *33*
12:23, *122, 165*
25:19, *33*
30:6, *207*
32:8, *55*
33:3, *56*

Joshua
1:15, *33*
24:15, *192*

Judges
9, *37*

1 Samuel
4, *148*
8:5-7, *148*
14–15, *148*

2 Samuel
7:1, *60, 62*
7:1-11, *117*

1 Kings
8:27, *117*
8:56, *33*
11, *148*
21, *115*

2 Kings
25:4, *56*

1 Chronicles
17:4-6, *51*
22:9, *33*

2 Chronicles
6:18, *51*
36:21, *116, 183*

Nehemiah
3:15, *56*
9:28, *58*

Job
1:6, *55, 56*
2:1, *55*

15:8, *56*
39, *46*
40:15–41:34, *46*

Psalms
1, *37, 40, 76, 82, 194*
1:1, *76*
2, *162, 240*
2:1, *27*
2:4, *60, 162*
2:7-9, *148*
7:14-15, *161*
8, *51, 54*
8:1-6, *148*
9:8, *60*
17:7, *26*
22, *163*
22:1, *27*
25:7, *26*
29:10, *60*
41:7, *33*
50:9-13, *53*
50:13, *128*
51, *139*
51–100, *240*
51–150, *34*
51:10, *139*
51:12, *139*
51:16-17, *53*
51:17, *139*
55:19, *60*
74, *49*
74:12, *49*
78:25, *202*
82, *55*
89:5, *56*
89:7, *56*
90, *239, 240*
90–92, *240*
90:12, *240*
90:14, *240*
90:16, *240*
90:17, *240*
91, *240*
92, *8, 23, 29, 31, 32, 34, 35, 36, 37, 38, 39, 40, 43, 63, 171, 194, 224, 239, 240*
92:1-5, *32*
92:2, *37*
92:3, *240*
92:4, *32*

92:5, *32, 240*
92:6, *35*
92:6-11, *33*
92:7, *35, 36*
92:8, *36*
92:9, *33, 35, 36*
92:10-11, *34*
92:11, *35*
92:12-15, *37*
92:13, *37*
92:15, *37*
93, *34*
95, *178*
95:7, *176*
95:11, *60, 177*
98:8, *141*
102:12, *60*
110, *148*
111:5, *78, 93*
118:22, *161, 200*
119, *97, 197*
130:4, *128*
132, *60*
132:8, *37*
132:14, *37, 60*
133, *51*
133:1, *25*

Proverbs
3:11-12, *69, 74*
9, *76*
27:20, *76*
30:15-16, *76*
31, *78*

Ecclesiastes
1:4, *70*
2:24, *101*
3:5, *211*
3:11, *20, 32, 216*
6:12, *142*

Song of Solomon
8:6, *157, 166*

Isaiah
1, *139*
1:10-17, *53*
1:11, *174*
1:13, *116*
6:2, *69*
8:14-15, *161, 200*

10:5-19, *230*
25, *174*
25:8, *174*
27:9, *138*
28:16, *200*
40:6-8, *39*
45:18-19, *48*
55, *153, 174*
55:1, *174*
55:1-5, *152*
55:2, *174*
55:12, *141*
58:6, *152*
61, *146*
66:1-2, *96*

Jeremiah
4:4, *207*
7:4, *96, 117*
7:23, *27*
11:4, *27*
12:1, *27*
23:18, *56*
24:7, *27*
30:22, *27*
31:1, *27*
31:29-30, *164*
31:31-34, *127*
31:33, *27*
31:34, *138*
32:38, *27*

Ezekiel
11:19, *117*
11:20, *27*
14:11, *27*
16, *165*
18, *164*
20:12, *112*
20:20, *112*
20:24, *116*
28, *56*
31, *37, 194*
36:26, *117*
36:28, *27*
37:23, *27*
37:27, *27*

Daniel
7, *148*
7:13, *55*

Scripture Index

Hosea
4:8, *96*
6:6, *26*
8:2, *244*
8:7, *161*
10:8, *244*
11:8, *244*
14:2, *245*
14:9, *246*

Amos
3:6, *102*
8:5, *116*

Jonah
4, *194*

Haggai
2, *143*

Zechariah
4:9, *143*
8:8, *27*
9:11, *127*
13:9, *27*

NEW TESTAMENT

Matthew
3:2, *146*
4:1-4, *68*
4:4, *204*
5, *236*
5:3, *150*
5:3-12, *180*
5:13-16, *214*
5:16, *188*
5:48, *130*
6:21, *13*
6:25-33, *152*
6:25-34, *60*
7:7-11, *152*
7:13-14, *65, 168*
7:15-20, *211*
10:26-31, *59*
11–12, *153*
11:3, *144*
11:27-30, *151*
11:28-30, *12*
12, *150, 152*
12:4, *223*
12:6, *51, 57, 118*
12:7-8, *26*
12:8, *55*
12:11-12, *58*
12:50, *147*
13:31-32, *103*
13:33, *168*
14:6, *167*
14:16, *152*
16:18, *250*
16:24, *184*
17:20, *103*
18:6, *186*
18:20, *198*
18:21, *82*
18:23-35, *129*
19:28, *57*
21:42-43, *161*
22:32, *96*
23:9, *220, 249*
25:1-13, *111*
25:31, *219*
25:34-36, *219*
26:6-11, *235*
26:24, *186*
26:45, *159*
27:6, *164*
27:27-31, *162*
27:46, *163*
28, *59*
28:19-20, *207*

Mark
2:5, *128*
2:7, *128*
2:26, *223*
2:27, *135*
2:28, *55*
3:35, *147*
6:37, *152, 167, 212*
8:24, *37*
8:34, *184*
9:42, *186*
10:23, *178*
11:12-25, *58*
12:10-11, *161*

Luke
4, *146*
4:4, *204*
4:16-21, *146*
4:18, *152*
4:18-21, *149*
6:4, *223*
6:5, *55*
6:20, *150*
6:45, *246*
7:36-50, *236*
8:21, *147*
9:23, *184*
12:15-21, *108*
12:22-31, *152*
12:34, *13*
12:37, *149*
12:42, *94*
12:49, *146*
12:50, *194*
12:56, *211*
13:24, *168*
14:21, *186*
16:1, *94*
17:2, *186*
19:9, *115*
20:17-18, *161*
21:1-4, *236*
23:30, *244*
24:21, *144*

John
1:12-13, *80*
1:13, *196*
1:14, *54*
1:29, *138*
1:36, *138*
2, *137*
3, *165*
3:3, *80*
3:16, *166*
3:16-18, *54*
4:7-15, *195*
6, *165, 202*
6:32-33, *202*
6:33, *203*
6:35, *202*
6:53, *205*
7:21-24, *105*
8, *196*
8:21-30, *162*
8:39, *54, 195*
8:39-58, *54*
9, *133*
10, *162*
10:34-36, *55*
13:1-5, *219*
13:34, *184*
14:3, *167*
14:6, *4, 167, 196*
15:12-17, *184*
15:15, *57*
16:33, *230*
18:37, *79*
19:30, *157*
20:17, *79*

Acts
2, *86*
4:11, *161*
6, *249*
7, *249*
7:48, *51*
8, *249*
14:22, *230*
15, *121, 205*

Romans
1, *73*
3:23, *66*
4:3, *103*
5:3, *230*
5:4, *231*
6:4, *194*
8, *229*
8:18-20, *230*
8:19, *142*
8:19-21, *72*
8:20-22, *142*
8:21, *22, 142*
8:23, *229*
8:26-27, *231*
8:28, *223, 229*
8:29, *55, 79, 167, 184, 198*
8:35, *230*
8:37, *90, 184*
11:17-21, *82, 177*
12:1, *140*
12:2, *192, 229*
12:17, *161*
12:21, *161*

1 Corinthians
3:2, *212*
3:10-15, *231*
3:12-15, *172*
3:13, *188*
3:13-15, *239*

3:15, *185*
5:5, *69*
6, *184*
6:2-3, *85, 184*
6:3, *57*
10:16, *166*
11:1, *209*
12:7, *210*
13, *239*
15:24-26, *163*
15:49, *79*
15:55, *187*
15:58, *188*

2 Corinthians
3:3, *117*
3:18, *79*
4:17, *230*
5:20, *188, 193*
6:1, *230*
6:1-2, *176*
6:16, *27*
9:8, *188, 234*
9:10, *234*
9:11, *234*
9:12, *234*
9:14, *234*
9:15, *235*
12:9, *162*

Galatians
2:19, *90*
2:20, *164, 184*
3:6, *103*
3:7, *197*
3:11, *197*
3:16, *107, 145*
3:19, *145*
3:24, *67*
3:24-25, *97, 130*
3:26-29, *107, 197*
4:19, *210*
5:6, *207*
6:2, *115, 148, 152, 207*

Ephesians
1:4, *29*
1:4-5, *197*
1:10, *199*
2:10, *188, 198, 228, 229*

4, *232*
4:15, *199*
4:28, *204*
5:2, *139*
5:16, *152, 178*
5:25-33, *71*

Philippians
2, *27, 149*
3:10, *184*
3:10-11, *90*

Colossians
1:15, *219*
1:20, *200*
1:24, *184*
1:28-29, *210*
2, *153*
2:8-23, *162*
2:12, *194*
2:17, *98, 153*
3, *229, 238*
3:3-4, *166*
3:10, *79*
3:22-23, *238*
3:23, *232*
3:23-24, *232*

2 Thessalonians
2:17, *188*

1 Timothy
5:10, *188*

2 Timothy
2:21, *188*

Titus
2:14, *188*
3:1, *188*

Philemon
8, *237*
9, *238*
16, *237*
19, *237*

Hebrews
2:14, *165*
3:6, *177*

3:7-9, *176*
3:8, *177*
3:11, *177*
3:13, *176, 177, 179*
3:14, *177*
3:15, *176*
3:19, *177*
4, *60*
4:2, *179*
4:7, *176*
4:8, *147*
4:9, *118*
5:8, *178*
6:1, *146*
6:1-2, *135*
7:16, *163, 205*
8:10, *27*
8:12, *178*
9, *134*
9:2, *223*
9:14, *178*
9:22, *134*
9:26, *134, 178*
9:28, *178*
10:1-10, *181*
10:5-7, *178*
10:10, *163*
10:18, *178*
10:20, *160*
10:24, *188, 198*
10:24-25, *179*
10:25, *178, 198*
11, *180*
11:4, *80*
11:10, *4*
11:13-16, *180*
11:16, *4*
11:40, *179*
12:1, *179*
12:2, *181*
12:5-6, *69, 74*
12:6, *198*
12:7, *180*
12:14, *181*
12:15, *181*

James
1:2-3, *180*
2:17, *196*
2:23, *103*

1 Peter
2:4-8, *200*
2:7, *161*
3:19-20, *158*
3:21, *193*

2 Peter
3, *36*
3:9, *102, 183, 184, 188*

1 John
2:2, *163*
3:17, *207*
4:9, *54*
4:12, *184*
4:17, *184*
4:18, *71, 184*
5:17, *132*

Revelation
3:19, *198*
5, *173*
5:6, *172*
5:10, *173*
5:12, *148*
7:9, *173*
7:17, *173*
11:15, *172*
14:13, *175*
15:2, *173*
17–18, *122*
18, *171, 175*
18:4, *175, 178*
18:22, *173*
19:7-9, *174*
19:8, *175*
20:4, *57*
20:14, *185*
21:3, *118, 173*
21:4, *174*
21:6, *174*
21:8, *185*
21:22, *118, 173*
21:25, *185*
22, *194*
22:1, *194*
22:12, *188*
22:15, *185, 186*
22:17, *174, 175*